SO-AZZ-011

$11.48

ALSO BY NINA BARRETT

I Wish Someone Had Told Me

The Playgroup

A TRUE STORY

OF LIFELONG FRIENDSHIP

THE GIRLS

NINA BARRETT

SIMON & SCHUSTER

SIMON & SCHUSTER
Rockefeller Center
1230 Avenue of the Americas
New York, NY 10020

Copyright © 1998 by Nina Barrett
All rights reserved, including the right of reproduction
in whole or in part in any form.

SIMON & SCHUSTER and colophon are registered trademarks of
Simon & Schuster Inc.

Designed by Ruth Lee

Manufactured in the United States of America

10   9   8   7   6   5   4   3   2   1

Library of Congress Cataloging-in-Publication Data

Barrett, Nina.
    The girls : a true story of lifelong friendship / Nina Barrett.
      p. cm.
    Includes bibliographical references.
    1. Middle-aged women—United States—Psychology.
  2. Middle-aged women—United States—Attitudes.
  3. Female friendship—United States.   I. Title.
HQ1059.5.U5B35   1998
305.244—dc21   98-19420
                                   CIP

ISBN 0-684-81370-X

For Joan

CONTENTS

PROLOGUE

This is a book about a group of women—the Girls—now in their mid-forties, who became friends more than thirty-five years ago in the late 1950s at their Catholic elementary school. They are real people (though I have changed their names and some identifying details) whom I came to know quite well over the course of two years of interviewing them and sometimes just hanging out with them as they drank wine and diet soda and wove comedy routines out of the fragments of their shared past. They already looked like a book when I found them—a book whose dust jacket we could all visualize. The front cover would feature raised foil lettering framing some fanciful, strategic cleavage; the back, a list of characters, dramatic feminine archetypes with boldfaced names: **Carole,** the suburban housewife, June Cleaver in running shoes, only . . . *restless.* **Maude,** the feminist idealist determined to construct a life of meaningful love and work . . . *with or without a man.* **Betsy,** struggling to reconcile her Earth Mother instincts with the passionate ambition that drives her toward . . . *a career.* **Donna,** engaged in a lifelong battle with appetites she cannot quite control. **Tammy,** the fast girl, the slut, apparently headed for the disastrous fate that inevitably awaits *that kind of girl* in books like this. And **Cindy,** the outsider, haunted for a lifetime by secrets she cannot admit, *even to herself.*

I'm sure you recognize the genre. Its mother was *The Group*, by Mary McCarthy, and its better-known daughters have included the novels *The Best of Everything* by Rona Jaffe, *Braided Lives* by Marge Piercy, and *Waiting to Exhale* by Terry McMillan, among others, as well as the nonfiction saga *Loose Change* by Sara Davidson. In fact, this ensemble-cast format is so well established in women's literature that I often wonder why there is no corresponding tradition of books about groups of men. But I suspect the explanation lies in the difference between what men and women in our culture expect (and what books often suggest we continue to expect) from our lives. In books, men find their identities through solitary struggles with Nature, or with the Devil, or with Civilizing Forces, or even with Money, but rarely in relation to other men, unless they're at war. In books, men don't often stop to view their friendships intimately until they're all stuck in foxholes depending on one another not to get their heads blown off.

Women, accused so often of being the Civilizing Forces against whom men must heroically struggle, have not traditionally been expected to have to struggle with Civilizing Forces themselves. A continuous flow of best-selling literature has been based on the premise that women are meant to spend most of their psychic and physical energy civilizing themselves and everyone around them. Such literature typically informs women that there are Rules for a happy and successful life, and that it is the job of the woman not to decide what her own Rules will be, but to *buy this publication* that will tell her exactly how to (pick one or all) lose weight, attract men, be spiritually serene, raise smart children, cook like a chef, dress for success, hide the gray, tighten the abs, etc. Women may not completely buy into these Rules; many of us are even consciously aware of the fact, so eloquently articulated by Betty Friedan around the time the Girls in this book were entering puberty, that these Rules are constantly reinvented by men on Madison Avenue with an eye toward civilizing us, or making a buck off us, or preferably both. Yet it's a rare woman who manages not to let the Rules invade her life anyway. They segue too neatly into her secret, passionate fantasy that someday, something will finally transform her into a creature who is gorgeous and perfect and . . . *loved.*

We are fascinated by stories in the *Group* tradition, I believe, because they play with the idea of Rules, and of women who live by them and women who break them, and what happens to both. We get excited in real life, too, when we think we see women for whom all the Rules have worked. That is the underlying premise of the celebrity profile that permeates our magazines and our television broadcasts: *Here's a beautiful, famous woman who has men in love with her and lots of money and everything!* We get even more excited when such a woman breaks the Rules, or when it turns out that despite having followed them to the letter, she secretly *isn't happy after all.* But then, just to complicate things, we keep changing the Rules. When I went looking through old magazines from the fifties, sixties, seventies, and eighties for material to use to sketch in the historical backdrop of the Girls' lives, what jumped out at me were the particular women singled out for celebrity at a particular time. These were not just the women's magazines, mind you, but also the stately newsmagazines like *Newsweek* and *Life* that claimed to document serious social issues. There, in 1967, was ninety-one-pound Twiggy, an instant supermodel portrayed enthusiastically as "the mini-girl in the mini-era"; and Mia Farrow at twenty-two, buying her husband, Frank Sinatra, a London taxi cab as a souvenir and explaining that it was okay for him to be married to a "career girl" because any number of women could have just "stayed at home and cooked his spaghetti for him." There, in 1971, was Gloria Steinem on the cover of *Newsweek*, hailed inside as "A Liberated Woman *Despite* Beauty, Chic and Success" (italics mine). In the end it was a gallery of such celebrity women—rather than an abstract history of their times—that found its way into this book, to frame the stories from the Girls' own lives. For it is through the public conversation that we have about celebrities' lives that we attempt to define and understand what is possible, or desirable, for all of us privately. It is through the lives of the fictional and the famous that the culture delivers to us our marching orders.

And then there is the other place women have, where they decide whether they are going to march, or not, and that is in the privacy of their friendships. I wanted to write about the Girls because they weren't fictional; they were real women who were born into the same set of Rules and then hit over the head, at various points along the way, with the fact that those Rules were not going to work. I wasn't a novelist; I wasn't going to get to decide who got a happy ending and who didn't. I was just going to go into that little foxhole with them for a while and see what it had looked like while they had hidden there throughout four of the most turbulent decades in American women's history, and counted mostly on each other to make sure that when they walked away from Operation Fairy Tale, they weren't going to get their heads blown off.

I

Once Upon a Time . . .

1960–1967

Fractured Fairy Tales

One day in 1926, a young woman named Gabrielle kissed her father good-bye in the anteroom of a Belgian cloister, pulled on the short black cape of a postulant, and began the process of transforming herself into a Bride of Christ.

Behind her was a broken heart. She had had a true love, but her father, an eminent doctor, had warned her not to marry him. The boy's mother had died in an insane asylum, so her father said there was too great a chance that children she had with him would inherit madness. Her father hadn't liked the idea of the convent much better, but broken-hearted women are usually eager to be transformed into almost anything else, and if they can't count on love to get them out of the house where they are daughters, they are going to seek, wherever possible, some other way. Perhaps it cheered her father that there was a good chance that after she finished her religious apprenticeship, the order would send her for medical schooling. More than anything, she yearned to be a missionary nurse in Africa, but she had to be careful how she wished for this because as a nun it would be unholy for her to wish anything for her own satisfaction—only that she be an instrument God might use in any way He saw fit. However, her father must have understood that it was more likely she would follow in his professional footsteps as a Bride of Christ than as the childbearing bride of a mortal man.

But first there would have to be that transformation: the process by which the convent would break down the individuality of a smart, high-spirited girl into the uniformed embodiment of selfless serenity that was a nun. There were many ancient steps for this process, contained within the Holy Rules of the order, which dictated every detail of convent life, from the times at which prayers must be said to the particular fashion in which nuns going down stairs must lift the backs of their skirts in order to avoid dragging them along the stone steps and wearing out precious fabric. The sisters who had most perfectly mastered all these details were referred to within the order as "Living Rules," because it was said of them that, were the written record of the Holy Rule ever lost or destroyed, it could be reconstructed simply by observing such a nun's comportment.

It would take a year and a half of learning, constantly observing the behavior of the Living Rules, and being subject in return to their constant surveillance, before Gabrielle and her fellows passed through the pupa stages of postulant and novice and were finally allowed to don the black scapular and veil of the fully vested nun. They practiced the silent, gliding walk that reduced nuns' bodies to flickering shadows in the cloister passageways; the downcast eyes that must never flutter to seek the source of external distractions; the meditational interior silence that neutralized mental and emotional intrusions; and the interpersonal silences that were supposed to create space for prayer and prevent the development between any two nuns of a "particular attachment." They learned to leap instantly from bed in the four A.M. winter darkness at the sound of the shrill morning bell, falling directly onto their knees in prayer no matter what their level of exhaustion. They learned that when the evening prayer bell rang they were again to respond instantaneously, interrupting any act—even as small as a gesture or an unfinished sentence—to report for prayers.

As a symbol of the shedding of her worldly self, after the six months as a postulant Gabrielle shed her worldly name and became known thenceforth as Sister Luke. Gabrielle, a mere girl, had had strengths and weaknesses; Sister Luke aspired to be— and was required to be—perfect. Imperfections, in the convent, were not aspects of character, but acts committed. A nun who committed an imperfection must note it down in a little book she carried around especially to keep track of this, and confess her list publicly at the end of each week. Then she must atone. There were the public atonements: the humiliation of begging soup from the half-eaten portions of the other sisters at dinner; going around the refectory while they ate, kissing each one of their feet. Or the semiprivate one of applying to her own flesh, in the only partial privacy of her curtained-off sleeping cell, the mortification of the whip with the five small chains attached that each ended in a small metal hook.

But the hardest struggle for Sister Luke was to avoid "singularizing" herself. Singularizing meant drawing to yourself any attention that distinguished you from your other sisters—all of whom were supposed to be interchangeable in the eyes of God. Schooled from childhood with her father's microscopes and medical instruments, Sister Luke possessed not only an unusual level of scientific talent and accomplishment, but an unfortunate, stubborn pride in the high quality of her work. The Mothers Superior of the order tried to help her—for the sake of her soul—stamp out that selfish pride. Once, when she was clearly near the top of the class in tropical medicine she was required to take before being assigned for missionary duty, her Mother

Superior suggested that she flunk her final exams as proof of her humility before God. Once, when she instituted a time- and man-power-saving innovation at her short-handed medical post, her Mother Superior rebuked her because the resident surgeon went out and bragged about it, and it got back to the Sisters that she was being mentioned in public by name.

And then there was the lure of that great singularizing force, so much to be hoped for outside the convent and so absolutely inadmissible within: erotic love. The surgeon, an accomplished seducer of women, seemed at times to see straight into her soul—her woman's soul, the one she was by now supposed to have extinguished.

But it was none of these experiences that critically challenged her conviction of her vocation. It was the morning in Belgium when she looked up to see parachutes floating down from the sky with Nazi soldiers dangling from their strings. She remembered that during the Great War of her childhood, German soldiers had come looking for her father, whom she only later discovered had been hiding out and working for the resistance. Now, as a nun, she was bound to remain neutral—not just in her behavior, conscientiously attending to the health of the Germans who wound up in her hospital, but even in the privacy of her own soul.

But this proved to be impossible. She tried going through the motions, nursing the war wounded and hoping that God would intervene and, in some miraculous fashion, recalibrate her heart. But all that happened was that one day she ran across an issue of a secret resistance newsletter. It reported that her father, the well-known Belgian doctor, had recently been gunned down by Nazi planes while treating refugees trying to escape the country on an open road.

After that, Sister Luke decided she could no longer be a nun. Though she knew she could serve the resistance effectively under the cover of the convent, she felt that to do so would be a hypocrisy in God's eyes. She would leave the order, and serve the resistance as the old self, Gabrielle, whom she now understood she still was. When her petition for release was finally granted, her Mother Superior acted swiftly, for what Sister Luke was doing was shameful and should not be witnessed by any of her Sisters. She was sent in her habit to a school building a mile away from the convent, where she was shown by a stranger to a room in which there was a pile of worn, secondhand women's street clothes. Slowly she pulled off each item of her habit: the veil, the scapular, the dress, the heavy, square-toed shoes, the undergarments with the number sewn into them—1072—that was her identity as an interchangeable soul in the convent's stream of instruments-of-God's-will. The number had belonged to a nun stabbed to death in the Congo two months before Gabrielle had arrived that first day at her convent; now it would be reassigned to a new postulant.

She folded the garments carefully, according to the Holy Rule, and slowly pulled on the ill-fitting blue suit that had been left for her. She tried to smooth down the short hair that had just begun to grow in after seventeen years of being fully shorn. It had been seventeen years since she had last seen herself in a mirror, or paid any but the scantest attention to what fashions or hairstyles women were wearing in the streets. She was fluent now, in those Holy Rules that told nuns right from wrong, but that alone had not seen her through, and now as she left that room there was no one to witness her departure, no one to bid her farewell or advise her on how one survived out there in the world, knowing right from wrong or virtue from vice, as a normal woman.

Most of the rest of the story of Gabrielle/Sister Luke is lost to us. But the preceding part was made familiar to millions of people the world over, because in 1945, a few months after she had left the convent and was working in a displacement camp for Polish refugees, "Gabrielle" met an American writer named Kathryn Hulme. Hulme, then forty-five, had never married and had led a remarkably adventurous life for her day. She had attended Berkeley and the Columbia University School of Journalism, and had then spent years abroad, writing short stories in Paris and publishing two books based on her travels in North Africa. With the beginning of World War II she had worked for a while as an electric arc welder at a shipyard in Richmond, and after the war's end had gone to Germany as deputy director of UNRRA field teams in the U.S. occupation zone. She had helped organize the refugee camp in Bavaria to which Gabrielle had found her way as a nurse.

"Gabrielle" may have discovered that she was not the same preconvent Gabrielle after all, for apparently at this time she was going by the name "Lou," short for Luke. Kathryn befriended her, and brought her to Los Angeles in 1951, where they lived in an apartment together for some years while Kathryn turned Lou's convent experiences into her third book. She published the work as fiction rather than biography, apparently because it told the story from Lou's perspective rather than from that of an "objective" observer, but perhaps also to avoid unnecessarily singularizing the real woman.

The book was a smash-hit best-seller. Published in 1956, *The Nun's Story* became a Book-of-the-Month Club selection, sold more than three million copies in the United States, and was translated into twelve languages. In 1959 it became a hugely successful movie starring Audrey Hepburn. In June of that year, *Life* magazine featured Hepburn on the cover, smiling in her tropical white nun's costume. The accompanying article included a photo of Kathryn Hulme and the real former Sister Luke in their Los Angeles home.

It's easy to see what deep chords *The Nun's Story* must have struck: To an audience still very freshly traumatized by World War II, it portrayed a heroine who had given up everything else she believed in to face down the Nazis. To a population of world Catholics just beginning to reexamine the basis for many Catholic practices and beliefs, it revealed the emotionally harsh and clearly undemocratic reality behind the romantic notion of a vocation. And, in retrospect, we can guess at another way in which the story must have resonated. A whole new generation of women was just then being coached by an emerging mega-industry of magazines and TV advertisers to form themselves into uniform Betty Crockers with wedding rings, Cross-Your-Heart brassieres, and Frigidaires. Those women, and their daughters, knew the daily tension of struggling to achieve a per-fection that, while improving you, somehow erased you. They strove—as they were constantly admonished—to obey; and yet silently they longed to become singularized. They may not have known why they identified with Sister Luke, for they had all the things she had had to give up—sex, babies, Frigidaires, love—and their culture insisted that these should make them happy, and they didn't yet have any inkling that a whole culture could change its mind and insist that these things should make them miserable. Or that one day when this still embryonic debate had ultimately subsided, they were just going to have to figure the thing out for themselves.

Real Life

Maude Chester begged her mom and dad to take her to see *The Nun's Story*. She and her two best friends in third grade at Holy Innocents Academy, Betsy Wolniak and Tammy Flanagan, des-perately wanted to grow up to be nuns. Already, they did not want to grow up to be like their mothers, and nuns and mothers were as far apart as you could get and still stay a woman. Nuns were virgins, which meant they wouldn't have to get married, which would be great because although at nine they were old enough to have felt the vague inner stirrings of childish crushes, they were also still young enough to wonder disgustedly why you would ever want to get your saliva mixed up with someone else's saliva, something being a virgin allowed you to avoid. (Later they found out from Donna DeMarco, who had heard it from her mom, that after seven years of marriage you became a virgin again, a puzzle they assigned to the category of Catholic mysteries and miracles including transubstantiation and the loaves and fishes.)

Mothers had no great knowledge to impart, just a set of restrictions, criticisms, and commands like *clean up your room* and *write a thank-you note* and *that skirt's too short*, while nuns were their teachers, and knew everything. The nuns spoke to them of life's profound mysteries, which they debated among themselves on bedroom floors scattered with Barbie dolls and accessories, and later in rec room basements with stolen cigarettes. For instance, how could the pain of hell consist of *the absence of God*, when what would really hurt you would be flames, or snakes and spiders, or Maude's nightmare vision of tons of fecal matter you would be made to shovel? The nuns wore long, romantic gowns—brides' gowns, only black, that you'd get to wear every single day and not just on your wedding day. They lived in a big house, all together, with no moms or dads or bratty little brothers, and Maude imagined them in there, floating around in little clouds of spiritual serenity. Betsy thought they must never be lonely in there, living together like a big happy family. But Tammy, the most down-to-earth of all the Girls, the one who always said exactly what she thought and no more and no less, just came right out and asked Sister Anita: *What do you guys do in there?* And Sister Anita told her: *We correct papers,*

*and every night one person is in charge of dinner, and some-
times we watch TV and we always say our prayers before bed.*
Pretty dull, thought Tammy, but she followed up: *And are you all
bald?* Sister Anita reached under her wimple and tugged out a
gray lock. *No, I got hair.* Tammy told Betsy that she had changed
her mind about becoming a nun, because, after all, the outfits
were pretty ugly, even uglier than their blue school jumpers that
Tammy couldn't wait to change out of when she got home, and at
least now they could pick out their own shoes.

But Maude begged and begged, and finally even though they
thought she was too young, her parents took her to see *The
Nun's Story.* It was fine, Maude thought, till the scene with the
priest in the leper colony. The priest had gone to the leper colony
to do the work of God's healing, even though he knew he would
eventually catch this disgusting, horrifying disease from the lepers, and it was Sister Luke's job to test him periodically to see if
he had come down with it yet. The scenes of the wasted, muti-
lated lepers' bodies haunted Maude for months afterward and
gave her nightmares. It was one thing, Maude thought, to want to
be perfect for God, and quite another to be willing to let Him
turn you into a dying monster.

So Maude began to lose interest in becoming a nun, but that
was okay, because she was still young and had her whole life before her and assumed eventually she'd get out of her parents'
house the way most normal teenage girls got out of their parents'
houses: She would fall in love.

Gerry Fitzgerald, with his dirty-blond crew cut and a pair of remarkably brooding, romantic dark eyebrows, was in love with
Maude in third grade. She knew, because he rode his bike over to
her house after school practically every afternoon, and after a
while he invited her back to his house. "To look at my army
stuff," he said, and that's exactly what he showed her, a couple of

green helmets and some little plastic guys in camouflage uni-
forms. Maude acted interested, but privately she thought he
ought to have *known* that a girl would be bored stiff, and this set
an automatic limit in her mind for how long she would allow
Gerry to go with her, because even though she didn't yet understand the meaning of the word "sophisticated," she still knew
somewhere deep inside that she was waiting for a boy who
would know better. A prince, who would treat her as the princess
she was.

Maude knew she was a princess because her parents told her
so, which wasn't as peculiar in the dawning sixties as it would
sound today. Even though the Chesters and most of the other
families in their small suburban town were economically blue
collar, with a hand or two grasping at the lower rung of the middle class, they stood mentally on the same magic democratic
springboard as everyone else in America, which might vault
them or their children right to the top at any moment, with
the help of an industrious attitude and a good, solid, Catholic
education. They watched the same black-and-white situation
comedies, with the understanding daddies who called their
curly-haired daughters "Princess." They wore the same princess
dresses, and their older teenage daughters, like Betsy's sister,
Patty, got to whisper to their boyfriends at night over Princess
telephones. There were some girls at school who weren't
princesses: the ones who got all A's but who you wouldn't think
to invite to a party because they were dull; the purely dumb ones
and the troublemakers; and the ones who (in Tammy's book,
anyway) were forced to wear ugly big brown orthopedic shoes.
Being a princess wasn't about being smart or dumb or rich or
poor exactly, but about having that distinctive spark called *personality* that showed you knew you deserved the world's attention and knew how to attract it.

That's what had drawn Maude to Betsy the first day they sat

next to each other in Sister Mary Teresa's second-grade class. Maude took one look at Betsy and thought of her forever after as the Smiley Girl because of the big grin she wore that seemed to say she was ready for anything. Everything about Betsy shone, from her glossy black hair that ended in a neat flip at her shoulders, to her dark sparkling eyes, right down to the shiny black-patent-leather Mary Janes on her feet. After Gerry Fitzgerald eventually gave up on Maude, Betsy was the very next girl he decided to show his army stuff to, and, just to be fair, it should be said that over the years there were many boys who went with Betsy first before moving on to Maude.

Now, in fairy tales, there's never room for more than one princess—one *good* princess, anyway. If a princess has sisters in a fairy tale, they always turn out to hate her, and if she has friends, they are bound to be either furry woodland creatures or supernatural spirits. But in real life there was nothing about being a princess that said you couldn't have other princess friends, and the whole point of a girls' clique, after all, is that you wouldn't want to have any other kind. Maybe that's why the princesses in fairy tales are always so desperate to be rescued by princes, because they're so lonely and isolated and bored. The Girls were expecting princes, of course, because nobody ever questioned that that was the way the story went; but they never felt desperate or isolated because they were usually giggling together over some private joke they had invented or a new dirty word someone had picked up and shared.

The main reason princesses in fairy tales can't have girlfriends, really, is that fairy tales assume that when a princess feels envy for something another princess has, the envy makes her furious and destructive; whereas in real life it is often envy of what another person has that makes us invite her into our lives as a friend. We aren't equipped to carry with us everything that is worth being or treasuring, as Maude was not equipped temperamentally to possess Betsy's perpetual sunniness, nor Betsy to possess Maude's dramatic romanticism. But with friends around we always know we can borrow and lend.

Besides her sunniness, Maude might have liked to borrow a bit of Betsy's remarkable industriousness. Maude did well in school because she had the kind of mind that could absorb big chunks of material easily, whereas Betsy did well because she was by nature thorough and hardworking. She didn't seem to expect anything to come to her easily, and maybe nothing ever had. In her family, at least, Betsy seemed to be sort of a self-made princess. No one seemed to fuss over her or have plans for her. Betsy's mother did basic maintenance work, like running a strip of tape across her forehead once a month and snipping along underneath to make sure Betsy's bangs were exactly straight, and buying her a rainbow of ribbons so that she never had to appear anywhere without a big floppy bow in her hair that exactly matched her blouse or skirt. Once Betsy was clean and shiny, though, her mother seemed to consider herself absolved from any further obligation. Though she didn't have a job, like Maude's mother, she was never in the kitchen baking cookies after school, as Maude imagined mothers without jobs did. She was always just out. And even when she wasn't, she didn't encourage Betsy to have friends over, so Betsy spent a lot of afternoons working on little arts and crafts projects alone in her room, or at Maude's house, or at the Egans' house down the street from her where there were seven daughters and everyone knew they were still trying for a son.

Wherever Betsy's mother went when she was out, at six o'clock each evening, as Betsy's father came banging through the front door, her mother would suddenly come bustling through the kitchen door with a tuna casserole in her arms. Her lipstick would be fresh and her jet-black hair dyed and styled, and they would all sit down at the dining room table just like a TV family, only the rule was that neither Betsy nor her sister nor her mother could talk until Daddy finished telling about his day at the construction site. This could take up the whole meal, since his accounts were very detailed, and he would use the salt and pepper shakers and the silverware as props to dramatize where all the heavy equipment had been positioned.

Sometimes Betsy's grandmother—her mother's mother—would be living with them, too. She was pretty much like everyone else's grandmother, Betsy thought: a crotchety gray-haired old lady who complained a lot and insisted on watching *Lawrence Welk* on Saturday nights when she got stuck baby-sitting for Betsy and Patty. An old lady you couldn't imagine having much of an interesting past. But there were old, yellowed photographs that showed her in the twenties, all dressed up in flapper outfits, at a time when she had apparently run her own newspaper and candy store in the train depot of a sleepy nearby town that had since been swallowed by suburban sprawl. "I was quite the flirt," she would declare smugly on the days when you could get her to retrieve coherent memories from the murk of her old-lady mind. But when Betsy tried to get more details from her mother, her mother would glare at her and snap, "She doesn't know what she's talking about. She was flighty and irresponsible. She couldn't take care of me; she gave me to her mother to raise."

Betsy would have liked to know more, but her mother's anger silenced her questions. Betsy wasn't sure she believed her, actually. It seemed ridiculous to imagine that this feeble, withered woman, whom both Betsy's parents treated like a baby, could ever have been powerful enough to do anything that could have made her mom that mad. Betsy herself would have been happy to have had that pretty, flirty flapper-businesswoman for a mother, and she felt sure the woman in the pictures would have appreciated Betsy's cheerfulness and industriousness more than Betsy's own mother, who didn't even seem to notice she was there.

"I'm going to have my own business when I grow up," Betsy announced one night at the dinner table after her father had finished his recitation.

"Good," said Patty. "Because no one's ever going to want to marry you, anyway."

"That's ridiculous," said her mother. "Of course you'll get married. And then you'll have children. And then you'll have to take care of them. You're not giving them to me to raise, that's for sure."

"Maybe I won't have kids," Betsy said. "What if they turned out like Patty?"

"Shut up," said Patty.

"Both of you, shut up," said her dad, taking another spoonful of mashed potatoes.

"You could teach," said her mom. "Then you can stop when you have children, and you know you'll always have something to fall back on."

Fall back on? Betsy wondered. In case of what? But she didn't ask, because she had the idea it had something to do with a mistake her mom had made, which Betsy herself wasn't going to be stupid enough to make. In her head she was already following the flapper, and she was cheerful and confident and competent, and not the type to worry about ever falling.

"That Betsy has so much get-up-and-go," Maude's mother said approvingly when she heard that Betsy, at thirteen, had already gotten herself a job as the shampoo girl at the beauty shop on the main shopping strip. "You could do with a bit more of that, Maude, instead of spending half your time with your head in a book. That's never going to help you get ahead in life, you know. It's too bad you've had it so easy. If you'd grown up like me or your dad, you'd have a different attitude. . . ."

Well, off she goes, thought Maude. Maude knew this speech

by heart, and once her mother launched into it, there were only two options. Sometimes Maude would interrupt, with a crack about how you'd think she was Shirley Temple or Elizabeth Taylor from the fuss her mother made, but this was likely to be rewarded with the whack of her mother's hand across her mouth for sassing back, and a further lecture. But if Maude could just remember to swallow the sass, her mother would eventually work her way through the sermon and into the story of her Forebears, the iron-willed women who had left their homelands and braved poverty and humiliation in America to bring lucky Maude to the throne of privilege—a vinyl-upholstered dinette chair—in which she sat today.

Maude loved to hear about the Forebears. They lived in her imagination like a race of Amazons, except that on her mom's side they were Polish and shaped, her mother said, like little fireplugs. Little Amazon fireplugs. Maude got her bush of wild, flaming hair and her own elongated frame from her father's Irish clan, which her mom said was also to blame for her dreaminess and moodiness, because on her mom's side the women were practical and resourceful and capable of crossing oceans and frontiers to get ahead. That's what her mom's mom had done, all by herself, at the age of nineteen. She had lost her own mother at two or three, and when at the age of six she had walked off to the village school by herself to see if she could learn to write her name, her father had beaten her and warned her never to go back again, because girls didn't need to have an education. Eventually he had remarried, and her new stepmother had treated her like a servant, just like the stepmothers in fairy tales, and to escape she had somehow managed to buy herself passage to America.

In America she'd had two or three husbands, the last of whom was a miner who eventually ran off like the others, and she built a farmhouse with him where she raised four children, grew all the family's fruits and vegetables, and ran a boarding-house for single mine workers. She did this with indomitable strength, which Maude's mother admired, and a marked lack of warmth, which Maude's mother did not seem to have noticed. She drank a shot of whiskey in her coffee every morning, and she didn't like her dinner interrupted at night, so if one of the children spoke without being spoken to first, she just leaned over the table and whacked them across the mouth with the back of her spoon.

Maude's mom, Anna, had married a good-looking but useless man just to get out of that house, but when the man turned on her and started beating her, she ran back to her mother and her mother stood up for her. When the husband came looking for Anna, her mom said, "Tell me vat you vant."

"I'm looking for my wife."

"Yah, yah, she's here. You come in, sit down."

So he sat down at the kitchen table, and Anna's mother went and fetched the broom handle she kept handy in the event of burglars or intruders, and this little Amazon fireplug just whacked this six-foot-tall man all around the head and shoulders and screamed at him for beating up her daughter until he was ready to apologize.

But, to back up a bit, around the time the Great Depression hit in the early thirties, Gramma had decided to send Mom's older half-sister Bertha, who was only thirteen, into the City to find a paying job. She put Aunt Bertha on a train with five dollars, one change of clothes, and the address of some distant cousins she probably hadn't even seen since before Bertha was born. Aunt Bertha got to the City and rode the streetcar around all day, partly because she kept getting lost but also partly because she'd never seen a streetcar before and thought riding around on it was fun. When she'd finally located the cousins, they'd taken one look at this miniature bumpkin fireplug and said, "Well, you can stay here tonight, but tomorrow you'll have to find a job."

So Aunt Bertha got a job as a nanny with a rich family whose father owned a restaurant. One day, he was short a waitress, and told his wife, "Sorry, I need to borrow Bertha for the day." The next day he told his wife, "You'll have to find a new nanny. I'm keeping Bertha at the restaurant—she's fantastic."

And by the time Bertha was eighteen or nineteen, she was making enough money to send for her mom and brothers and sister and set them all up in an apartment in the City. She married a busboy, and eventually they opened their own restaurant together; when they retired fifty years later, they had enough money to buy a house in Florida and travel all over the world. And when Maude's mother finally decided to leave her abusive first husband, it was Aunt Bertha who took in Maude's four-year-old half-brother, Paul, and raised him with her own kids while Maude's mother got a job in a factory to support herself.

It was at the factory that Maude's mother met her father, a calm and careful man who, possibly in reaction to the storminess of his own clan, rose at five-thirty every morning and fixed his own toast, and never took seconds at dinner; the prince who rescued Maude's mother from the chaos of her life, allowed her to be reunited with her son, and provided this new, good, suburban safety into which Maude, feeling entitled, had been born.

So this was how Maude had come to be the princess she was, and she was never for one moment to forget how lucky she was, even if she didn't have hair bows as pretty as Betsy's or riding lessons like Tammy. And that was why, out in the backyard, where all the neighbors had the useless ornamental lawns they devoted whole Saturdays to grooming, and Tammy's family had a swimming pool, Maude's dad still had a victory garden that produced most of her family's fruits and vegetables. And that was why her mom insisted on having a job, even though her dad periodically reminded her that most of his coworkers' wives stayed home and they could really afford for her to, too. "You wanna go live in some dark little apartment in the City?" her mom would shriek, as though he had just proposed a quick slide back into the primordial slime from which they had all just clawed their way up. "You wanna give up your beautiful garden and not be able to send your kids to Catholic school, and have nothing for when you retire?"

No doubt about it, Getting Ahead wasn't over yet, and even if you were a princess living in the lap of luxury you were expected to pull your weight, like Betsy washing hair for money, in that family where no one ever nagged her about getting ahead in the first place. Like Maude should be doing, instead of escaping into her fantasy world of books, or the colorful land of her Forebears, those women who had not been born princesses, yet lived lives of such challenge and adventure that by comparison an existence filled only with Gerry Fitzgeralds or the regular Saturday night gatherings of her parents' bridge partners could never cast even the slightest glimmer of enchantment.

Tammy Flanagan just really envied Betsy's shoes, those pretty black-patent-leather Mary Janes. And there wasn't a single reasonable explanation she could think of for why she shouldn't have them, because most of the time it seemed like it was her mom's major religious principle in life to make sure her three daughters never left the house without looking like a set of matching fashion dolls. No new department store was far enough away to discourage Thelma from packing them all into the car and killing an entire Saturday afternoon—when maybe Maude and Betsy had even asked her to go roller-skating—making them try stuff on to see if she could find an ensemble she liked in all three sizes. And for Christmas and Easter they needed accessories, too: matching hats and purses, and those little white gloves that were so skintight you could barely bend your fingers.

School days were different, though. You had to wear the same outfit as every other girl at Holy Innocents Academy: blue jumper, white short-sleeved blouse, and white ankle socks. The only choice you got to make was in shoes. And Thelma insisted that she wear penny loafers. "You're so hard on shoes, Tammy, you'd ruin a pair of Mary Janes in a week," she said, but she was wrong about that, because the ugly brown penny loafers didn't have a dent in them—*didn't even look broken in*—by the time she outgrew them.

Oh, well, what were you gonna do? After a while, Tammy made a joke of it, not with Thelma, who didn't have much of a sense of humor, but with Betsy. Every so often when the Girls put on a new record and danced around somebody's rec room, Tammy would remind Betsy not to dance with her, because she had Big Clunky Feet that could slay a pair of Mary Janes in a week. Other than that, Tammy didn't make a big deal about it, because she hated the kind of people who made a big deal about things.

Like Bobby Leopold. Bobby Leopold had gone with all of them—Maude, Betsy, and Tammy—and once Tammy had actually had kind of a crush on him. But then one day in sixth grade he had sidled up to her in the hallway and said, "I know somethin' about you that I'm not tellin' you."

"Yeah? Like what?"

"I told you, I'm not tellin' you."

"Yeah? So then why're you tellin' me you're not tellin' me?"

"Okay, I'll tell you, but you gotta promise not to tell that I told you."

"Okay, what?"

Bobby paused for full dramatic effect, and looked around to see if anyone else was within earshot. Then he leaned so close to her that she could smell the tuna fish on his breath, and whispered, "I heard you were—*adopted.*"

Tammy gave him her scathing look, her where-were-you-when-they-handed-out-the-brains look, and said, "Yeah, so?"

"What—you mean you already knew that?"

"Well, Bobby, it's not the kind of thing your mom and dad just, like, forget to mention."

After that she wouldn't give Bobby Leopold the time of day. It wasn't like she'd ever tried to hide the fact that she was adopted, it was just that she didn't think about it enough to think of mentioning it. Her parents seemed to want to make a big deal about it, too, not all the time, but just every couple of years when it occurred to them it was time to sit down and have a Big Talk about it. The point of the Big Talk was always that she should feel free to talk about it, if she wanted to, and if she decided when she grew up that she wanted to know more about her natural parents, her mom and dad would be happy to help her find out.

But Tammy pretty much doubted the part about being happy. One afternoon she came home from school to find her mom and dad sitting at the kitchen table, looking all pale and wrung out, like they'd been crying. Between them on the table, like some kind of radioactive bomb they were afraid to touch, lay a big brown mailing tube.

Thelma pointed to the tube, and said, "It's from Nashville."

"Oh, cool," said Tammy. "It's my Elvis Presley poster that I sent away for."

"Show us," said Thelma. Then, when Tammy had Elvis unfurled across the kitchen table, Thelma burst into tears and said, "We saw the return address, and we thought you had gone behind our backs and contacted the agency for information about your mother."

Well, it was true, her mom and dad had briefly lived in Nashville, and that's where they had gotten her from Catholic

Charities, because a doctor had told Thelma that she would never be able to have any children of her own. To Tammy it seemed perfectly natural that babies came from Catholic Charities, rather than from the stork, because she could still very clearly remember the day they went to pick up her little sister Dorothy. She remembered getting to hold Dorothy in her lap on the car ride home, really carefully, so she wouldn't break her, and having the grown-ups ask what Tammy thought they should name her, and Tammy thought of her favorite TV jingle about a miraculous laundry detergent, and suggested they call her Blue Cheer.

And then later, when against all the odds Thelma actually had gotten pregnant and had her youngest sister the regular way, Tammy and Dorothy turned the whole thing into a joke. "Mom got *stuck* with you," they would taunt Edie when she was acting like a pain. "She *chose* us."

But Tammy could not think of words to explain to her parents why this was a much bigger deal to them, apparently, than to her. Her attitude was, if somebody just takes their baby over to the adoption agency one day and says, "Too bad I can't take care of you, hope you have a nice life somewhere else," then it's a pretty clear sign they don't want you. So, while you were off having a perfectly nice life with somebody else, it would be pretty much the height of stupidity to go chasing after those people with your tail wagging. Making a big deal out of it.

That's the kind of thing Maude would have done. If Maude had been adopted, the entire world would have had to know about it, and there would have been some dark, possibly tragic tale behind it that would have made Maude look mysterious and alluring, instead of just unwanted. Maude was that rare kind of person who could make a big deal out of practically any minuscule thing and get away with it. Things that would have made other people self-conscious, she would dramatize. She was probably a full head taller than any of the boys in their grade, but did she stoop over the refreshment table at dances like the misfits? No way. She couldn't even dance for shit, but there she would be, out in the middle of the dance floor all evening, her frizzy red head bobbing above everyone else's, having the time of her life.

Tammy had to admit, grudgingly, that she admired that. That it took a certain amount of gutsiness that maybe Tammy thought she could use a teensy bit more of. When Maude's hand went shooting up in class as it always did at the first possible sign that the teacher was about to ask a question, Tammy would just sit there convinced that whatever answer had just popped into her head was pretty sure to be wrong. And then the answer in her head would come out of Maude's mouth, and it would turn out to have been right, and Tammy would just sit there thinking, *Next time, I should raise my hand.*

But next time she wouldn't, because face it, she was basically lazy. And because she didn't want to have called attention to herself if it turned out she *was* wrong. And anyway, why make a big deal out of it?

At the beginning, of course—in elementary school—they had no idea they were making friends for life. They made no pacts or vows, and they all had other best friends who came and went, like Ellen, who went riding with Tammy, or the Egan sisters down the street from Betsy. You could make or lose a best friend overnight, it was just like changing outfits; the world didn't stop over that. You kept growing up and changing, and change was a wonderful thing, it was tugging America into the Space Age. President Kennedy said we were going to reach the moon, and it almost looked like we could get there in the new bowling alley where Maude and Betsy and Tammy spent so many Saturdays: a big squatting aquamarine pavilion that looked as though it could have landed on their local hillside after fleeing the site of the upcoming 1964 New York World's Fair. They bought lipsticks and rock 'n' roll 45s and still believed it when the nuns said they would go to heaven if they were good. And then one day Sister Mary John came on the PA system and told them all to go home because President Kennedy had been shot, their own Catholic president who was going to heaven without reaching the moon. And for a few days, the world did stop. And then when it finally began turning again, they were in high school before they started to notice that now it was spinning faster than ever before.

Maude, Betsy, and Tammy entered St. Mary Magdalen High School in the fall of 1965 and found a whole new crop of girls who'd been to other elementary schools in different parishes. The first day Sister Agnes thought it would be nice if they could all get to know each other.

"Let's go around the room," she instructed, "and you can each tell us where you live, where you went to school last year, and why you chose to come to St. Mary Magdalen."

Well, one by one, in alphabetical order, the girls stood up and recited the requested information, and of course Maude gave an entire speech about how she'd chosen SMM because Catholic high schools "educate the mind, body, and spirit." When they got to the D's, up stood a heavyset girl with dark curly hair and wonderfully exotic dark gypsy skin and eyes, and she announced, "My name is Donna DeMarco, and I'm here because my parents made me come."

There was some scattered tittering, and Donna looked briefly pleased for the slight fraction of a second before Sister Agnes ushered her out of the room and down the hall to Sister Mary William's office. Donna thought Sister Mary William looked like she had one or two things on her mind other than helping make sure Donna felt fully at ease in her new environment. What Sister Mary William said, with one wrinkled hand poised on the receiver of her big, black telephone, was, "Perhaps you would like me to phone your parents and explain to them that there is another school you would prefer to be attending."

Donna, whose two best friends from eighth grade had been allowed to attend public high school, got the feeling that after a phone call from Sister, her parents might not let her live long enough to attend high school, period.

"Oh, no, Sister," she said smoothly. "That won't be necessary. You see, I think Sister Agnes just misunderstood what I meant. What I *meant* was, my parents *convinced* me that St. Mary Magdalen was the right place for me, and now that I'm here, I can really see how right they were."

Donna understood that Sister Mary William's half smile of satisfaction was a four-year sentence. But she also drew hope, from the admiring glances she got from several girls back in the classroom as she sat down, that she and her big mouth might find a way to make the best of it.

Carole Bourquin deeply appreciated the kind of mouth Donna had—that Maude Chester had, too, and even Tammy, though hers stayed clamped shut in class and you had to get to know her personally to understand her capabilities in this department. Carole herself had the kind of mouth that seemed only to be capable of squeaking out sincerity. There shouldn't have been anything wrong with that; there shouldn't have been anything wrong with being a true and honest girl who knew her own heart, could not dissemble, believed in the essential goodness of human nature, and spent every Thursday afternoon tutoring ghetto children under the auspices of her Christian Youth group.

But she knew there *was* something wrong with it. Look, if you were a person who was so caring that you would reach inside your own chest and pull out your beating heart and hand it to someone who needed it, you would have done something glorious, like the saints and martyrs they learned about from the nuns, but also you would be dead. This was the kind of thing you could get Maude to talk about for hours: Would you rather be dead and have your name live on forever, or alive and completely unappreciated? But of course, Maude didn't have it in her to go five minutes unappreciated, dead or alive, whereas Carole could give so much of herself away she sometimes wondered if what was left was a self at all.

Carole wanted a couple of things that saints and martyrs don't. In addition to being alive, for example, she wanted Vince Pastorino, a friend of her older brother Greg, who was quarterback on the high school football team and displayed his excellent athlete's physique at the public swimming pool most of the summer when Carole was fourteen and working the hot dog concession there. But it was so far out of the realm of Carole's imagination that Vince would actually notice her that the afternoon she finally saw him bearing down on the hot dog stand she raised her hand to her head in consternation and realized she had come to work with all her long, wheat-colored hair up on big pink rollers. Girls did that in those days, before there were curling irons and blow dryers, because they couldn't always spare the time to sit under one of those huge glass helmets or the king-size shower caps with hot-air hoses coming out the back. It was the kind of thing you did, like wearing falsies, but didn't want to be caught doing, particularly not by someone like Vince Pastorino, who was perfect in every way.

"Oh, geez, Suzie, don't let him know I'm here," she squealed to the other attendant as she dropped down under the counter. And she squatted there, in the duck-and-cover position they had been trained at school to use in the event of nuclear attack, until he was gone.

After that, of course, she was very careful never to wear

curlers to the pool again, and by the end of the summer, Vince had, miraculously, asked her to the movies. And she had just stood there for a moment, gaping at him, waiting to see what kind of answer was going to come out of her mouth. The truth? *I'm sorry, my mom and dad think I'm too young to date, could you come ask me again in a year or two?* Well, Carole was very, very honest, but she was *not* a loser. She was not going to pass up the once-in-a-lifetime chance for a date with Vince Pastorino. So she did what any normal girl her age would do, only she did it badly. She was stammering and she could feel her face going all red with the strain of it, but she gave Vince a time to pick her up when she knew her parents would be out at their regular Saturday bridge game.

So then the date was like something out of the antics of *I Love Lucy,* with her parents leaving late and barely out of the driveway by the time Vince pulled up in his Chevy. She could barely hear the soundtrack of the movie they went to because her heart was pounding away so violently the whole time, and she couldn't tell whether it was her hand or his that felt so revoltingly sweaty. At the point when she should have been sitting there thinking, *Is he going to try to kiss me?*, all she could think of was, *Is he going to get me home before them?*

Vince never asked her for a second date, which was fine since once you'd been out with him you could see that he wasn't completely worth dying of a premature heart attack for. But Carole was haunted by the thought that another girl might have handled the same situation with a little more style and confidence.

Like Maude Chester. Freshman year they were both elected to student council, along with Betsy and Donna, and Carole got the impression watching her with the nuns that she could talk her way into or out of anything. The first student council meeting let out a little earlier than planned, and Sister Mary William told all the girls to go back to their last-period class, but Maude tapped

Carole on the shoulder as they left and whispered, "Let's go hang out in the locker room and talk. I bet they won't catch us."

So they walked, coolly, to the locker room, and sat down on a bench, talking and watching the big hand on the clock tick closer and closer to the hour of the final bell. Carole wondered what Maude could possibly say if they were caught. But that whatever it was would work just fine Carole never for a moment doubted, and she was almost disappointed when the bell sounded and they were free to go. She had looked forward to learning a thing or two from Maude—the kind of thing she understood instinctively was going to be very important in getting what she wanted from life; the secret of a girl's education that a nun would never be willing or able to teach.

From the moment Sister Mary William announced in sophomore French class that she would be taking a group of students to France for six weeks in the upcoming summer of 1967, Maude just knew she would find a way to go. And from the look on Betsy's and Carole's faces, she knew they were going to find a way, too.

It wasn't an obvious thing, though, the sort of idea any of their parents were likely to encourage automatically. Nobody's family just had seven hundred dollars lying around, and if they did, it would not have occurred to them to spend that kind of dough sending teenagers to Europe to get some culture. Older relatives still vivid in their parents' memories—if not actually still in their dining rooms every Sunday for meat loaf and creamed corn—had just *left* Europe dreaming of little private bungalows like theirs as a goal that might always remain financially beyond their reach.

But Maude was desperate to grow up, to acquire the polish and sophistication she was sure a trip to Europe would provide. She was already so tall and well developed that adults—and,

more important, boys—often mistook her for older than her fifteen years. It wasn't like you wanted to look thirty or something—just old enough for people not to hold you to little kids'
rules. You wanted to be a full-blown teenager as fast as possible,
and stay that way forever, because this was the Golden Age of
the Teenager, and they all understood that perfectly well even at
the time. You could be brilliant and famous and at the top of your
profession, like Peggy Fleming, women's world champion figure
skater at eighteen; or like Twiggy, turning the fashion world upside down at seventeen; or like Janis Ian, at fifteen already the
"next Bob Dylan" and writing a really cool confessional column
with no capital letters in it for *Seventeen* magazine. Of course,
Seventeen's stodgy editors went ahead and added their own capitals to Ian's prose. That bothered Ian, of course, as well as the
fact that the column "won't come out for another three or four
months and by then I'll be a different person. . . ."

What had always been the great weakness of adolescence
was becoming, in the 1960s, *the whole point:* You were unfinished, unstable, in flux. That didn't make you immature, it made
you flexible, spontaneous, open. It meant you could wake up any
morning whatever woman you decided to be, like Audrey Hepburn as Holly Golightly, transforming herself from a country hick
to a New York sophisticate in *Breakfast at Tiffany's*. Or like
Twiggy herself. Up until just two years ago, according to
Newsweek, she had been "just another gawky school kid in drab
West London" with the pedestrian name of Lesley Hornby. Then
she had started dating a decorator named Nigel Davies, who had
made them both over, himself into a promoter-manager named
Justin de Villeneuve, and her into "The Face of 1966." Suddenly
she was all over *Vogue, Elle, Seventeen*, even *Ladies' Home
Journal*, defining the New Look in fashion with a five-foot six-
and-a-half-inch, ninety-one-pound body that *Newsweek* alternately described as "meager as a wartime British ration book"

and "just a few calories this side of visible starvation." Instantly, it seemed, she had become a Living Rule.

> Back in England [*Newsweek* reported], Twiggy shops dot the London department stores. Girls have shorn their hair à la Twiggy, affected her knock-kneed stance, starved themselves to her 91 pounds, decked their eyes with three tiers of false eyelashes, all in imitation of their idol. So cosmic an image has Twiggy become that Madame Tussaud's famous wax museum is readying a figure of 5-foot, 6-inch Twiggy that will stand on an even footing with life-sized replicas of Napoleon, Churchill and Stalin. . . .
>
> Whether the Twiggy look will now sweep across the U.S., emaciating American teen-agers as it goes, remains to be seen.

If you didn't like who you were, or who you *looked* like, there was always plenty of advice around for changing it. *Seventeen*—Maude's private guide to the kind of worldly sophistication you didn't get from your mom or the nuns—suggested in its January 1967 issue—the one with the Janis Ian column—that you "Have a Beauty Happening." It pictured several teens whose own spontaneous Beauty Happenings had transformed them into something the magazine suggested was definitely more gorgeous—yet still more deeply *themselves*—than they had been before. Janet Trigere had had 150 hairs individually plucked from each eyebrow. "I can't say it was fun," she commented, "but what a difference it made." Barbara Neil "just decided one day I was tired of long hair and being quote pretty unquote and looking like everyone else. So I went to a hairdresser and said, 'Start cutting and I'll tell you when to stop.' "

Luckily, the resulting "wonderfully striking look" worked well on Neil, who just happened to be "a teen-age English model visiting New York [who] has the well-shaped head and well-behaved hair needed for this cut."

Because that was the catch: While you wanted to express
yourself by the way you looked and acted and dressed, you
didn't want to end up acting or looking—well, stupid or dorky.
Some things were just obvious, like that if you were a Climber—
as the Girls mostly were—you wore madras and penny loafers,
and you didn't rat your hair and wear leather like the Greasers.
But who else besides *Seventeen* was going to give you authorita-
tive answers to your embarrassing, intimate questions, such as
"Is a girl who's only thirteen or fourteen too young for a tampon?"

There were ads that suggested which fantasies might be
within a young girl's reach, and (though we only see this clearly
in retrospect) which weren't. "Someday when I marry," a girl
with long, straight hair in one ad told herself, gazing heaven-
ward, "I'll make him so proud of me . . . and of our very first
home. It will be filled with lovely, enduring things. I'll have flowers in my dining room and we'll dine by candlelight . . . my table
set with the most beautiful china and crystal in all the world. By
Lenox, of course . . ." In another, a pretty blonde model wearing
heavy dark spectacles low on her nose in an apparent intended
visual satire on the possibility of her being brainy, squealed, "Me,
a girl psychologist? Crazy!" The ad copy confided: "Crazy like a
fox. Suppose you were a stewardess with United Air Lines. You'd
have to be a psychologist. And a good one. Of course, you'd have
to like people, responsibility, challenge, and travel." Also, the ad
said, you'd have to be between 5'2" and 5'9" and weigh 140
pounds or less, and you'd have to report to the modern Stewardess Training Center in suburban Chicago, where you would
"learn beauty secrets and tips on poise and personality from experts."

You found other nuggets of crucial information, too, for example: **"A candid comparison of French and American
girls. Conclusion? THERE IS A DIFFERENCE."** Eighteen-

year-old Charles McConnell from Cresskill, New Jersey, who had been an AFS student in France the year before, informed *Seventeen* readers:

> French girls are just as moral as American ones, but they seem more sincere about expressing their feelings. I can't imagine any French girl not kissing a boy good night because she "knows" she's not supposed to on a first date. A French girl will show a boy exactly how she feels. And why shouldn't she? In her country, a date is a way to appreciate and enjoy the company of a boy; it's not a necessity, an achievement, or a way to be "one of the crowd."

Hmmm. Maybe there were some things not even a magazine could teach you, some things you just had to go and see for yourself. This, Maude intuitively understood, was what was so important about getting to France. It wasn't about conjugations or idioms, it was about the way things would *be* there, in that old, romantic country where people ate and drank and kissed, well, somehow *differently* from how they ate and drank and kissed in America. Maude didn't know exactly *how* it would be different, but she sensed that if you got there you would magically absorb part of that way of being and it would stay inside you forever and transcend the sturdy prose of your merely American girlhood.

So for once Maude pulled her red head on its spindly stalk out of the clouds, and proposed a deal with her parents that her mother immediately approved: She would pay half the cost of the trip if they let her get a job shampooing in the beauty shop where Betsy worked. She worked Fridays after school till nine and all day Saturday for $1.25 an hour plus tips till she had earned her half of the France money, and proved to her mom that she did so have what it takes to get ahead in this world.

*   *   *

On July 3, 1967, the Girls' school group flew to New York City, where they were to do a day's sightseeing, spend the night, and then catch a flight to Paris from JFK the next day. "Bopped around 42nd & Broadway," Donna noted in her "Diary of Time Spent in Europe." "Cruise → Statue of Liberty."

They stayed at the Times Square Motor Hotel, giving the twenty-one high school virgins and their two chaperoning nuns an optimal view of the city's nerve center of sin. Because there wasn't room to house them all on the same floor, Sister Mary William sent the most mature and trustworthy of the group—the Girls—to a room on another floor. Carole sat at the window gazing wide-eyed at the flashing neon and the chaos of the street traffic. "I'm going to go to sleep as soon as I can count to ten and not see a derelict walk by," she thought. She was up late.

Maude and Betsy sneaked out in search of a couple of sailors Maude had flirted with in the lobby earlier. Donna was horrified; she'd had no idea Maude was that fast. Then, while somewhere in the bowels of the motor hotel, Maude sat on the lap of a nineteen-year-old sailor, kissing, while Betsy sat on the floor with another one smoking cigarettes, the phone rang in the Girls' room.

"Donna, how are things going?" said Sister Mary William. "I'm about to come down for a bedtime check."

"Oh, Sister," Donna whispered into the phone. "It's a good thing you called. The Girls are all sleepin'. I was just doin' my meditation for the evening. If you're comin' down, do you want me to wake 'em all up?"

"Oh, no no no," Sister said. "They're all sleeping?"

"Yeah, I'm the only one up."

"That's good, Donna. Well, then, I guess you can get yourself to bed. Sleep well, Donna."

"Yeah, Sister."

*   *   *

In Donna's private opinion, this whole France trip was a waste
of time. She was not, that she could see, in any particular need
of having her horizons broadened. She already knew exactly
how big her universe was, because her dad had explained it to
her more than once, and her dad was the kind of guy people listened to.

"This is me," he would say, holding up his hand with the
thumb sticking out. "And this is your mother," he added, flicking
out his index finger. "And your brother and your sister and you,"
he said, as the three remaining fingers popped up. Then he
would curl them slowly into a fist as he concluded: "And we're
like this. And nothin' gets in, and nothin' gets out."

So. Apparently there were things you didn't say, questions
you didn't ask, questions you didn't even think. Like: Why is
Daddy so scary? And why is everyone so scared of him? And
Donna had a problem that nobody else in their very tight family
apparently had: She didn't fit. She was too big for that fist,
from the moment she arrived, and her tiny mother even exagger-
ated the problem. "My ten-pound baby," her mother called her,
though she had actually weighed in at nine pounds and one-half
ounce. She was bigger than the other kids always, and then
when she was eight she started to get her period and from that
moment on her parents acted like it was just a matter of time till
she landed herself—and somehow, by implication, them—in Big
Trouble. If she tried to sit in her father's lap, he peeled her off,
saying she was too old for that kind of crap; if she tried to go
down the street in a tennis dress, he called her back and told her
to get some goddamn clothes on. Whatever attention her sultry
Mediterranean face and precociously curvaceous body were
earning her, it didn't seem like the kind of attention really worth
earning. "Make somethin' of yourself, Donna," her mom would
mutter, stirring some big vat of spaghetti sauce on the stove.
"Don't get married, like I did. I shoulda never got married. I don't

know what the hell I married your father for. And I shoulda never had you."

What she really needed, her parents seemed to agree, was shrinking. So at thirteen—5 feet, 7 inches tall and 210 pounds—Donna was taken to a diet doctor, who gave her magic shots that made her lose her appetite. She'd gotten down to 140, but by the time they left for Europe she had bounced back up to about 180.

Her father had one story about her he liked to tell over and over: How, one day when she was two, he came home from work, and at that time they were still living in the City, in an apartment that was drafty, so there were space heaters around. Donna was just sitting by the space heater playing with a toy, and her father said, "Hey, Chicken, get away from that space heater, you're gonna burn yourself." Donna ignored him. So he said, "Hey, you hear me? I said, get away from the heater." And still, Donna didn't move, she just sat there staring at him with these big soulful brown eyes under their thick dark lashes. So he started walking toward her, saying, "You little shit, I *told* you . . ." But before he could get to her, she, quick, reached out and put her hand *directly on* the heater.

He told this story to everyone with great relish, though what the punch line was supposed to be, she couldn't exactly say. It had something to do with his semisecret admiration for how she was willing to hurt herself just to prove this big bully couldn't boss her around. He admired her spunk, her spirit—but that didn't mean he was ever going to allow her to win.

There was something else in there, too; but whether it was his curse on her or a simple foreshadowing, would take years to determine: If she ever tried against his explicit warnings to get out of her father's house she was going to get burned. Next time more badly.

So even though the nuns had somehow convinced her mom that this trip to France would be a good idea, Donna wasn't looking to see any more than she had to. She wished she hadn't seen Maude acting like an idiot. But, having seen it, she was going to manage the situation. As for the sights and sounds and smells of Europe, she wasn't going to get too excited. "Left for airport at 8:00," went her Diary. "Plane 2 hrs. late. Took of [*sic*] at 2:00 a.m. Ankles swollen."

Maude had religiously followed *Seventeen*'s instructions on "How to choose double-time travel clothes." The idea was to pack the fewest number of items in mix-and-match colors so, for example, a simple dress could become three different outfits: alone, it's casual for daytime; then a jacket "turns it into a suit; on its own with a change of accessories, the dress whirls off for an evening's entertainment."

Maude bought a navy blue cotton blazer with gold buttons. Then, working within her tight budget, she sewed a matching navy shirt and a red skirt and a red-and-white-striped top that could go with both. Then, for the dress, she picked a lime green paisley fabric with swirls of blue and green and yellow that she could just imagine whirling off by themselves for an evening's entertainment, and sewed it into a long-sleeved shift whose hem came down to just above the knees. Finally, with the leftover scraps, she created a matching headband.

She wore the green dress the day they boarded the flight at JFK, which turned out to entail an unexpectedly arduous journey across the airport. No wonder Donna's ankles hurt. There was no direct boarding from the waiting area. Instead, they had to walk outside, through a rainstorm, to a bus, which drove them around the runways till it found the jet, and then they had to get off the bus and walk again through the rain to the staircase leading up to the plane and the friendly stewardess, standing there full of poise and personality. By the time they got onboard, they were soaked to the skin.

A while after settling into her seat, Maude noticed that her hands had turned green. When she pulled the paisley headband off her sodden hair, her companions pointed out, giggling uncontrollably, that her ears were green, too. As soon after takeoff as she was allowed to leave her seat, she hurried to the bathroom, where she discovered that the dye from her wonderful new dress had run all over her body, and her underwear was now green, too. Damn! She hadn't thought it would make a difference if she just skipped the step in the directions that told you to prewash the fabric, but for the whole next six weeks, the water in the little dormitory sinks where Maude rinsed out her travel clothes was tinged with green.

That was the thing about the instructions you found in those magazines, though: You were never quite sure, when the instructions did not seem to produce the desired result, whether there was something wrong with the instructions you were trying to follow, or whether there was something wrong with you.

They stayed the first three weeks in a nondescript suburb about half an hour outside Paris, in the dorm of a boarding school on summer vacation. Tammy got a load of the low-budget accommodations and the daily study schedule and nearly flipped. A trip to France should be luxurious, right? She'd been thinking: croissants on little silver trays, and snails in butter sauce, and maybe a midnight cruise down that river that passed right by the Eiffel Tower.

And here's what *this* was like: They dragged you out of bed at six in the goddamn morning, like there was some good reason you had to be up with the roosters, and then all they served you was *continental* breakfast. A loaf of bread, a dish of orange marmalade, and this huge bowl of—eeeew—coffee. None of them drank coffee. Tammy tried it black, white, sweet—still it was eeeew. As she wrote home to her parents, who were funding this whole escapade: *You're paying all this money so we can have bread and water for breakfast.*

Then there were *hours* of French classes, which might have been bearable had she been in class with Maude and Betsy, passing notes and stuff. But since normally she didn't take French at home, like they did, she got dumped into the slow class with the younger girls, which was not only boring but humiliating to boot.

Then in the afternoon they'd put you on a bus to go sightseeing, with a box lunch that was probably a thin little slice of ham and cheese on a roll, not even on a croissant. Tromping through Notre-Dame, Les Invalides, the Tuilleries. Versailles was pretty cool; Tammy could imagine living there if you fixed it up a little. But you got thirsty from all this walking around, and it turned out there was nothing cold to drink in all of France. Everything was room temperature. Even the milk was lukewarm, which made you think of dangerous bacterial diseases. But wait—hadn't Marie Curie been French, hadn't they sent pasteurization over to us, had they forgotten to keep it for themselves? Anyway, Tammy never did make it up to the top of the Arc de Triomphe with the other Girls, because on the way, right across the street, she discovered an American drugstore that served milk shakes. Icy-cold milk shakes.

Maude learned to call what they put on those box-lunch sandwiches *jambon*, which made it a whole lot less like the Sunday leftovers you might get in your lunch box and a whole lot more like a delicacy you might obtain from the quaint local *boulangerie* if you could just manage to make the proper request trip off the tip of your tongue in casual French.

"*C'est une voiture*," Carole wrote painstakingly in her *L'orthographe du Francais*, "*Voilà une dame.*"

One day Carole ran out of deodorant. Donna went with her to the drugstore, to help.

Hopefully, politely, Carole recited potential brand names to the man behind the counter: "Arid? Mum? Ban?"

The man regarded them blankly.

Donna poked her elbow into Carole's side. "Show him your pits, Carrie, show him your pits!"

Sweetly blushing crimson, Carole slowly raised one arm and pointed with her other hand.

"Ahhhh," said the pharmacist, nodding vigorously. "Day-o-der-aunt!"

In France their group merged with high school groups from around America, and though of the total about 120 were girls, there were 20 or 25 boys, enough to make things interesting if you added them to the small throng of French boys who hung around the front gates of the school like insects sensing pollen. Technically, they were forbidden to talk to the French boys, but there wasn't much the nuns could do to stop the Girls from taking daily strolls around town, trailing French boys in their wake. In their pajamas in the dorm at night, the Girls thoroughly discussed the implications of its being called *French* kissing, and how this was something you certainly needed to experience, like French pastry, where there were specialists. So it was that on at least one trip to the local patisserie, they detoured into some French boy's basement rec room to play Ping-Pong and sample the native kissing techniques.

But these flirtations paled next to their interactions with the American boys, which they considered to be real *relationships*. With so many interminable bus rides into Paris, and summer evenings so much longer than were necessary to conjugate five of the day's verbs, and so little adult supervision, there were extraordinary opportunities to pour your heart and soul out to another person, as you might not be inclined to do at home in the McDonald's parking lot even on a long summer night. Maude poured out her soul to Hank the Hunk from Detroit, who might or might not have been listening, and to nice Freckle-Faced Jim—who undoubtedly was. And to Rod, who had a physique like an adult man and who listened to all the girls pouring out their souls that summer, as Maude eventually discovered. But, really, the whole first three weeks she was almost exclusively devoted to Lester Wojciechowski, who had smoldering dark eyes and toppled over in a dead faint at the Bastille Day parade in Paris because he hadn't eaten any breakfast.

The medics came with a stretcher and carried him to the first-aid tent, where they revived him with orange juice and croissants. Maude, who followed along, had a premonition of the way history becomes engraved on a soul, as she was now seeing it engraved on a country. "I will remember this moment forever," she thought with total clarity, even as she vaguely understood that Lester would soon disappear from her life as completely as a misplaced lipstick. She had always seen herself as a very Modern Girl and taken for granted that that was the only *cool* thing to be: very hip, very trendy, like *Seventeen* with a brand-new issue every single month, full of new looks and new ideas, whose entire claim to beauty was often only that they were new. America was like that: a whole culture focused on getting to the moon and getting there first. What was old was dingy, fuddy-duddy— your parents.

But in France there was such a sense of oldness as *antiquity:* castles and palaces that, even crumbling, were so much more breathtaking than any buildings America had produced; cities and cobblestoned streets that had stood for more than a thousand years; countryside where the Romans had carved roads and raised aqueducts. In America beauty could only be etched on a blank white page; here beauty was the layers history deposited by rolling in like an endless flow of tides. She would always remember how she had stood that day—before Lester's spectacular collapse—

sweating in the heat, wondering when the floats were coming, the majorettes and marching bands and Cub Scout troops. Whereas all that unfolded were column after column of uniformed soldiers and jeeps and tanks, and overhead, bomber jets flying in formation.

It was a grim parade, an unwelcome reminder of how history left scars as well as beauty as it swept past. Twenty-three years ago, Maude knew, this city had been occupied by the Nazis. To her that was a historical war, a dead war from the unreal era before her own lifetime, but here you could see in this humorless, charmless show of military force that its memory was still alive. Of course, right now America was sending young men off to war, but that, too, still seemed unreal. As an American, you had this sense of invulnerability; you knew it wasn't possible you'd have to watch the Viet Cong march through Washington, D.C. Back home, public protest against that war was only just beginning to gain momentum, and no one could yet foresee the way a war could invade a country's television sets and cause wounds equally deep and lasting.

July 27, 1967

Dear Carole,

I am writing this note while supper is cooking. Your brother went for his physical exam for the army today and was classified 1-Y. I guess that means he won't be going. I am so happy, and I know Greg is, too. It would be so terrible for them to get married and then be separated right away.

From the tone of your letters it seems that you are in better spirits and not quite so homesick. I am glad because I want you to enjoy every minute of your trip.

I'll say good-bye now and will try to write again tomorrow.

We love you very much and sure do miss you. Even your brother looks for the mail when he gets home. Take care of yourself and write to us often.

Love,
Mom, Dad, and Greg

Carole wasn't sure how badly she had really wanted to come on this trip. The other Girls were going, so it might be a good idea, and she had casually let it loose, a trial balloon, at the dinner table one night, even though she knew they didn't really have the money.

"You know we don't have that kind of money," said her mother.

"Maude's going," said Carole. Her parents liked Maude.

"Well, I think maybe we can swing it," said her father.

"*What?*" said her mother.

But then they must have talked it over, and decided it would be good for Carole to get out of the house. Carole's heart had been broken that year. She'd been going with a really nice boy all year, and then suddenly he'd dumped her.

"But, Mom," she'd wailed in her mother's arms in the kitchen, day after day, "he said he *loved* me. How could he love me and then just break up with me?"

Her mother knew no words that could relieve this kind of pain. Fresh-baked cookies and homemade lasagne were a comfort, of course, but you didn't want to ruin a girl's figure nursing her through heartbreak. Maybe this trip, with those girlfriends Carole had who were all so nice . . .

That was the thing about the Girls: The parents all liked them because they were so nice, and they all liked each other because they weren't. Whatever forbidden feelings might be just awakening in your teenage soul, you knew you could share them safely and secretly like smuggled cigarettes with the other Girls. And the Girls, just by being themselves, suggested options. You could contemplate the treachery in boys' hearts till your own grew weak and timid, or you could check out Maude over there, bouncing from boy to boy as though her heart were a pogo stick, and obviously having a great time.

So even though Carole had sworn never to fall in love again, she did slowly find herself spending more and more time in France with a very cute, clean-cut boy named Dave, from New Jersey. He'd brought his guitar with him, and the other Girls all liked him, and they spent many a summer's evening sitting outside in a circle, singing Beatles' songs, and everyone agreed that Carole's voice was particularly clear and sweet.

After three weeks in the Paris suburb, they all got on a train for Evian, a village in western France just across Lake Geneva from Switzerland, where they would stay in dorms in an old castle for the second three weeks. It was on that overnight train ride that Maude and Freckle-Faced Jim stayed up for hours talking and discovered they were soul mates, so that by the time they got to Evian, Maude had pretty much forgotten about Lester. But Carole and Dave were already trying to figure out a way to get back and forth for each other's junior proms the next spring. And as the trip began drawing to a close, instead of feeling so overwhelmingly homesick, Carole began to anticipate the regret of parting from Dave. This time, geography would administer the heartbreak, just when she'd found exactly the sort of nice boy you'd be safe settling down with, if you were the kind of girl who didn't really think leaving home was such a good idea.

Betsy had come along to France because all the other Girls were going, and she didn't want to be left behind. If she had stayed home, she would have felt lonely, in that strange, scary way that she didn't think other people felt lonely. The way your own family could make you feel, when your sister was being mean to you again, or when you came home from an evening out and discovered your parents had gone to bed without even leaving the porch light on. To Betsy, the Girls were real sisters, the sisters she would have had in a big house like the Egans' down the street that always smelled like something baking, and where there was always noise. And to have them around all day and all night, instead of for only a Saturday afternoon, was like a big sleepover that never ended.

But on the other hand, if Betsy had stayed home, she would have had Billy. Sometimes it was hard to keep smiling all the time when you noticed out of the corner of your eye that Maude was holding hands with Jim, or that Dave was looking deep into Carole's liquid brown eyes. Betsy and Billy were definitely going together, and he had promised to be waiting for her when she got back, but if she'd expected long soulful love letters, well, Billy just wasn't the poetic type.

> We had a wienie roast tonight [she wrote in her diary]. It was a lot of fun, but everyone seemed to have someone else, and there I sat all by myself. Everybody sat around and sang. Lake Geneva was extremely rough, and the lights on the other side were sparkling clearly. I was so lonely. I wish everybody could be here with me.

Evian was paradise compared to the dingy suburb. The castle was renovated inside, quite comfortable, and it sat right on the shore of Lake Geneva, with its own private beach. On clear days you could see the picturesque little Swiss towns on the other side of the lake, and Evian itself was so much more beautiful than where they had been, and the patisseries so much more inviting you could never decide what to choose.

But Tammy was still looking for something cold to drink. On the dinner tables each night were bottles of the Evian spring-

water that was not yet an international status symbol. Tammy
tasted it: Yeah, so it was water, and it was *warm*. Tammy wrote
home: *Send Kool-Aid*. So for the last week, the Frenchwomen
who served their dinners looked on aghast as the Girls emptied
envelopes of brightly colored powder into the water bottles.

One of the last nights, there was a talent show. Carole sang, accompanied by Dave, and afterward they all passed around their
French exercise books, like autograph books, to sign.

[From Carole's notebook:]

To Carole—The girl with the best voice on campus.

                                        Lester

To the Girl! I had a lot fun this summer, thanks to you. Good luck.

                                        Love
                                        Rod

My feelings toward you cannot be put to words. I liked you from the first
time I saw you. I'm sorry that our time together was so short, and believe
me, I have never said that to any girl before.

    I'd like to keep up our relationship as long as possible but please
don't feel obligated to me, just let me know how far you want it to go,
or, if you want to end it, just say so.

    If you do want to keep going, remember that where there's a will
there's a way, and there's a will on this end. You're not really that far
away, and I'm positive we'll get to see each other again, if we try. So,
until you get a letter from me

                            votre toujours,
                            with love,
                            Dave

Dear Carrie,

I'm so glad you came on this trip—for your sake & mine. Never give up
loving—it's the best thing goin! We've all grown & changed during this
trip. I know you'll grow—but please don't ever change. I'll never forget the
confidences we've shared. We'll be friends forever because of that and
so many other things. I love you like a sister—don't ever forget you can
come to me for everything & anything—I promise I'll never let you down—
and we will meet again—in that free society we know will come to be.

Love forever & ever

Maude

When their plane touched down back in America, the Girls let
out a big cheer, except Maude, who burst into tears. Everyone
else, she thought, had a good reason to want to be home: Tammy
and Betsy were coming back to steady boyfriends; Carole had
missed her parents so badly; and Donna was just relieved not to
have to negotiate every single goddamn day with strange people
who insisted on conducting all their business in that incompre-
hensible language.

But Maude had nothing calling her home. She had crossed an
ocean now, just like her Forebears, and her soul had expanded,
just as she'd hoped it would, to encompass the subtleties of
l'amour and ripe Brie cheese, and now it was going to have to
contract again, to the proper size for a plain old American
schoolgirl. If all the world was a stage, then Maude had just discovered that the stage was much bigger than she'd ever dreamed
possible. Home had shrunk to the size of a doll's house, and
somehow she was going to have to cram herself back into it. Until she could come up with a way to get out. For good.

First Comes Love

1967–1971

Fractured Fairy Tales

At the moment in December of 1967 when the marine band in the East Room of the White House struck up Mendelssohn's "Wedding March," all America—at least according to *Newsweek* magazine—breathed a collective sigh of relief. For "Lynda Bird Johnson's wedding day had come at last, and come in triumph." The president and Lady Bird looked on fondly, along with five hundred guests, as handsome marine captain Charles Spittal Robb and the president's daughter exchanged vows and were pronounced "man" and "wife." What made this $63,000, celebrity-studded wedding so triumphant, *Newsweek* explained, was that it was a day, "not only for Lynda, but for all the solemn, bypassed older sisters who ever kept a tremulous upper lip while a kid sister dashed to the altar ahead of them."

For a long time, tall, overweight, self-conscious Lynda had been upstaged by her younger, prettier, flightier sister, Luci, who, at twenty, had not only already snagged a handsome mate but had also, just that spring, produced the president's first grandson. When she had been only eleven and Lynda fourteen, Luci had introduced herself to at least one acquaintance by saying,

"Hi, I'm Luci and this is Lynda, my older sister who doesn't go steady." President Johnson, *Newsweek* reported, had once told friends that he "had no worries about either of his daughters, since pert, vivacious Luci would always have a man around to take care of her and solemn, serious Lynda could always make good in a career. That stung, friends say. . . ."

Lynda had gone through school and college "with her cap set on a straight-A course," which the magazine implied highlighted her failure to find anything more romantic or feminine to do with her time. "She was a tall girl who never quite learned how to carry herself," the magazine quoted an unnamed former college acquaintance as saying. "At school she never had clothes that fit her nicely, and she didn't know how to put a comb in her hair and make it look like something." It was to escape her awkwardness, according to *Newsweek*, that Lynda sought "consolation in books and bookishness." Meanwhile, vivacious Luci "squeaked through school with remedial reading help and special tutoring," merrily baking brownies out in the kitchen while Lynda studied, and "it was generally Luci who had the boyfriends."

It didn't seem to count somehow that as Lynda moved from academic success into a job as a columnist for *McCall's* magazine, she had actually been involved in a steady stream of press-documented romances with attractive, accomplished men. The clock was ticking, and, as far as anyone knew, no one had ever proposed. It appeared that the president's daughter was, at twenty-two, headed very publicly into the pathetic Land where women were No Man's.

Then, in the nick of time, a Fairy Godmother intervened. In late 1965, deeply tanned movie star George Hamilton, then only twenty-seven, began dating Lynda, and, according to a family friend, "took her under his wing and made her over." Literally. Early in 1966, Hamilton booked her an appointment with George Masters, "one of Hollywood's leading makeup artists," who had worked with Marilyn Monroe, Rita Hayworth, and Mia Farrow, among others. Masters himself reported—in a special boxed feature accompanying *Newsweek*'s wedding coverage—that he had "shaved her eyebrows and waxed her hairline to change the shape of her face. Then I raised and arched her eyebrows to open her eyes and I used two and a half sets of eyelashes. I shaded her nose to make it look smaller and to soften the lines around her mouth. And I shaded her cheeks."

Whooosh went the magic wand, and not a moment too soon. The newly glamorous Lynda was Hamilton's date for the nationally televised Academy Awards ceremony. As the TV cameras "picked her out of the audience, there was a collective gasp of admiration from the Johnson family watching in Washington. And no one was more thrilled than Luci, who dashed to the phone to tell friends, 'That's my sister. Isn't she gorgeous?' "

According to another unidentified friend, "That climaxed the remaking of Lynda." Everyone, apparently, was quite relieved that "for the first time in her life she let a man take the lead, take care of her, tell her what to do." But, unfortunately, Lynda began to see that Hamilton, like all his predecessors, "had no intention of letting a good time turn into marriage."

But it was just at this point, before she had fully broken off the relationship with Hamilton, that Chuck Robb, a junior officer at Washington's marine barracks, came into her life. A "tall, bright, athletic young man . . . of wit, manners, discretion and slender good looks," Robb had been one of the "hand-picked bachelor officers who double as table mates and dancing partners for the unattached at White House parties." Clearly, he looked and behaved like a Prince. Even if he was neither a president like her father, nor did he send her 365 roses for Valentine's Day, as Hamilton had, nevertheless he did offer her "at least two months of married life together in their rented split-level home in Arlington, Va., before Chuck reported for a year of active duty in Vietnam."

And so, there in the "lambent gold and glitter of the East Room," everything ended happily after all. "The handsome young infantry officer turned to his bride, kissed her and whispered, 'I love you.' " Then, after a final blessing, "Captain Robb led a radiant Lynda through an arch of gleaming swords into the future."

Real Life

Tammy had given Eddie a blow job on their first date, in the summer of 1966, a year before the Girls' trip to France. She had been fifteen, he sixteen. It wasn't a very Catholic thing to do, and she couldn't even blame it on his being a Public, because he wasn't. (The nuns had warned them that the Publics were dangerous because to them the body was not *a Temple*. Therefore they did not respect the progression of physical steps by which flirtation could lead inexorably to eternal damnation.) The fact was, Eddie went to the Catholic boys' high school and should have known better than to ask. And when he *had* asked, she should've slapped him; after all, he wasn't even chasing her, she'd had to call him first. They had met at CanTeen, where local kids were encouraged to come on summer nights and listen to music and play Ping-Pong so as not to fall into delinquency (as though Ping-Pong and delinquency were mutually exclusive, a mistake in adult logic you caught on to after you knew Eddie for a while). But that night no one was really getting to know anyone, it was just big gangs of boys and girls checking each other out. Afterward, Eddie called up her friend's sister June. He took her out on a date to one of those carnivals that spring up in the parking lots of shopping centers, and she threw up all over him on the Tilt-A-Whirl, and he never called her again.

Meanwhile, Tammy had decided she wanted a boyfriend. But she wasn't going to make a big deal out of it, the way she thought most girls did, where it was all they could talk about. The way Tammy looked at it, it was kind of like a question of economics: how much energy you wanted to put into it versus how much good you were going to get out of it. The good was obvious. If you had a boyfriend, you knew all year exactly who was taking you to the prom. How much energy to put in was kind of a variable, though, and Tammy got a little queasy in math class when they started talking about variables. Frankly, Tammy had started getting queasy in math as soon as they had started on fractions, in fifth grade, and if you stopped paying attention for just the teeniest while, next thing you knew the teacher was flipping them upside down and multiplying them, or adding the bottoms without adding the tops—or was it the other way around? Anyway, Tammy probably would have been sunk that year, even in the dumb math class, if she hadn't happened to have ended up sitting next to Russell Hyatt, who everybody said was the dumbest boy in the whole school because, Christ, the kid ate paste and *crayons*. But he wasn't dumb about everything. One day as they were exchanging math homework, which saved Sister Martha the trouble of having to correct each paper herself, Russell whispered, "How many you want wrong?"

Tammy caught on right away. "Three," she whispered back. "How about you?"

He held up one finger.

Tammy rolled her eyes. "Are you *crazy*? She'll never believe that. She'll catch us!"

Russell reconsidered, then held up four fingers. The rest of the year neither of them even bothered taking math homework home; they just filled each other's papers in with what they figured was a reasonable number of mistakes as Sister Martha called the answers out from the front of the room.

So here's how the boyfriend thing was like math. You could do the whole complicated process, with all the variables, which was what Tammy felt like girls did endlessly at slumber parties and recess: *Does he like ME, or does he like HER? How do I get him to like me? Is it Puppy Love, or is it Real Love? Why did he dump me?* You could pick yourself apart, break your own heart into little pieces and then wait for them to mend.

Or, assuming you were decent-looking, which Tammy with her sky blue eyes, milkmaid skin, and pert, upturned nose figured she was, you could find a shortcut, and save a little precious energy. So Tammy called up Eddie for a date, and then she did what most girls wouldn't have been willing to. She knew a Magic Wand when she saw one, even if she never *had* seen one—let alone touched one—before that particular night in Eddie's car. There in the front seat in the dark lot where teens came to steam up the windows, Tammy stuck her neck out a little and opened her mouth wide.

And she must've been a natural, because after that Eddie started calling her up for a date every Saturday night.

Betsy had met Billy the same night Tammy met Eddie—Billy and Eddie were buddies, actually, and their whole gang was at Can-Teen that night. But Betsy didn't pay much attention to either of them. There was another guy there she had her eye on, and he called her for a date right afterward. But her parents wouldn't let her date till she was sixteen. *Please call back when I'm sixteen,* she told him, *please please.* And then, right after her sixteenth birthday, it was Billy who called, and she never heard from the other guy again.

Oh, well, not that there was anything wrong with Billy. He was really good-looking, and one of the best athletes in the boys' school, the kind of boy your parents referred to as a "fine young man." They had fun out on their dates, and other than that Betsy frankly didn't think much about him, because most of the time she was far too busy to think. High school offered so many challenges and opportunities, there was hardly a moment of her life that didn't have an activity scheduled into it; besides homework, there was student council with the other Girls, and tutoring ghetto kids one day a week, and a pen pal she corresponded with in Germany, and her job at the beauty shop, and going out with the Girls on Friday nights if Billy was going out with the boys, and in the rare event of a moment when she found herself actually at home with nothing to do, there was always a book she was in the middle of reading, and some kind of little crafts project. She especially loved paint-by-numbers kits. Unguided, she had no visual imagination; she could barely draw stick figures freehand. But she liked filling in those numbered outlines with colors, being careful not to mess outside the lines, and then watching the finished, perfect pictures emerge like magic from her merely competent fingertips.

She and Billy double-dated a lot with Tammy and Eddie. They went to drive-ins and roller rinks, parties at other kids' houses, pro hockey games where the boys bought two-dollar standing-room-only tickets and they climbed about half a mile up to the very top of the arena, under the rafters, where you could barely even stand up straight and the players looked like ants gliding around on the big white patch below.

Junior year both Billy and Eddie talked about wanting Corvettes, so for Valentine's Day Betsy and Tammy decided to make them little Corvette models. They went to a hobby shop and got model kits, and special paints so the miniatures would be the same colors as the cars the boys wanted for real, and then for a week they rushed home from school and called each other on the phone to talk each other through the assembly process.

"Betsy, what's this little part here? It looks like a cylinder with a lemon on the top."

"I don't know, Tammy. I don't have one of those."

"You *gotta* have one of those, we're makin' the same thing."

In the end, Tammy got impatient and kind of slapped hers together, coated it with paint, and hid a bunch of pieces she hadn't been able to figure out what to do with in the back of a desk drawer in case Eddie happened to notice they weren't there. But Betsy followed the instructions to the letter, taking pains with every tiny piece, until the little red car was perfect.

The boys seemed to like the cars. They laughed, like they got the joke. But then on the Fourth of July, Billy got the idea of tying a firecracker to the top of his, and they blew it up.

That's what Tammy said, anyway. Billy never mentioned that particular incident in front of Betsy.

Tammy got to take riding lessons every Sunday from fifth grade on. By high school she was jumping. She would leave the house at eight-thirty in the morning for her lesson, and then she'd stay on to help with the beginner class, and then she'd help cool down the horses and groom them. Often she wouldn't get home till three. This was her private life. It got her out of the house, where Thelma and Dorothy and Edie were constantly engaged in either all-out nuclear family warfare or periodic cold war intervals. Thelma had very definite policies about things, and sometimes these were as clear as any of the other laws of nature (for example, no straw hats or white gloves until Easter) and sometimes, well, if you couldn't figure it out for yourself, it was gonna *break Thelma's heart* to have to explain it to you. While you tried to figure it out, Thelma would withdraw into a hurt and furious silence that might last for days. Meanwhile, she phoned and visited with her own mother *every single day*, as a living model of the kind of selfless devotion that, her silences made clear, her own children failed to demonstrate.

Tammy's dad, who as a traveling sales rep was usually out of town during the week, came home on weekends never sure whether Thelma was speaking to him or not. He lived in a perpetual state of hoping that whatever had set her off last time had blown over by now and that some new cause would not yet have arisen. What the cause ever was, though, he had not the slightest idea, nor the slightest desire to find out.

Tammy got mad sometimes, thinking about the way Thelma ignored him. His job wasn't dangerous, but it required him to fly around the country on the kind of little airplane that had a tendency to crash in nasty weather, and there were several stories of flights where he had been told to loosen his tie and put his head between his knees in the crash position. Did Thelma act glad to see him when he got home alive? Well, if she was speaking to him at all she was most likely to leave the house Saturday morning with a reminder not to smoke his smelly cigar inside, and then fly out of the driveway toward the department stores with her mom in the front seat next to her and Dorothy and Edie yelling at each other in the back.

Tammy would get herself excused from the expedition by volunteering to accompany her dad on his weekly trip to the barber. So the two of them would drive off in silence—not that loaded feminine kind of silence her mother perpetuated, but a rich, companionable, masculine kind of silence, like you found at the stables very early Sunday morning. Those were the two moments of great peace she experienced on a regular weekly basis, and so the sweetest comforts of her childhood were both intimately entwined with what other people regarded as stinky smells: the stable's aromatic mix of sweaty horses and old hay, and the rich blue smoke of her father's Saturday morning cigar.

The first time he saw her on a Sunday, Eddie made a face, pinched his nose between his fingers, and said in a dramatic nasal voice, "Peee-eeeew. You smell like a horse."

Uh-oh. A variable Tammy had neglected to factor into her formula for boyfriend math: Now her body was no longer hers alone. It was disgusting enough, the smells the magazines said a girl's own body produced: Bad Breath, Body Odor, Smelly Feet, and something feminine-related that came from you-know-where. Who wanted a boyfriend going around telling people you stunk?

Tammy quit riding.

After that, Eddie started picking her up even earlier on Sundays, some ungodly hour like seven A.M., and they'd go over to the drag strip where a bunch of his friends raced. He'd spend all morning in time trials and tinkering with the engine, while Tammy sat on the grass with the other girlfriends and smoked cigarettes. Then races took all afternoon.

He'd drive her home around five, dirty and sweaty and reeking of gas and motor oil, but if he ever noticed that cars smell worse on a person's skin than horses, he never said anything. And neither did she.

That same summer, Maude started dating Ron, who worked in a record store in the shopping center and played guitar almost like a professional musician. He was eighteen and had already graduated from high school, a full grown *man* rather than a kid like the boys her friends were dating. Of course, on dates they did pretty much the same things the other girls were doing: movies, the beach, cheap burgers. They kissed with their mouths closed. It was quite sophisticated, Maude felt, without being actually loose.

Maude, still only fifteen, had been forbidden by her parents to visit the bachelor pad that Ron shared with his two high school pals, Mike and Brad. Mike and Brad were good-looking bad news. They worked nights for an airline, cleaning out planes, and then slept most of the day away. They had parties with wild girlfriends and drank a lot, and when they drank, they'd start cooking up schemes for pranks they could pull, things they could steal. The entire apartment was furnished with tables and chairs and lamps they'd smuggled out of the hotel where Mike used to work. At Christmas they festooned the place with blinking lights and nativity displays they'd stolen off neighborhood bushes and lawns during their drunken midnight crusades.

Maude felt demeaned by her parental prohibition. She felt it implied that she did not have the maturity necessary to take responsibility for her own behavior. Really, if she and Ron wanted to get into trouble, they could do that in his car, or in a hotel for that matter. The point was, she had no intention of doing anything immoral and neither did he. So what was the harm of stopping in sometimes and being entertained by the outrageous antics of Mike and Brad?

Brad was also an outrageous flirt. It was his true gift, as Ron's was music: He could pick up a woman the way Ron picked up a guitar and play her till she was beautiful, regardless of what she had looked like or felt like before he came along. One day at the apartment he pulled Maude aside and said, "What are you doing with Ron? He's so boring." Then his eyes narrowed and he made a whistling noise between his teeth and said, "And you're just gorgeous." And then he kissed her.

Oh dear. That was the end of Ron. What was Maude supposed to do? She'd come home from school in her high school uniform—a plaid skirt now, with a white blouse and a blue blazer—that kept the girls so innocent and anonymous, camouflaged their ripening bodies and made them appear almost as identical and selfless and sexless as the nuns, and she'd get a call from Brad: "I'm taking you into the City for dinner Friday. Wear heels." And he would whisk her off downtown to some restaurant where candles flickered in Chianti bottles on the tables and buy her an expensive dinner, and for that one night she would be magically transformed into what neither the nuns nor the Girls had the power to make her: *a woman.*

The trouble was, he didn't always call, and she was pretty sure why. In the car at the ends of dates, his hands roamed freely on her body, man's hands out hunting big game, not boy's hands on a little fishing expedition. She was nun-trained. Sister Agnes had actually locked the classroom door before imparting the delicate metaphorical information the nuns thought the girls needed to protect themselves: Your virginity is a gift, she told them, a gift you will give your husband on your wedding day. Now, would you give someone a present that had already been unwrapped by someone else? There were other acts, other intimacies, that were also appropriate only in the marital relationship. If you merely technically preserved your virginity, but indulged in these other acts with boys you dated, then it would be as if on your wedding night you presented your husband with a package whose ribbons and wrappings were soiled and ripped.

It wasn't that these acts would not be pleasurable to you. You would be tempted, and that's what made this hard. But it was your responsibility to slow the boy down, Sister Agnes said, launching into a new metaphor, because your sexuality was like an iron, which, once plugged in, heated up slowly. Whereas his was like a light switch: On, and Off.

So when Maude felt herself warming—going from, say, Delicates to Cottons—she would sit up abruptly and switch Brad to Off. In the beginning he was pretty good-natured about it, but she suspected this was because he had other outlets. And then, after a while of this, he told her that he loved her but just couldn't go on seeing her.

She cried, and wrote sad love poems that didn't rhyme about how he was the one true love of her life and she would never get over him. Then there was Mark, and then Fred, and then Tom, and after a while she'd almost forgotten that she would never get over Brad.

But once a year or so, Brad would call and ask her to spend a

day with him, and she would go, and every time she would magically turn for those few hours into the mature alluring woman he
saw in her, the person no other boy was powerful enough to
make her become. Then he would disappear for another year. He
seemed to be checking on her, the way you would check on a
cake in the oven, pressing your fingertip lightly into the top, to
see if it was done yet.

Junior year, Tammy, for whom going to the prom was more or
less the whole payoff for maintaining a boyfriend, was crest-
fallen to hear that Eddie would not be allowed to attend his own.
A disciplinary act of some kind on the part of the school; as
usual, Eddie was in trouble. It was particularly upsetting since
Tammy had heard that The Bojangles were playing and she really, *really* wanted to hear them. Luckily, a week before the
prom, she met another boy at a dance at her school who asked if
she wanted to go with him, and she said, "Sure."

Eddie flipped out when she told him. He hung up the phone
and raced right over to her house, where he probably would've
started yelling and screaming, except that since her mother happened to be sitting right there at the kitchen table, he didn't.
Instead, he gravely warned her mother not to let this *jerk*—
whoever he was—take Tammy out of the house if he had liquor
on his breath. Her mother had a good laugh about this after he
left, which apparently meant she had noticed that Eddie had
liquor on *his* breath about 75 percent of the time.

And even though they weren't going steady, Tammy felt guilty
enough about the situation that instead of going somewhere
with the guy after they'd left the prom, she told him her parents
had insisted she come right home. Was it possible that Eddie
could've been spying on the house? Because she could swear
she had not been home more than five minutes before the phone
started to ring and ring.

*   *   *

Nobody asked Donna to the prom junior year, and that was embarrassing, because Donna was class president. Finally the Girls fixed her up with someone. "Hey, thanks for takin' care of me," she said afterward. "I never forget a favor."

The truth was, Donna was a born politician, the old-style kind who knew instinctively how to consolidate grassroots power and get things done. When the junior girls complained that they couldn't get their public school boyfriends into the gym for dances, Donna didn't go plead with Sister Mary William to change the rules. She just stationed herself at the back door of the gym for the next dance and quietly let the girls with Publics in that way. Sure, Donna had spunk, but she'd learned in a million small ways by now that confronting authority didn't usually get a girl anywhere. At home, her dad no longer found their power struggles cute.

"Dad, you can't yell at me like that, because I have rights."

"Whaddya mean, you got rights? You got no rights in this family. You got the rights I tell you you got."

"That's not true, Dad. For instance, parents aren't allowed to hit kids."

"Hey, come over here and tell your mother what you just said. Hey, Irene, come listen to this little *Communist* we got here. You know, Donna, you got too much goddamn education for your own good."

The question was, what was all the goddamn education supposed to be for? One day her mom would be warning her not to waste her life: "Don't be a secretary, Donna, be the boss. Don't be a nurse, be the doctor." And the next she'd be saying, "Whaddya wanna go to college for? You're gonna get married and have kids anyway, so don't waste anybody's time and money."

The nuns acted like the girls were all destined to grow up to be brain surgeons. There was a saying painted on the wall outside

Sister Mary William's office in Day-Glo orange lettering: PEOPLE
HAVE THE NEED TO BE WHAT THEY HAVE THE ABILITY TO BE. But what
the nuns really wanted—just like their parents—was obedience.

Ironically, at that exact moment in history, nuns all over the
world had begun to challenge the authority of the Catholic
Church. In December 1967, the week after it covered Lynda Bird
Johnson Robb's wedding, *Newsweek* ran a cover story entitled
"THE NUN: A Joyous Revolution." Like women everywhere,
nuns had apparently decided that they didn't want to grow up
just like their Mothers. Nor did they want to do what their Fathers told them to. These days, *Newsweek* reported, "the purely
masculine way of running the church no longer seems to work
so well." Nuns were making themselves over: "The tall head-
dresses, starched wimples and flowing robes that long symbol-
ized the nuns' 'no' to secular society are beginning to disappear,"
the magazine reported. "As the cloister door swings open, there
is a new sense of sisterhood—of feminine love—toward the human family. There is also a refreshing militancy." Nuns were de-
serting their orders in droves—two thousand in the previous
year alone—and those who remained were questioning everything from whether the all-male hierarchy was exploiting them
as a cheap and "convenient labor source" for the Catholic school
system, to whether their ancient vows of "poverty, chastity, and
obedience" should be edited down to a vaguer "total availability
to God and people."

But in the halls of St. Mary Magdalen High School, no one
seemed to find even mild militance refreshing. When the junior
girls came to Donna complaining that Sister Mary William
wouldn't give them class rings till senior year because she said
they hadn't really earned them yet, Donna thought, Maybe Sister
doesn't realize how much the rings mean to everyone. So by the
next morning's eight o'clock bell, she had three hundred student
letters on Sister's desk.

At approximately 8:10, Sister's stern voice came over the PA system: "Donna DeMarco, please report to the office."

The good news was, Sister gave in about the rings. The bad news was, she was furious with Donna. She bawled her out and told her never to pull a stunt like that again, and the next year at graduation when Sister gave out awards to the class's outstanding leaders, Donna didn't get one. Of all the things she learned in school, it was probably this lesson in how the world didn't really need Donna DeMarco's opinion that stuck with her, and made her think that her brain, like her overdeveloped, overpadded body, was going to function as an enormous danger zone in her life, if she couldn't somehow cut it down to be like everyone else's.

On the way home from a party one night, a car full of boys flagged down the car full of girls Donna was riding in, and they all pulled over and exchanged phone numbers. Typically, after a couple of double dates, the guy who'd paired up with Donna— Ralph—lost interest, but the guy who'd paired up with Donna's friend Gail was still calling her, and so was another friend of Ralph's, a scrawny, hungry-looking boy named Stan. One night they both called Gail for a date, and Gail, giggling, called Donna to ask what she should do.

"Have 'em both over together," Donna said gamely. "I'll come over and eat popcorn and watch."

But then a miracle occurred. The scrawny boy, the friend of Ralph's, just kept staring at Donna with this stupid smile on his face till finally he got her alone, and then he asked if he could hold her hand.

"Hey," said Donna, "I thought you wanted to date Gail."

"No," said Stan. "I've been in love with you since before I met you."

"Eat shit and die," said Donna. "What are you talkin' about?"

"Aw, Donna, please don't use that kinda bad words. Listen, Ralph showed a bunch of us your picture, and the minute I saw it, I knew you were the girl for me."

He meant it, apparently. He kept calling and coming over to visit, even though all Donna talked about in the beginning was how broken up she was about losing Ralph. He'd listen to her go on about how crazy she was about Ralph, and then he'd go on about how crazy he was about her, and after a while it got through to her that he either didn't understand or didn't care that she was too big and too smart and too smart-ass for a guy like him.

Her mom and dad didn't like him. He was poor and hadn't lived next door for twenty years and he wasn't all that bright. What he did have was a kind of dumb animal persistence and a deep unconditional adoration of Donna. After her father had twice refused them permission to marry, Stan told her: "I'll ask him one more time, and if he says no, you better run away with me."

"If he says no," said Donna, "there ain't no way I'm gonna run away with you because he'll come after us and kill us both."

But on the third try, Donna's dad relented. "Donna," he said, "when you walk into a room, his face totally lights up. Anyone who worships my baby like that is good enough for me."

So it was settled, just like that, the efficient transfer of Donna from father to husband—a relief to all of them. Senior year Donna pretty much retired from both her extracurricular and social lives, in what should have been the triumph of her engagement, but she felt a bit mysteriously and disappointingly numb. No point in political struggles with the nuns now, since they didn't appreciate her leadership abilities anyway. No point in studying too hard, since she wouldn't be going on to college. Why bother, when Stan was putting himself through truck-driving school so they'd be able to get union wages and union insurance? No point, really, in even spending time with the Girls. She'd always felt herself to be an outsider to the core group of

Maude, Betsy, Tammy, and Carole. She'd always felt dumber than them (well, maybe not dumber than Tammy, but Tammy had a kind of social cool that made up for her lack of academic talent). She'd never felt as naturally, effortlessly popular. She'd always felt they understood some secret she did not, the secret of being the In Crowd, the secret of belonging. For a while, she'd hoped that by attaching herself to them, she'd become like them. But that didn't seem to matter so much anymore, now that she belonged to Stan. It was more of an achievement to have a boy pick you out, any boy, than to be picked out by even the most popular of girls, and no one—not her family, not her friends, not even herself—had ever really dared hope it would happen to her.

She spent almost all her free time now with Stan. On Friday nights, they'd buy a pound of bologna and a loaf of white bread and just go sit somewhere, at a playground or on a park bench, and talk for hours. Actually, Donna did most of the talking. Once in a while, she'd pause and look at Stan and ask, "Do you know what I'm saying here?" And Stan would just *beam* at her, like she was Einstein himself, and say, "Sure, Donna." He was never much more specific than that, so Donna was never quite completely convinced that he *did* understand what she was saying, but so what? It was the beam that counted. It was the beam that bathed Donna in the glow of an uncritical adoration she had never gotten anywhere else. What was Stan getting out of the conversation? she wondered from time to time. Maybe he was just sitting there politely waiting for the making out. But that was okay, because Donna liked that part, too; it was its own sort of beaming: the adoration he lavished so uncritically on the big body she herself hated. It was a potent combination, the adoration and the making out, potent enough to render her parents' standing offer of four years at a Catholic girls' college preposterous.

Still, her parents made her wait two years after high school graduation to marry him, hoping she'd somehow change her mind. But she never doubted the wisdom of letting herself be chosen for wifehood. By the time of the actual wedding, she hadn't heard from any of the Girls in so long that it didn't even occur to her to invite them. High school was history to her by then, and girlfriends but a frivolous circumstance of youth.

The night before the wedding, she and Stan were out in his car in front of her house, and she surprised herself by telling him, "Ya know, I think I'm gonna be a baby factory."

Now, where had that come from? She had never in her life either played with a doll or imagined herself growing up to have babies. But Stan was clearly pleased, and was trying to tell her so when midnight struck and, like a cuckoo, her mother shot out of the house and onto the porch and yelled, "Get in here, Donna, it's twelve o'clock."

Donna rolled down the car window. "For Chrissake, Ma, I'm gettin' married tomorrow."

"Yeah, that's tomorrow. This is NOW. Get your ass in this house."

Donna came in, wondering why her mom was so angry. "You know, you're throwin' your life away," her mother said as she headed up the stairs. "You coulda had the world if you'da stayed single. We woulda sent you to college, we woulda sent you back to Europe . . ."

"Yeah right," said Donna. "You'da kept me in prison."

"Donna," said her mother, with a look full of bitterness and gall, like a crone spitting out her final curse, "you're on your way to prison right this very second."

Sometimes there was magic, the kind that made you think against your better judgment that everything was going to work out fine. In the winter of junior year, Sister came on the PA system one morning and said, "Just a reminder, girls, that the senior ski trip is scheduled for this weekend, and as yet we have no snow on the ground. So, girls, pray for snow."

Well, if three hundred letters on Sister's desk could derail the straight and narrow of Sister's judgment about class rings, just imagine what four hundred earnest pleas direct to heaven could produce in terms of snow. Friday morning the flakes started dancing daintily down from low gray clouds, first tentatively, then with more conviction, and by early afternoon so hard and fast that school had to be dismissed early because the municipal snowplows couldn't keep up. By Friday night there was so much snow on the ground that Sister actually had to cancel the senior ski trip because there was no possibility that the buses would make it through.

Nothing got through. Cars parked on the streets were buried under great drifts, and Tammy's aunt, who had been invited for dinner Friday, had to leave her car on the main drag five blocks away and pick her way slowly through the Siberian landscape. Inside it was cozy and warm. Tammy's dad said, "As long as we've got booze and cigarettes, and milk and bread for the kids, we'll be okay." They played cards and watched TV, and when late in the evening the doorbell rang, they all looked at each other in surprise: Who the *hell* would come out on a night like this?

Well *surprise!*, it was Eddie, with Betsy and Billy, all bundled up like refugees, laughing and throwing snowballs and singing Christmas carols, and Tammy went out with them into the unreal brightness and stillness of the snowy night, to stamp deep footprints across the nearly erased neighborhood.

But as time went along, Eddie only got more Eddie. When he found out Tammy was flirting with some other guy who hung around Maude's house, he followed her there one evening, drunk, and stood pounding at the front door, yelling, "Tammy, get out here. Get the fuck out here."

Maude pushed the other boy into the bathroom and then opened the front door and faced Eddie down: "Whatcha screamin' about, Eddie? There's nobody else here but us girls."

Later, when Eddie was sober and somewhat calmer, Tammy told him, "Ya know, we're not goin' steady. I can see other people."

So, about a week later, Eddie came over and casually pulled something out of his pants pockets to show her. "I got my class ring," he mumbled.

Tammy turned it over once in her hand and then gave it back to him.

"Well, that's nice," she said.

He looked at her like maybe she was deaf or retarded or something, and finally said, "You don't want it?"

Aw shit, she thought. How about something a little . . . like . . . *finesseful*? One part of her wanted to say, "Do whatever the hell you want with it." But something stopped her, a little voice that whispered that he had picked her out and maybe she should be grateful. That maybe she wasn't such hot stuff, maybe no other boy would be as dogged in his pursuit of her. Who or what would she be holding out for?

So she said blandly, "Well, sure."

After that, it somehow got easier and easier just to sink further into the relationship, even though the episodes with Eddie's drinking and his temper got worse and worse. Once, out driving drunk, he hit a tree—then kept on driving till the police caught him. The cops got to know him. Another time, on a particularly frigid winter night, when they'd gone out for a bite to eat after a school dance and were sitting in Eddie's car in the now empty school lot waiting for the engine to warm up, the cops came along and, recognizing Eddie, hauled them both into jail for curfew violation.

He threw tantrums when she wouldn't do what he wanted.

"Let's go to the movies Saturday."

"I can't. I gotta go to my gramma's house."

"Whyncha just tell your mom you don't wanna go?"

"I can't tell her that," Tammy said, casting about for a legitimate reason. But all she could come up with was, " 'Cause, actually, I wanna go."

"Oooooh," said Eddie triumphantly. " 'Cause I guess *they're* more important to you than me."

Well, DUH, thought Tammy, I *have* been living with them my whole life, but she didn't say that. Now he wouldn't call her for a few days just to punish her, like she really cared. Actually, she accepted these silences as normal, because they were just like Thelma's long, accusing ones. The difference was, with her mother it was always Tammy who had to go begging for forgiveness, to patch things up, whereas Eddie always eventually broke down and came begging to her: "Aw, come on, let's forget about it, okay?" He would promise, swear, that whatever it was that had happened—which sometimes he couldn't exactly remember, because he'd been too drunk—would never happen again. This was exciting in the beginning, because boys never apologize. They must really *seriously* love you if they're willing to apologize. But then eventually she discovered that the apologies were empty, that whatever-it-was would always happen again, no matter what he'd promised.

The one time she refused him—the one time she told him outright that she was breaking up with him—he stopped his begging and pleading, and his eyes grew cold and mean, and he said, "Tammy, if you do that, I'll make sure you're blackballed in this town, I'll make sure nobody ever dates you again."

Could he do that? Would he tell people she was dumb? Would he tell people she stunk? Would he tell people what it was they were up to *now* under the cover of darkness and behind the steamed-up windows of his secondhand car? And would he tell people that *she liked it*?

So they picked out an engagement ring. It came with Green Stamps. So they picked out a card table and chairs, the centerpiece of a married social life.

A couple of weeks before the wedding, there was another incident, another fight, and after Eddie stomped off, Tammy felt a sudden surge of hope, the condemned prisoner's last-minute glimpse of reprieve.

She grabbed her coat and said to her mother, "If he calls, tell him I'm not home."

"Where should I tell him you went?"

"I don't care. Tell him I went crazy. Tell him I went to the moon."

Her mother snapped: "Oh, no, you don't. There's *money* down on this wedding. We paid a deposit on the hotel, on the band. . . ."

Tammy covered her ears and ran out of the house. From a pay phone she called Betsy, who came out to meet her at the Howard Johnson's the Girls referred to as St. Howies, because they often met there on Sundays for coffee when their parents were under the impression they had gone to Mass. Betsy was home on Christmas break from her freshman year of college. She was spunky, Betsy. She had enrolled in the college of business management, which was all guys, instead of the college of business education, where girls usually enrolled because a career teaching typing and shorthand was much more flexible. You could always abandon it on short notice when you started a family.

"So," said Tammy, stirring cream and sugar into her coffee. "That place must be crawlin' with cute guys. Ya gettin' any action?"

Betsy frowned, then reached into her pocket and brought out a ring with a small but definite diamond.

"Hey, Billy finally came through," said Tammy. "So, how come you're not wearin' it?"

Betsy shrugged, then slipped it on her finger. "I do wear it," she said. "Usually."

Tammy wondered what that meant, but she didn't ask. Betsy didn't always tell you everything about everything, the way some of the Girls did, and Tammy understood that because she didn't either.

"So, what *are* you gonna do when you start a family?" Tammy asked.

Typically, Betsy was prepared. Betsy had a Plan. "Well, I don't think it would be fair to get a job with a company right after graduation and have them invest their time and money in me and then have to leave," she explained. "So I think I'll probably get pregnant senior year so I can have the baby as soon as possible after graduation, and then we'll probably have another one within two years. I don't think you should have more than two, because there's such a population problem. And then when they're both in school most of the day, I'll still be pretty young and that's when I'll get started with a company."

"Sheeesh," said Tammy, a little wistfully. "I wish I could get it all thought out like that."

"Well, you could still go to college. It's not too late, you know."

"Aw, Christ, I couldn't do that," said Tammy. "I'm too dumb and too lazy. Besides, they wouldn't send me anywhere but a girls' college, and who needs that once you've—you know. . . ."

Betsy looked at her shyly and said, "Tammy, in high school, when you used to tell me in the hall that you'd got your little 'friend' this month, were you saying that because you and Eddie were already . . . um . . . ?"

Tammy shrugged and said, "Well, sure, aren't you guys?"

Betsy shrugged noncommittally. At college, she knew, girls all around her were doing it all the time, which had pretty much disabused her of the idea that God would find out and send you straight to hell. More terrifying, though, was the possibility that the college would find out, or that your parents would find out, or that you'd get yourself pregnant and have to go off in secret somewhere to have the baby, and that would be the end of your Plan. She admired Tammy, who didn't seem to need a Plan, who didn't seem to need to be always kicking just to keep her head above water, as Betsy did; who just seemed content to float along on the surface of life as it was.

"So, you'll be married this time next week," said Betsy.

"I guess," said Tammy. "I mean, we got money down on the hotel, and the band. . . ."

A week later, on the morning of the wedding, Tammy's sister found her in the kitchen in her ratty bathrobe, with big pink curlers in her hair, munching on a bologna sandwich.

"Whaddya doin'?" her sister asked.

"Whatsit look like I'm doin', I'm eatin' a baloney samwich."

"You're gettin' married in a coupla hours and you're eatin' a baloney samwich? Aren't you too excited?"

"Aaaaagh," said Tammy, who was about to cleave unto Eddie in a union the Catholic Church said could *never* be torn asunder. "It's no big deal."

Betsy, Carole, and Maude all came home from college for Tammy's wedding—Maude from Downstate, where a scholarship had led her, and Betsy and Carole from Upstate, whence they had been led by—um—love.

Betsy's Billy had started at Upstate in 1969, the year the Girls were still high school seniors. That was reason enough for Betsy to follow, without needing to think too seriously about other schools. You were talking efficiency, here: This way, she wouldn't have to delay or forgo college for marriage, as Tammy was doing. This way, instead of working some crummy job till you had children, you'd be working toward a degree that would make you more marketable somewhere down the line, when you got to that step in the Plan.

Frankly, the Plan hadn't originally been built to accommodate marriage or Billy. It had been incubating inside Betsy's head since she was eight or nine, when she had realized—though she would not have phrased it in exactly these words—that a Fairy God-mother probably wouldn't ever come for her. It was a nice idea, it might work for lucky girls: Up gallops the horse with the wealthy, handsome prince who takes care of you and loves you for the rest of your days. But honestly, in Betsy's experience, you were in this thing alone, what you got in life you got for yourself. Billy's insistent pursuit of her surprised her. Despite the swarm of boys usually buzzing around her, she never felt that she had fallen in love with anyone. She expected that if she were capable of it, it would have happened by now, the way it had happened to all the other Girls. She probably did love Billy and just didn't think about it that way, and anyway, if he really was going to stick around, there was no reason she couldn't alter the Plan in order to include a house she had sometimes dreamed of, a house as full of life as her own childhood house had been empty of it, with all the kids from up and down the block visiting and cookies in the oven.

Unfortunately, just as Step One of the Plan was ready to go into operation—just as she was preparing to leave home for the first time to join Billy at Upstate—Billy got kicked out, and had to come home. He had flunked practically everything freshman year. You could hardly blame him, he said. It had been pretty time-consuming to come home and visit her every other weekend, what with the four-hour drive each way. It had really eaten into his study time. Now he would have to live with his parents and take courses at the local junior college till he got his grades up enough to get readmitted.

Meanwhile, instead of their being together at Upstate that year, now Betsy was catching a ride home every other weekend to visit Billy. The drives *were* very long. Luckily, through a notice on a bulletin board, Betsy was able to make a regular arrangement with a guy named Howard who needed to make weekly trips back to the City to help his recently widowed mother run the business she'd suddenly inherited.

Betsy liked Howard. Because the possibility of romance had been ruled out from the beginning—obviously, Betsy told Howard first thing about the reason for all these trips home— they developed an easy friendship. Betsy realized she'd never actually just *talked* to a boy before. Somehow, she had always felt they were all too busy sizing each other up. There were all kinds of cute, pert, witty things you would say to intrigue guys, even if you didn't need them, even if you didn't want them, just for the satisfaction of ensuring that they were interested in you. But no one could keep up that level of flirtatiousness for four hours straight, twice a weekend, two times a month. Instead they talked about whatever came into their heads: books they were reading, classes they were taking, stuff that happened in the dorm. Eventually, she even told him about the Plan. He told her about his mother and the business and what it was like to step into his father's shoes at this young age. Like me, she thought, he's going it alone.

Then, over Christmas break, Billy produced an engagement ring. He actually got down on one knee and asked to marry her, which was touching. Of course, she said. Then, just before Howard's car pulled up to her house to pick her up for the drive back to campus, Betsy slipped the ring off her finger and into her pocket. And when Howard said, "How was your Christmas break?" she told him all about Tammy's wedding, but not about Billy's proposal.

It was very cold that winter, and the old car's heater didn't work well, so they got in the habit of sitting close together on the front seat for warmth. By now they had also gotten in the habit of sup-plementing their long car conversations with long phone conver-sations on dorm pay phones, and one day they were talking about a movie that was showing on campus that they both wanted to see, and it seemed natural to make a plan to go together.

But when they met, there was a weird tension between them that was never between them in the car. Howard took her hand and said solemnly, "This isn't just a movie, is it? It's a date." And Betsy, whose engagement ring was at that moment in a little box in the bottom of her underwear drawer back at the dorm, didn't know what to say.

She called Billy and broke off the engagement.

"Are you in love with this guy?" Billy demanded.

"I don't know."

"Are you in love with *me?*"

There was a pause—too long—before Betsy replied, miser-ably, "I don't know."

Then all hell broke loose. Howard stopped calling her, or re-turning her phone calls. Billy's parents called her a few days later, hysterical, to report that Billy had disappeared.

"He took our car and closed out his bank account," his mother said. "It's not like him. He's not erratic."

Finally, a Valentine's Day card arrived from Billy. He wrote that he was camped out in a friend's dorm at another college. The card was sitting on her dresser when Howard finally showed up at her room, saying he needed to talk to her. Howard picked up the card and read the message Billy had scrawled: "I'm just not willing to share you."

Howard put his arms around Betsy. He told her that he'd been in love once before, and the girl had been taken away from him by some other boy, so he knew what that felt like.

"And there's no way," he said, "that I can do to some other guy what that guy did to me."

Then he kissed her and walked out.

Betsy felt numb. She had the sense of finding herself in the middle of a tightrope with the safety net yanked suddenly away. Don't panic, she thought, and whatever you do, don't look down. Down was empty, there was lots and lots of nothing there: raw time where first Billy, then Howard, had been, and now no one was, not even her. Maybe this was it, the big empty place her mother had once alluded to, where you would fall and there would need to be the thing for you to fall back on. But now she could sense, without even really looking, that this place was much deeper than that, and that not even the Plan would be big enough to fall on safely, if she really just lost her grip and fell. There was just the perilous nothingness, and the necessity of not falling, and her certainty that she would never feel normal again.

So she didn't object when Billy called and said he wanted to come see her. On his visit, they got reengaged, and the night they did he took her to a hotel because he said he needed to know for sure that she loved him, and anyway, if they were definitely going to get married, it would be okay.

In the middle of that night, there was a fire in her dorm. It injured no one, and the firefighters got it under control before it could do much more than smoke damage to most of the rooms. But all the girls had to be evacuated and accounted for, so the college could assure the parents that everyone was safe. The phone lines were knocked out, which was unlucky because it took Betsy's roommate hours to get through to her at the hotel and tell her to hightail it over to the campus to get counted, but lucky because it also took hours for her parents to get through to inquire about her whereabouts.

Betsy took that fire very personally. She had come THIS close to getting caught. One little false move on her part, and God had blown the whistle. It didn't seem fair, when all around her girls were doing much worse, and evidently getting away with it, while Betsy was, by and large, just following this extremely mature and responsible Plan. Still, Betsy vowed to start being more perfect, so this nitpicking vindictive God would never have another excuse for hassling her.

In December 1970, a year after Tammy married Eddie, Betsy wed Billy. Instead of the traditional wedding march, they used the love theme from the smash-hit tearjerker *Romeo and Juliet,* about doomed teenage lovers, and everyone cried.

The night before the wedding, at the bachelor party, Tammy's Eddie and Betsy's Billy, boyhood best buddies, had some kind of a fight. The girls were never able to find out from either of them what it was about, but Eddie and Billy never spoke to each other again, and Eddie came home drunk and told Tammy, "You ain't goin' to that weddin' tomorrow."

"Whaddya mean I'm not goin'? She's one of my best friends. I'm goin'."

"Yeah? If you go, don't bother comin' back."

Tammy was a wife now. She had chosen this man, so she guessed she had to stick by him, even if he was nuts. Also, she had learned to do what she could to stop his tantrums before they escalated out of control. So she ended up missing Betsy's wedding, and she never could even explain to her exactly why.

But Carole was there, beaming, on the arm of the man she had now been married to for exactly one week. Maude, radiant, brought the man who would within hours—as though perhaps ignited by some sentimental wayward spark from the wedding's cozy glow—propose. Both girls were madly, deeply in love.

[Class notes from a page in Carole's school notebook, early
1968, the winter after her trip to France:]

Constitution

Preamble
   Legislature
   Executive
   Judiciary
               Dave
               David Matthew Peterson

last legislative clause

Each night I pray that what blossomed this summer won't die away,
but, as I pray, I know that my love for you could never die, just grow.

[Letter from a friend:]

July 4, 1968

Dear Carole,

I've had your letter on my mind since the morning I received
it. I'm so glad your summer is full of happiness. Dave is truly
poetic, and, Carole, I think you're really lucky. I'd envy you
horribly except that I think you deserve him. The poem is
beautiful, something so sensitive that it must have come
from one who loves you very much.

You must *really* be unbelievable this summer. You were
making people happy even before you felt you had a "purpose."
Just came naturally, I guess. I've taken to astrology ever since
I noticed this "boyfriend horoscope" I found in a magazine,
which told correctly the characters of four boys I knew rather
well. You're a Cancer:
      sensitive with a capital "S"

lacks security

love (for a Cancer) can never be a game; it is a deep, sincere, even painful experience

very vulnerable

overemotional

many colors, moods

Cancer is ruled by the Moon (patroness of chastity)

tenacity & patience, maternal love, understanding of others, extreme sensitivity & introversion. Very gentle.

influence spheres of moon: the feminine principle, the soul, the psyche, the mother, the wife, the family

influence spheres of Cancer: wealth of feeling, parenthood, the quality of "attachment"

spheres of influence of fourth (Cancer) house: the residence, place of birth, houses, landed property . . .

[From Carole's notebook:]

August 14th, 1968

Thank you for my friends:

for Maude and her deep faith, her "Sara Bernhardt" acts, her romantic nature, her ease for falling in love, and her complete honesty.

for Betsy and her hopes and dreams, her slim figure in spite of how she eats, and her intelligence.

for Tammy and her "unphoniness," her unspoiled way about everything, her coolness in any situation, and her love of her Eddie.

In these and all the friends I have, i am *heartily* grateful.

[Undated note:]

I want to say "I love you" but I want to hear it first.

SELFISH

December 9, 1968

am i really feeling inspiration or do i just think i should feel inspired
because i'm in love? or do i just think i'm in love because i'm so
physically attracted to him? it's Christmastime—time for dreams to
be realized or shattered. am i afraid that my dream will be shattered
again?—yes, but why am i so afraid? always on my guard? do i know
something that i'm afraid to tell myself? it's not that i'd rather kiss
him than talk to him, it's just that i'm afraid he'd rather kiss me than
talk to me. and i have to want what he wants or—or what?

[Undated note:]

To be anything but human would be blissful—not to feel the hurt at a
boy ignoring me, not to be misunderstood by my friends, and not to be
doubted by those i love most. If only i could be an insensitive animal,
whose only pain is physical, I would give the world. I'd be a hawk, and
i'd fly up as high and as far away as i could. When i'd come down, i'd
only be able to watch people—not feel anything for them. I'd never get
attached to anything or anyone because i would be unable to experience
any emotion . . .

June 1969

Dear Carole,

I don't know if writing this letter is going to help you as much as
it will me, but I hope it will show that I care very much for you.
Please don't misunderstand. I realize there is nothing I can do or
say to make up for what I did to you. That's not the purpose of
this letter. But I must explain what caused me to do it.

   Before I start I want to make it clear that I have never spent
a day without thinking of you; there was always some little

thing to bring back memories of the wonderful happiness you gave me. I know this sounds phoney, but I've never lied to you before, so I'd like you to put the faith you once had in me to use again and believe me when I say that when I stopped writing to you I created an emptiness that has never been filled, or ever will be, by anyone. I have felt very alone and very guilty for about seven months now.

But the question still remains, why? Maybe it was another girl? No, that's not the reason. Until April, I was never out with the same person more than twice. When the prom came up, I asked someone and have been going out with her ever since. I don't love her, and I think she realizes it. It's more or less a security arrangement on my side—someone to take to parties and dances. But that lonely feeling remains.

Did I stop loving you? I don't think I ever could.

Then what was the reason? You were. Your happiness and future. For a long time, I struggled with the belief that you were giving up too much. I did not want to believe it, but when I went to see you in August, reality hit me in the mouth. You weren't doing the things, or having the fun, of being young. You're a very loving girl, and very sensitive. You needed what I wasn't able to give—unselfish, constant love.

You'll never realize the misery I went through knowing that if I didn't let you go, I might be ruining your life, and if I did cut you off, I'd be cutting off part of my life. What I decided is obvious . . .

You've got to understand that if I had written like this before, it really wouldn't have really ended it. Writing this letter may also be a bad move . . . I feel that I shouldn't send this, that I should just let the issue lay closed, for you, anyway. I guess reading this will be opening old wounds.

Oh God, Carrie, I'm just hoping this letter will make it easier for you to understand my feelings and the reason for what I've

done. I don't expect an answer so don't worry about writing.
I'm sorry. I love you. Please forgive me.

Dave

[Undated note:]

God, help me to find something in me good enough to share with
   others.
Let my friends know my faults and help me to overcome them.
Let them see my love for them and let them love me.
And, God, if i find that i have nothing to share, let me die.

For i was born to love and be loved and if i can't do either i have no right
   to live.

When they were still high school seniors considering college
options, Betsy took Carole along on one of her visits to Billy at
Upstate. That weekend, in the glow of a bonfire at an outdoor
party organized by Billy, Carole met Josh Kaplan. With his beard
and long curly black hair and his head full of radical politics, he
struck her as dashing and exotic: an intellectual, where she was
used to good-natured jocks; a Jew, where she was used to dutiful
Catholics; from a family where the mother not only worked (as
did Carole's) but was an Artist. He read great literature and
wrote stories and poems; he was a member of the Merry
Pranksters and organized to stop the war; and he was, though
Carole didn't find out till later, tripping on acid when they met.

Anyway, it was 1969 now and the whole world was psyche-
delic. The adorable mop-top Beatles were singing hymns to
drugs, and there were neon Flower Power daisies stuck to everyone's class notebooks, and head shops right on the main street of
the little college town that reeked of patchouli and sold ten different varieties of bongs. If you weren't turned on, you were

hopelessly out of it. How exciting, to abandon her safe, cozy, conservative suburban nest for Josh's incense-permeated bohemian crash pad—a quick radical makeover of the soul, reflected outwardly by long dangling beaded earrings and bell-bottomed hip-hugger blue jeans. She applied to Upstate without looking any further and for the rest of the year she caught weekend rides with Betsy.

She let Josh, for the first time, get her stoned.

"So, you feeling anything yet?"

"Noooooo. But look up there. When the moonlight comes shinin' through the trees, doesn't it look like there's snow on all the branches?"

"Hey, Carrie—congratulations! You're fucked up!"

She fell headlong in love with him, and for the first time she was sure she was ready to share herself with someone, physically. But, of course, there was the explicit understanding that they were getting married. Taking on the outward form of a very cool hippie chick didn't automatically obliterate the superstructure of the obedient Catholic girl underneath. Also, Carole had been around the block by now, and harbored in her heart a dozing consciousness that not even the sweetest love could be relied upon to stand fast, as long as he was single.

Maude thought one of the best things about going away to college was being liberated from the dorky Catholic school uniform. Kids all over America were confronting school administrations over their right to *be themselves*, whether that meant wearing blue jeans embroidered with daisies or taking classes that were "relevant." Boys were growing their hair long, to show their nonconformity with the culture's oppressive notions of masculinity. Girls were rejecting the teased-hair-and-lipstick notion of femininity in favor of the *natural* look.

The irony, for anyone following the progress of the Natural

Look in the women's magazines, was that it wasn't something that you could attain *naturally*. It required at least as many products to cover up your body's flaws and odors and still look natural as it had before, at least if you weren't planning on repelling the opposite sex by, for example, growing fuzz all over your legs and underarms. There was Love's Baby Soft line of lotions and powders to keep you as soft and sweet-smelling as a baby (an advertising agency baby, the kind who didn't poop or spit up); Ten-O-Six or Revlon's "Natural Wonder" lotion to "discipline your complexion" invisibly; Summer Blonde by Clairol—"the gentle hair lightener you just shampoo in"—to "lighten your hair like the sun does"; and Psssssst, the miracle chemical you could spray into your hair to make it *look* clean when it wasn't.

The other flaw nature might have handed you was your native resident flesh. Voluptuous feminine attributes that might have seemed perfectly natural in the fifties, such as assertive breasts, no longer worked in the unbound aesthetic of the braless look (which, incidentally, had started appearing in the magazines purely as a sexy and provocative fashion innovation several years before it was redefined as a manifestation of hostility toward men on the part of "bra-burning feminists"). Hips and thighs that might have rested quite comfortably underneath a petticoat and an A-line skirt were now ruthlessly exposed and outlined by the miniskirt and fishnet stockings. So whatever weight you might have been carting around from a previous era had to be dropped as fast as possible. *Mademoiselle*'s January 1969 issue suggested that you take the "Bone Test" that would determine whether you were merely beautiful, or *"bone-beautiful."* If you failed, though, you could still "relax" because there were ways the look of the "naturally" bone-beautiful models in the magazines could be forced, for example, diet, exercise, pulling your tummy in, and, of course, bone-showcasing makeup ("Try a shimmering pale highlighting cream along the collarbone, slick a bit of moisturizer on elbows, wrists, and knees . . .").

Seventeen's October 1969 "Special Shape-Up Issue" urged you to "Rate Your Weight." Three very scientific-looking charts presented ideal weights, measurements, and calorie allowances for various figure types that were characterized as Slight, Ideal, and Stocky. Maude was dismayed to discover that at 140 pounds, she was 8 pounds over even the Stocky weight listed for her height of 5 feet, 7 inches. And even if she could slim herself down to the Ideal of 125, she'd *still* be a full 34 pounds fatter than Twiggy, who was only half an inch shorter. Maude invested 25 cents in a wallet-size card from the drugstore that listed the calorie counts of hundreds of "everyday foods," and embarked on what would become a largely ineffective 10-year battle to lose 15 pounds.

Of course, Maude had a few other ideas on what she wanted her life to be about. Ever since returning from France, she had begun to see that life as a whole was meant to be a sort of—Journey. And, while she accepted the notion that there were rules for how she ought to look on The Journey, she didn't for a moment believe that following these rules actually *was* The Journey. Somewhere deep inside she felt that if she kept looking, past the little suburb where the brick bungalows lined up block after block and were their owners' highest aspirations, someday she would find the magical place where all the people she read about in novels and poems and plays lived. Just as in France there had been baguettes and Brie instead of Wonder bread and Velveeta, so there must be somewhere she would find not boyfriends, but lovers; not keg parties, but cocktail parties; not a job, but a meaningful life's work.

Her only glimpse so far of such Elysian fields had been those enchanted but far-between dates with Brad, downtown. In the City, she thought, people must take all this for granted: exotic aromatic food, smoky late-night jazz, the differences between one bottle of white wine and another. That was probably where she should head as soon as she got herself through college and could pursue her great dream of becoming an actress. She didn't for a minute think that Brad himself would be the means to that life. He was essentially a suburban boy, and besides, he was far too *bad* to regard as husband material. In fact, during her junior year in high school, the law had finally caught up with him and his equally bad roommate Mike.

Another drunken inspiration, apparently: Brad thought the boat at his parents' summer house on the lake needed a bigger outboard motor; hey, why not just *steal* one from that big, well-lit showroom out on the highway?

Well, Mike's parents didn't have the money Brad's parents had, so after they got caught Mike ended up doing a year in jail and another on probation, whereas Brad's family hired a fancy lawyer who got him a break: *Four years serving your country, son, in the military outfit of your choice.* So off to the navy went Brad.

And Maude went off to Downstate. It was a very, very cool time to be in college, Maude thought. Student Power was sweeping the nation. Before her eyes, the campus she arrived at underwent a transformation from a relatively stodgy, frat- and sorority-dominated backwater into a hatchery for youth activists who were going to stop the war in Vietnam and rethink everything about education itself: what college was for, who was a good teacher, what the curriculum should cover, how the sexes should live together in the dorms—issues that until that very moment had always been considered the sacred province of grownups. When it turned out that the theater crowd at Downstate was cliquey and obnoxious, Maude dropped her career plans without much regret, because anyway, how could you make plans for what your life would be like out in the world when students were changing the world so much right now that nobody even knew what it would look like in four years? You actually felt sorry for those rather grim preprofessionals, like the premeds. They weren't spending their time getting to know people and having long philosophical conversations that went on all night, getting stoned and listening to Jefferson Airplane, and just seeing where The Journey took them.

Maude fell in love a few times freshman year, naturally, and finally went to bed with someone, and after all those years—all those boys she'd let get slowly closer and closer to unwrapping the package—sex itself was, well, initially quite disappointing. She slept with a couple of other boys just out of curiosity, but all that came of it was that, when she got home for summer vacation, she discovered she had gonorrhea.

She and Betsy both worked that summer at the candy factory where Maude's mother was also working, so they had to sneak out right under her mom's nose at lunchtime to go down to the VD clinic, in a part of town where they were the only white people, to get Maude a shot of penicillin. Still, everything would have been fine except that Maude had then written a quite vivid letter to a college friend about the entire experience—an account on which she worked hard and of which she was artistically proud, embellishing just the teeniest bit some extra-juicy details about the sexy older guys who lived in a nearby apartment complex where there was a swimming pool, which they all hung around while the guys served them drinks and gave them free dope. Then Maude went out for the evening, carelessly leaving the letter on her bed in an unsealed pink envelope.

Well, that very night, arriving home from said apartment complex, where these guys had been concocting some kind of rum punch cocktail that had required a great deal of mirthful taste testing, she was met at the front door by her parents. Her mother, holding a pink envelope in one hand, immediately sniffed her breath and demanded, "You've been drinking, haven't you?" Her father just stood there, shaking his head sadly.

"Well, yeah, I had a drink, it's not like you ever forbade me to drink. . . ."

"You need help, don't you?" her mom said. It sounded scarier somehow—more serious—than "You're in big trouble."

First, she was grounded for the entire summer. Next, she was sent to the old white-haired family doctor, who gave her another shot of penicillin and a horrible, humiliating, Victorian lecture about sex. Maude began to think that she did, indeed, need help, but not this "help" her parents thought they were offering. How could it be helpful when its obvious purpose was to clip your wings, bring you down, hold you back from The Journey? If she was going to take help at all, it was going to be from someone who'd actually *gone* on The Journey—probably the only person in history who had ever, without a shadow of a doubt, known what He was doing on this earth.

"That was Maude's mother," Thelma said, hanging up the kitchen phone just as Tammy arrived for their scheduled Wednesday shopping-and-lunch expedition. "She sounds very upset."

"Yeah? What's Maude up to now?"

"Well, Mrs. Chester says she's all of a sudden found Jesus. She's joined some kind of Young Christian group at college, and now she's writing her mother long preachy letters quoting passages from the Bible."

"Oh yeah?" said Tammy. "What happened to being an actress? What happened to her personally stopping the war in Vietnam?"

"Oh, Tammy," her mother sighed. "Can you imagine how they must feel about paying all that college tuition?"

Actually, Maude had belonged to Catholic youth groups all through high school, but so had practically all the other girls, because it was a kind of after-school social club that allowed you to fulfill your Catholic obligation to help the poor and suffering by tutoring and picking up trash in dirty neighborhoods. But now, sophomore year in college, she joined a prayer group of really *serious* students who analyzed Bible passages, applied them to relevant situations from their everyday lives, and prayed to the Lord for guidance. She threw herself in completely, with the romantic abandon she had formerly reserved for Love. (And being an actress. And being against the war.) It was definitely the most important thing about her now, that she was a Christian. It distinguished her radicalism from the plain old hippy radicalism of which her parents unfairly suspected her. The true hippies were amoral, they were dropouts looking for free drugs and sex. But Maude studied hard, and she paid for her pot. Usually. And she understood now, after numerous all-night discussions with the other young people in her prayer group, that yes, God wanted her to have sex eventually, he wanted her to have *great* sex, but he wanted her to have it within the context of holy matrimony, because only that provided the atmosphere of commitment and caring that could responsibly encompass the undeniable possibility of becoming pregnant.

It was just about this time that bad, bad Brad—now lean and tanned and muscular, and even somewhat chastened by the rigors of navy life—came home on leave, and evidently determined that the cake was done.

He was home for the whole month of December, he told her, and the first thing he wanted to do was visit her. Well, even with Jesus so much on her mind, Maude could figure out what *that* meant. She called up her friend James from the prayer group, to ask if Brad could sleep at his room, because he was planning on staying the weekend. James understood completely. He and his girlfriend, Amy, had been wrestling with the same issue, he told her.

As a matter of fact, the two couples ended up over at James's pretty late, and somehow James and Amy just went to sleep on the couch, so Maude and Brad crashed on the floor. And all through the night, every time Maude rolled over or woke up, Brad would be stroking her hair, consuming her with his eyes, murmuring, "Maude, you're SO beautiful. I love you SO much."

He drove back two weeks later to pick her up for her Christmas vacation, and he showered her with Christmas presents, and on the very last day of his leave, he went as her date to Betsy's wedding. His bus was pulling out at three A.M., so from the wedding they drove straight to the Greyhound station and sat in the parking lot talking and necking.

"I can't let you go," he told her. "I can't go back unless you tell me you'll marry me."

Maude, who after all the kissing and rubbing and sighing was now heated up to around Linens, pulled herself out of his embrace and tried to cool down. Finally, she told him, "Brad, you know I love you, too. And I'd really love to say yes. But I've prayed to God for a Christian husband, and I know that's what God's going to send me."

So Brad got on that Greyhound and went back to Virginia.

About a week into January, he called Maude up to share with her the good news: Brad had just found Jesus.

Once they had set the wedding date for July, they pretty much agreed that it would be okay now in God's eyes if they went to bed together. They said a private vow first: that their lives would be yoked, their finances and their families joined in the sight of God. Then they went at it.

And it was right in the middle of the act itself—with Maude sitting astride him—that Brad reached behind his head, under the pillow, brought out a little jeweler's box, took out the diamond ring, and put it on her finger.

From Brad and Maude's wedding program:

We thank You for loving us, Jesus, for caring about us, guiding our lives and giving them purpose. We thank You for the Life You have given us to feel for each other. We pray that we will always respect Your gift, and that our love will continue to grow. We pray that You will give us understanding and patience with each other and remind us always that the beauty, joy, and depth of our love comes from You. We pray that as we become husband and wife our lives will merge, and we will become one person. As one person we ask that our life, our love, and our marriage will give glory to You. We pray that every day we will look to You for guidance, and every day we will respond to your Will. Jesus, we pray that we will never lose sight of the fact that You must be the center of our lives, and that only You can keep our love alive. We ask You very humbly to bless our love, our wedding, and our marriage.

The bride and groom entered the church to Simon and Garfunkel's "To Emily Wherever I May Find Her." The men wore bell-bottomed tuxes, Maude had flowers in her long loose hair, and Carole played guitar and sang "We Are One in the Spirit." Afterward, they loaded up their new used VW bug and drove down to Brad's base in Virginia to set up housekeeping. Maude's parents were concerned, but she told them she was determined to return to college once Brad shipped out to the Mediterranean in four months.

It was 1971, and Maude, the last of the Girls to get married, had just turned twenty.

The Wives, the Babes, and the Bathwater

1970–1974

Fractured Fairy Tales

Pat was just waiting for something to happen. It was obvious that she and Bill couldn't go on like this forever, but they should probably try to hold out till all the kids had finished high school in another four or five years. Bill thought she should get a job, but she thought he was only hoping to get her out of his hair that way, so she refused. Now there was a new thing called Women's Lib where some women were actually complaining that they didn't "get" to work like their husbands, but Pat thought that was those intense neurotic East Coasters acting up again. Out here in California, people were mellower, they had religions and cults and alternative lifestyles, and maybe that gave women a sense of freedom they didn't feel in the uptight East. Anyway, the kids hadn't finished growing yet, and *that* was the job she had signed on for: Wife and Mother. And as far as she knew, she'd been doing a damn fine job at both. So she couldn't for the life of her figure out how exactly she'd come to be—as she suspected she was—in the process of getting fired.

Some days, at lunchtime, she went down to a local restaurant and sat at the bar. She'd order a drink and chat with the bartender till some guy came along who looked interesting. Not interesting like you'd want to marry him; just one-afternoon interesting. The men would be in the bar looking for exactly what she was looking for, so the little transaction would be over fast enough for her to get home and meet the school bus. She discovered a whole little subculture of perfectly nice-looking housewives who were all doing the same thing, and once she could have sworn she even spotted one of the kids' teachers.

Don't feel sorry for Bill, though. This whole thing had been his idea in the first place. Ever since what she thought of as The Night of the Files, back in 1966, he had been lecturing her on the problems of American Upper-Middle-Class Society, by which she understood him to mean: Us. The problem, he said, was too much Togetherness. The problem, he said, was that love and sex were really unrelated, but women got them mixed up and that made them jealous and possessive. He thought American marriages should be more like European marriages, where the couple wasn't really expected to love each other, and both were free to sleep around with other people if they felt like it (or was it that the couple did love each other but didn't confuse that with sleeping around with other people in a meaningless but fulfilling sort of way?).

The problem, in other words, was *her*. The problem was an oppressive society. The problem was an archaic institution that no longer functioned to support the individual's right to self-realization and personal happiness. The problem was everything but the fact that he had broken his sacred, Catholic promise to love and cherish her, and that for many, many years now had been sleeping around with a virtual harem of women. He didn't even bother to hide it to keep from hurting her; on the contrary, he left clues scattered around the house like an overlooked criminal whose wounded pride in his profession causes him to drag the cops straight to the crime scene. The clues had led her to his office where, on that Night of the Files, she and a friend had found files full of credit card slips, restaurant chits, hotel bills, plane tickets, and even photographs documenting all the details of Bill's extramarital adventures.

Ever since then, she'd been in a state of semi-paralysis, drinking too much, picking up the occasional lunchtime fling, periodically threatening to get a divorce. Not that that seemed to worry Bill. Why should it? He had a great income; he had girlfriends in every American city. She'd get the five kids she had no means of supporting, the big house whose mortgage she couldn't afford, and her own over-forty worn and shattered self, whom no man would probably ever find interesting again.

Several years slipped by like this, and then, one evening, the doorbell rang. The man she found standing on her threshold was not her knight in shining armor, exactly, because he didn't propose carrying her off to his castle and making love to her passionately and supporting her in the lifestyle to which she had become accustomed. But he did appear to be some sort of Fairy Godmother. There in her living room that first evening, he proposed a magical, once-in-a-lifetime transformation: He was going to take her, this unremarkable middle-aged housewife, whom no one, including her own husband, particularly cared about, and wave his wand over her, and make her *famous*.

The man's name was Craig Gilbert, and he said he was trying to make a documentary for public television about the "embattled" American family. It was fast disappearing, he said, and he wanted to document it before it became obsolete. A mutual friend had led him to Bill and Pat, and after spending an evening with them, he thought they would be the perfect subjects. All he needed to do, he said, was park a camera crew in their home for an unspecified length of time, filming everything that happened to all of them until, after a while, he said, "truths would start rising to the surface like dumplings."

Well, Bill and Pat were flattered. Each of them had a clear vision of the sort of truth that would rise to the surface of such a TV show. Bill later told *Newsweek* that he thought "the series would make them look like 'West Coast Kennedys.' " Pat, with the help of a professional ghostwriter, later wrote quite colorfully that she imagined "Bill's women [watching the TV show] . . . in their frowsy little rented rooms . . . Their bleached blond hair would be falling sloppily out of its hairpins and their enormous breasts would be falling equally sloppily out of their torn, spotty negligees as they clutched their glasses of Scotch and rested their fat ankles on footstools to relieve their aching varicose veins," while meanwhile, "There we'd be, all seven of us, a portrait of family solidarity, all interwoven by blood and love and time and mutual need and a thousand other ties those poor things couldn't even comprehend. And *good-looking, every one of us*—not a slob in the group. . . . *That would fix them.*" [Pat's italics]

But the filming did not progress exactly as planned. For one thing, after only a few days, Gilbert informed Pat and Bill that instead of filming one hour on each of five families, as he had originally intended, he now wanted to focus on their family for the whole five segments; in the end, he actually filmed three hundred hours of their life and edited this down to twelve hour-long episodes. The upshot was that cameras were around for seven months, far longer than Pat and Bill had anticipated when they had initially agreed to the filming. Then, quite early in the project, the camera crew accompanied Pat to New York for a visit to her oldest son, Lance, who, Pat now discovered as the cameras rolled, was homosexual. He took straitlaced Mom and the camera crew to a drag show, "which had the intended effect of shocking mom to her shoelaces" but hardly led to any illuminating conversation or insight about the revelation.

Eventually, with months of daily presence, the cameras began to fade into the woodwork, and the family's guard slipped down, and just as Craig Gilbert had hoped, another fat dumpling rose to the surface: The cameras were there and rolling as Bill returned home from one of his frequent "business" trips, and Pat informed him that she'd been to see a lawyer and this time she was serious about a divorce. She wanted him to move out. "Fair deal," Bill said with a shrug. "I won't have to unpack my bag."

And the crew stayed on another few months after Bill left, which Pat rather appreciated since it saved her from the loneliness a suddenly single mother of five kids might feel in the isolated splendor of a suburban house. But finally the crew left, and there was a whole year before the series was scheduled to air in early 1973.

Pat, once again, waited. "I don't know exactly what I thought would happen to *me* when the series happened to the whole country," she wrote later, "but I knew something would. I wouldn't just be sitting around by my plastic fireplace smiling and thinking the same old thoughts. In some way I would change . . . I suppose I thought that if Bill didn't love me, a lot of the viewers out there would. And that would fix him . . . The series was like a jury that was still out, and when it came back on January 11, I would be re-created out of the whole cloth [*sic*]. A new Pat, a whole new identity. And that, of course, was what I badly needed. Anybody with my life does."

An American Family became a nationwide sensation when it began to air on PBS in January 1973. Pat and Bill Loud became instant household names. *Newsweek*, which put the whole family on the cover, called the series "a starkly intimate view of one family struggling to survive a private civil war—and a scathing commentary on the American dream." Family members were invited on to all the hottest talk shows: Dick Cavett, Mike Douglas,

Jack Paar, Dinah Shore, and Phil Donahue. *The New York Times Magazine* and the *Atlantic Monthly* prominently dissected them. Anthropologist Margaret Mead called the series "a new kind of art form . . . as significant as the invention of drama . . . a new way in which people can learn to look at life by seeing the real life of others interpreted by the camera."

Pat, however, was bewildered and angry. Rather than transforming her into an object of envy, the Fairy Godmother had turned her into something scary, something ugly: a symbol of everyone's most secret fears and nightmares about what love and marriage had deteriorated into in the 1970s; the embodiment of why love and marriage could not save us from our existential loneliness, and our empty American materialism. *You've got it wrong,* Pat insisted, *we're not really like that!* "We weren't [portrayed as] people," she wrote later, in *Pat Loud: A Woman's Story,* "we were public targets to take potshots at, balloons being bounced around in the air by a lot of dopey children. . . . We didn't think we could hold onto ourselves, or God knows *I* felt that way. If this was what my personality transplant was going to feel like, I didn't want it. I'd grapple with old Pat just as she was, warts and all."

Ironically, the series did not appear to have the same effect on Bill. He told the *Chicago Daily News* in March 1973 that "My phone number is listed, and I get about six calls each evening from ladies who want to meet me. It's nice to talk to them. Last week one lady called from Boston and asked me not to marry until I see her. I told her to send a photo."

Warty old Pat got no such propositions—at least none she reported in her tell-all book. She did admit that, their finances wrecked by the divorce and a decline in Bill's business fortunes, the whole family now eagerly jumped at any opportunity to cash in on their public-television fame. And she unabashedly shared her newest fantasy, about moving to New York, where she imagined

she'd find some kind of job, after all, but mostly hoped to meet a
man who would see her as herself and not as—and here she drew
a distinction—"Pat Loud." The man would take her to superb
French restaurants, be "rich and successful," make love to her,
take her skiing and to the theater, and would be one of those men,
also, who would love the chance to have her teenage daughters
hanging around.

The women's magazines, by the way, did sympathize with Pat.
Ladies' Home Journal actually paid her $1,500 to "express her-
self freely" to its resident psychiatrist, Theodore I. Rubin, M.D.,
and he came to some "very interesting conclusions." He thought
she looked much younger than her forty-six years, that she
dressed simply "and wore little make-up . . . in keeping with her
direct, open, natural approach to the interview and to life in general." He thought she had married under the illusion that marriage would be a "beautifully romantic idyll," and had then
"assumed the dependent role (like her mother) to comply with a
cherished dream, and with what she perceived to be the requirements of the culture in which she lived." And that worked fine
until she began to feel "important stirrings within herself. These
stirrings were her need for personal growth—a need that, like
other women of her generation, she repressed in order to avoid
inner conflict and anxiety, until her intelligence and sensitivity
could no longer allow her to cover up what had become so obvious: that her marriage to Bill was not what she had expected."
What would become of Pat, now that she had left her marriage in order to confront the remaining blank pages of her
own existence just as the new revolutionary forces of Women's
Lib were exhorting women everywhere to do? Well, the last
that *Ladies' Home Journal* readers saw of her was later in the
same issue, in a photo spread headlined "A Beautiful Week
for Pat Loud." The beauty editors had shipped her off to spend a

free week at the fabulously expensive Maine Chance spa in Phoenix, where she toned up her figure and received a complete makeover. "I'm not very familiar with cosmetics," she said afterward, "but I really looked a lot better."

Real Life

The social upheavals of the late sixties and early seventies went roaring like a flash flood through the colleges where Maude, Betsy, and Carole were, sweeping everything up and then dropping it all somewhere else on its head. But they just trickled through the suburbs, like a hidden leak in everyone's everyday assumptions, so that it was only over the very long haul that they dripped steadily and heavily enough on anyone to erode her expectations.

Of course, Tammy hadn't actually ever had any expectations. She hadn't thought much of anything was going to change after she became Mrs. Eddie, except that she wouldn't have to worry anymore about whether her period was going to arrive each month, and she would have a bicker-proof excuse for seeing less of her mother. She didn't even see much more of Eddie, because she was working all day as a secretary for a trucking company, and his new job as an insurance salesman required him to be out most evenings on sales calls. She did see more of Eddie's mother, though, who continued to act as though Eddie were still bringing his dirty underwear and his paychecks home to *her.*

"Tammy, Tammy! Wake up!"

Tammy, thinking she must be dreaming, rolled over and pulled a pillow over her head.

"Tammy—" The pillow was snatched away, making Tammy reluctantly hoist her eyelids up and peer through the darkness at the pool of moonlight where a woman stood. *Delores?*

"You gotta get up, Tammy."

"Why?"

"Eddie's in jail."

"Yeah, so?" Tammy didn't even ask, *What now?* It was always drinking-related.

"So, he said he tried to call here, and there wasn't any answer, so he called me."

Well, it was none of Delores's business if Tammy occasionally went out on a Friday night by herself, especially when she knew Eddie was gonna stop by a tavern on his way home from work and maybe not make it the rest of the way home till three or four in the morning.

"Yeah, so?" Tammy repeated.

"So, we gotta get him out."

"Delores, I'm tireda goin' and gettin' him out. I'm in the middle of a good night's sleep right now. I'll go get him out in the morning."

HMMPF, went Delores. If Tammy wasn't even going to fulfill the basic requirements of the job she'd accepted by marrying Eddie, well *of course* a mother would have no choice other than to interfere.

"Then *I'll* get him out," she said, turning and stalking from the room.

"Do what you want," Tammy mumbled, retrieving the pillow from where Delores had dropped it on the floor near the bed, and pulling it back over her head.

Where Tammy usually went by herself in the evenings of that first married summer was over to the place of one of the other Girls who was home from college. Donna had pretty much disappeared; none of them had been invited to her wedding, and somehow they had all lost touch. Maude always had to be home early that summer because she was in BIG trouble with her folks, and it was just as well, really, because you woulda thought she was one of the original disciples, the way she would talk your ear off about Jesus Christ our Savior. But Carole's house was a real wild scene that summer, especially when her parents weren't around. Josh was usually there, and a crowd of his pals from Upstate, and Tammy thought a lot of them were pretty fulla shit, too, like they were gonna single-handedly change the world, like they knew what was best for everybody. But what they had that was special, and what they shared very generously with Tammy, was marijuana. And Tammy, from the first moment she ever got high, absolutely loved it.

Now, Eddie knew she went over to Carole's, but she didn't tell him exactly what was going on there because Eddie hated hippies. Some long-haired kids hanging around smoking outside the gas station one day had walked right in front of his car, flashing him the peace sign, and in return he'd given them the finger, and then he'd gone on and on: "Fuckin' hippies, fuckin' freaks, I'm out workin' for a livin', I ain't askin' nobody for handouts, *blah blah blah*." But, actually, Eddie *hated* working for a living, his whole family thought they shouldn't have to. His dad had died when Eddie was in sixth grade and his brother was only four, and Delores had gone around town doing this Poor Widow act and raising the kids with the idea that the world owed them something for making them practically orphans. Everybody else in the world were idiots except them. Especially Eddie's bosses. Eddie'd been out of high school three years and already he'd changed jobs like some people change socks; he was on his third or fourth, and he'd always quickly discover that his bosses were incompetent or stupid in some way that he'd get himself more and more enraged about till the day he'd come home from work and announce, "I quit."

"Yeah? You got another job you're goin' to?"

"Shit, Tammy, you know I couldn't work for that asshole anymore, you know what he said to me this morning, the jerk . . . ?"

Anyway, Tammy didn't feel like getting him started on the subject of jerks and assholes and idiots because he could go on pretty much forever, especially if he had a few drinks in him, which he usually did. So she didn't mention the hippies over at Carole's, and since he refused to ever go there with her because of the feud he was still having with Betsy's husband—*that fucker*—it seemed like this was going to be pretty much her secret.

Then one Saturday morning, after a Friday night when they'd been out separately, he got out of bed and said, "I got something to show you."

"Yeah?"

He came back and sat down on her side of the bed, flipping the top off an open pack of Marlboros and pulling out two lumpy, spindly joints.

"Hmmm, what's that?" Tammy said, trying not to let her face light up visibly.

"It's pot. I tried a little bit of it already, but I thought—ya know, we could do it *together.*"

"Okay," said Tammy, "we could try it."

There were a lot of old people in their apartment building and they didn't want anyone asking about the smell, so they went into the kitchen, where there was a little exhaust fan in the window, and they turned the fan on and smoked into it.

"Hey, it's like we're still kids sneakin' around our parents' house."

This thought struck them both as hysterically funny. They laughed and laughed, so hard they had to go back in the bedroom and fall down on the bed.

After that, they got stoned together all the time. Even when Eddie was out of work and the phone was shut off because there hadn't been enough in the checking account to pay the bill, they would scrape together enough cash for a baggie full of weed.

They came to look like hippies themselves, ripped jeans dragging on the ground, enveloped in a marijuana haze that clung to them wherever they went. Once, after they'd interrupted a Christmas shopping spree to get high in the mall parking lot, the girl behind the jewelry counter had sniffed a couple of times and then said, "You guys been smokin'? You might wanna stop over at the perfume counter and have 'em squirt you with a sample."

That was pretty funny, too. And that's what was so great about pot, it made everything seem funny—the jerks, the assholes, the mothers, the bills, and whatever little episodes of marital discord might sometimes bubble up between them.

Of course, at the beginning all the Girls were intoxicated with glee whenever they thought about how cleverly and completely they had escaped their parents' houses. It would have been Oedipal, if only Sophocles or Freud had been female and understood that while men might want to dispose of their fathers in order to sleep with their mothers, what women really wanted was to get rid of their mothers so they could have the house to themselves. Now the Girls all had houses of their own, and the only thing they had to do to prevent them from turning back into their mothers' houses was to make sure that they themselves didn't somehow metamorphose into their mothers—those angry, frustrated, bitter watchdogs of other peoples' lives. They were all extremely confident that they could manage this, because each one of them had a secret credo locked away deep in her soul, like a gem in a safe-deposit box, that she could check whenever she needed reassurance that she was, in fact, *definitely* not turning into her mother.

Donna's secret credo was: "I *like* being a wife and mother."

Being a wife was great because, first of all, you had regular orgasms. Donna wouldn't have even known what an orgasm was if it hadn't been for Stan. One night, before they got married, they had been lying on the couch in a friend's basement, kissing—nothing improper, though, he wasn't touching her breasts or anything, he just had one leg kinda wedged between hers—and he was moving against her real gently, and all of a sudden an almost unbearable feeling focused right in the middle of her spread throughout her body, and she began to tremble. And then she burst into tears.

"Donna, baby, what's wrong?"

"I don't know, I don't know, I just had this crazy feeling. . . ."

He explained to her, very tenderly, that this feeling was the climax, it was what you were supposed to feel when someone you loved made love to you.

Donna felt very grateful. It was so moving that he could give her this. Then she discovered that there were other ways he could give her orgasms, even more intense ones. He wasn't dirty about it either, the way some boys might have been. He referred to her crotch as His Little Girl, and he would say sweetly, "Can I talk to My Little Girl now?"

They were careful not to toy with her actual virginity, though, because if they had, her father woulda found out for sure, the way God the Father found out about everything, and he woulda killed them both in case God wasn't paying attention. So Donna wouldn't even let Stan put his penis between her legs till a week before the wedding. She just assumed that if she could have orgasms like that without his penis inside, then once he did get it in, it would be completely spectacular. Because by then in the magazines they were writing about the difference between *clitoral* orgasms and *vaginal* orgasms. Clitoral, like the kind he gave her by playing around with the part of her that stuck out down there like a little tongue, were nice, but vaginal—the kind you got only from intercourse—were supposed to be the most mature and satisfying climax a woman could have. But some women—for example, neurotic women who weren't well-adjusted in their feminine identity—couldn't have them. The magazines always ran quizzes you could take to find out if you were a neurotic woman who was not well-adjusted in your feminine identity, but anyone with half a brain could figure out what the right answers were just by the way the questions were worded, so it was pretty hard to take those tests without fudging to make your score come out right. Which meant you could never really be sure. Unless, of course, you turned out to be the kind of woman who couldn't have one of these vaginal orgasms.

On the first episode of intercourse, in their honeymoon hotel room near the newly opened Disney World, where Stan had wanted to come for some good clean fun, he seemed a little nervous, which might have explained why he was so uncharacteristically brief and businesslike. But then, on the second night, he was brief and businesslike as well.

"Honey?" she said, as delicately as she could, because it was embarrassing to have to admit that this *mature* business with his dick was not anywhere near as interesting to her as that other less mature stuff they'd been doing all along. "Could we go back to that—uh—touchy-feely thing?" He looked upset, like maybe he thought she was criticizing him, but the next night he went real slow and spent a long time kissing her and rubbing against her, and sure enough, when he put himself inside her and started to thrust, she could feel it take like a spark to dry wood inside her, and the heat flared up until she felt she was about to go off like a firecracker, which was great because she wasn't a neurotic feminine failure after all and she cried out in her excitement, "*Oh, Stan I'm gonna come,*" and slapped him on the butt—

"Whoa there," said scrawny little Stan. "Take it easy, you're gonna hurt me."

Donna withdrew as though she herself had been slapped, but it was too late. From that time on, Stan would come the moment he got inside her. "It's not your fault," he would say occasionally, which she took to mean that he thought it probably was. And it made sense, if you thought about this other topic you found in the magazines: the Sexually Demanding Woman, who wanted equal orgasms along with equal rights. Psychiatrists warned that this was a "frightening image for American males." And didn't it make sense, when Donna's other appetites were so outsized, that her appetite for sex should overwhelm poor skinny Stan, who was only trying to do his best, and very thoughtfully returned to making sure she had her orgasm before he entered her?

She kept her mouth shut, even when she started to run across articles that talked about "premature ejaculation," suggesting that his orgasms, as well as hers, were of dubious quality. She had unmanned him enough already. There didn't seem to be any tactful way to bring it up. So she never found out whether he, too, went along vaguely troubled by the sense that their sex life, despite all the orgasms, fell somehow short of the standard the experts had set for well-adjusted couples.

Meanwhile, Donna proved to be, as promised, a baby machine—though not really a well-oiled one.

Only a month after Disney World, she missed her period. Two months after Disney World, she was nauseated and miserable. Five months after Disney World, they flew off to Nassau in the Bahamas on a second honeymoon, because all the people at the wedding who had so urgently inquired as to when they were planning on starting a family were now knowingly admonishing them that they were about to forfeit their freedom forever, so they had better enjoy it while they still could.

Nassau was as beautiful as its travel brochures, with long white beaches, sparkling azure water, and deep-tanned women in very small bikinis. Donna was not feeling very good about her own bathing suit, however, since she'd piled on more pounds than were officially called for by the pregnancy and was now inching toward 280 on the scale—much more than she'd ever imagined weighing. Then one afternoon she found herself doubled over with stomach pain so severe that Stan rushed her to the local hospital, where they told her she had dysentery and gave her a shot of morphine for the pain and sent her back to the hotel. When she was back at the hospital again the next day, they advised her to fly home to her own doctors, and gave her another shot of morphine for the airplane.

Her doctors at home told her she was having a gallbladder attack and that her temperature, at 106 degrees, was dangerously high. They packed her in ice to bring the fever down, gave her a shot of penicillin, and told her they were going to have to operate. But first, *ahem*, they were going to have to abort the baby.

"*No*," said Donna. This was not the doctors' decision to make. This was going to have to be God's decision. "Give me an hour. I'll get the temperature down." She apologized to God for every single time she'd ever wasted His time with silly prayers about getting boys to like her or being skinny. But she was going to get this prayer onto His desk as surely as she'd gotten those three hundred letters about the class rings on Sister's, and He was going to listen. And after an hour, when the doctors were bothering her again because the fever hadn't gone down, she just told them, "One more hour," and they backed off.

It took another few hours, but finally the nurses started patting her on the hand and smiling and the doctors shrugged and said she was very, very lucky but they were all going to have to keep an eye on her. A few weeks later, she developed preeclampsia, and then toxemia, and she was hospitalized several more times and pumped full of medications and painkillers, until finally the doctors determined that the baby was two weeks overdue and that labor would have to be induced.

It was indescribably awful. The pain was literally unbearable, so that when, eight hours into it, the doctors increased the dose of Pitocin to try to get her to dilate faster, her body went into convulsions and her soul simply got up and flew away. It fluttered around the ceiling of the hospital room like a trapped bird, watching the body on the table writhe and contort while the doctors and nurses rushed around yelling about an emergency cesarian. She was going to die now. Maybe she was already dead. It felt much better to be dead, actually, to no longer be imprisoned in her body, to be flying. If only there had been a window, somewhere in the floodlit operating room, her soul might have slipped free into eternity.

But then, sometime later that night, she awoke to find herself back in her body like an escaped slave returned to the chains of the oppressor. The doctors said the baby *seemed* fine, except that his tongue was attached to the floor of his mouth and one of his feet was turned way in. The nurses kept coming in and examining her hands.

"What are you doing?" she asked finally.

"Well, the baby has simian creases," said the nurse. "But so do you, so that's a good sign."

"Whaddya mean, simian creases?"

"See this line on your palm that goes all the way across? That's called a simian crease. All people with Down's syndrome have simian creases, but not all people with simian creases have Down's."

"Are you sayin' the baby's retarded?"

"We don't know," said the nurse. "But you did take an awful lot of drugs during pregnancy . . ." Her sentence trailed off, leaving a slight suggestion in the air.

"I was *sick*," Donna protested.

"Yes, well even that alone, without the drugs, is sometimes enough to cause the baby to be—deformed."

*   *   *

"Oh, that's crap," said her doctor later. "He's not deformed, and he probably doesn't have Down's. I've clipped his tongue, and you may need to get him speech therapy when he's three or four, but otherwise he'll be fine."

"But what about his foot?"

"I'll show you some exercises you'll have to do with his legs three times a day, and in six months it'll be all straightened out."

So Donna took little Donny home. She didn't have any idea of what she was supposed to do with him. She didn't feel qualified to have him. She hated diapering him, she hated getting up in the middle of the night to feed him, and she was scared of the little withered stump of umbilical cord coming out of his belly button. She seemed to have no maternal instinct whatsoever. All she had was a sort of awe of him, that he was so alive and so complete in spite of her unworthiness to have made him. But she followed the doctor's instructions to the letter, and six months later his foot was straightened out. And six months after that, Donna was pregnant again.

This time she had preeclampsia and toxemia right from the start. So they drugged her up immediately with phenobarbital and, because she seemed to be hysterical about what deformities the phenobarbital might produce, Valium. The drugs made her woozy over and above her morning sickness, and she was afraid to carry Donny around because she thought she might drop him. So she took to keeping him in the playpen on the floor, feeding him through the slats, and talking to him in what she thought would be a comforting tone:

"I hope I'm not a rotten mommy, Donny. I hope I didn't fuck you up with all those drugs, and I hope I don't fuck up your little baby brother or sister either. I love you, at least I think I love you, sometimes I'm not sure, you're pretty cute but sometimes you're an awful pain in the ass, and please, please don't cry all night tonight. . . ."

Well, it sounded a little crazy, even to her, but it was much nicer than the things her mother had said to her, and at least she wasn't yelling like her mom always had. And if she was handling it better than her mom, she must like it better than her mom, so things were probably okay; so it did not occur to her, even as she gazed through the bars of the playpen at the baby thoughtfully sucking his thumb within, that her mother's prophecy had come to pass within less than two years.

In Betsy's house, unlike her mother's, there was going to be To-getherness. Technically, of course, she had missed the boat on Togetherness; the rest of the world had OD'ed on it in the fifties, and now in the late sixties and early seventies had moved on to Doing Your Own Thing. Betsy, the Smiley Girl, would never have said that her childhood had been anything other than completely happy, but still she was bothered by the vague sense that it had been the form, and not the content, of Togetherness that had been observed. There had been tuna casseroles on the table promptly at six so the whole family could eat together; there had been long destinationless Sunday drives with the mom and dad in the front and the two girls in the back, whining, "When are we going to *get* there?"; followed by the Sunday extended-family dinners where everything swam in a pool of brown gravy and, afterward, clothing around everyone's waists had had to be loos-ened an extra inch; and of course, Gramma had even lived with them on and off. But then there was the time when, at one of those dinners, the subject of the family plot at All Saints Ceme-tery had arisen, where Grampa had been eternally slumbering, God rest his soul, for the past twenty years, and Gramma had emerged briefly from her apparent senility to snap, "Don't you *dare* bury me next to that man. I *hated* that man."

So Betsy had spent an entire childhood longing futilely for the grown-ups to like each other as much as they pretended to, but suspecting that if she just stopped smiling for even so much as a moment, they would probably start hating her, too. There hadn't been anything she could do about it then, but now that she was setting up her own household she was going to make very sure that everyone in it was smiling because they had something genuine to smile about.

At the beginning, luck played along. Billy managed to get himself reaccepted into Upstate in time for the wedding, so that afterward they would have two and a half years left to finish together. At first they lived in married student housing and acted as the official Married Couple for all their single friends—particularly Billy's buddies who didn't have girlfriends, who would hang around hoping for an invitation to one of Betsy's home-cooked meals. Her kitchen became a rebuke to all the brown gravy and canned convenience foods of their childhood diets. Poring over the new hippie-influenced, back-to-the-land cookbooks with the same diligence she applied to her management textbooks, Betsy began producing homemade whole-grain breads that filled the apartment with the cozy aroma of warm yeast. Billy and his buddies sometimes went hunting on weekends, returning with duck, pheasant, squirrel, or rabbit. Betsy compliantly acquired a game cookbook and learned to dress the catch of the day, even the poor little dead bunnies who arrived frozen in something like the fetal position and made her long for the comparatively mute lumps of supermarket hamburger.

They needed money, though, because of course they were their own family now and not their parents' dependent children, despite their being barely twenty and still in college. So most evenings they worked—Together. She waitressed, he tended bar, and they hired themselves out as a team because they discovered that employers viewed them automatically as a responsible married couple instead of as potentially unstable college kids who might steal things or blow the job off with no warning.

Senior year, this happy work-and-marriage synergy culminated in an offer from a motel owner who wanted them to manage his motel in exchange for living there rent free. A long and perfect future stretched out before them: the congenial atmosphere of the small college town, where Billy would teach gym at the local elementary school while Betsy raised the two kids and the whole family managed the motel together. It was better even than the original Plan, because this way when Betsy went back out eventually to find herself a corporate job, the years of child-rearing would not have laid waste to what she thought of, like a muscle that needed exercising, as her Marketable Skills.

To celebrate, at Christmastime Betsy and Billy went into the bathroom—Together—and ceremonially flushed every last one of her birth control pills down the toilet.

Then, with as little warning or justification as life usually offers for that kind of thing, the whole framework crumbled. By the time they graduated in June 1973, the bank was foreclosing on the motel, whose owner had apparently abandoned the mortgage, and Betsy was four months' pregnant. With no jobs, no home, and no medical insurance to cover the cost of the impending birth, they headed instinctively home for the suburbs, where both their families lived, hoping their local contacts would pay off in a quick job prospect. Billy got hired almost immediately— as a substitute assigned to the "industrial arts" class, which his certificate in physical education gave him no idea how to handle. He hated the kids, and after a week, refused to go back.

Then the parents stepped in. Billy's sent Betsy to the kindly obstetrician who'd delivered Billy, who, in view of the circumstances, agreed to give them a break on his fee and get Betsy out of the hospital in twenty-four hours, assuming the birth went smoothly. The birth didn't go smoothly, but at least Betsy managed to head off an emergency C-section by valiantly propelling little Jeremy into independent life while she was still parked temporarily outside the operating room.

Meanwhile, Betsy's father pulled a few strings and got Billy on a construction crew. It was back-breaking work, but Billy was young and his back seemed unbreakable, and the money was good. The City was in the midst of a sewer reconstruction project that promised to go on indefinitely, so you might even say Billy's future looked bright, if you didn't listen too closely to the stories he told about the rats he'd seen scurrying around while he ate his lunch in the dark wet tunnel below the City, where other college graduates applied themselves in daylight.

But even if Billy were somehow to turn into her dad, that didn't mean Betsy would necessarily start turning into her mom. If she seemed to be doing what her mom had done—stay home to raise kids—that wasn't actually so, because Betsy was going about it in a very different way. Her mother's generation had tried to cope with the chaos of babies by imposing an artificial discipline and order. They bought child-care manuals written by orderly, disciplined male doctors who insisted on regular four-hour feeding schedules and strict deadlines for sleeping through the night. If the baby didn't go along, you simply let him cry till he got tired enough to acknowledge the reasonableness of what you were demanding. And you fed the baby with bottles, ostensibly because formula was more "scientific" than breast milk but really because orderly, disciplined male doctors tended to share a cultural disapproval of having female breasts come bobbing out in broad daylight where people other than lawfully wedded husbands might see them.

Of course, by now things were different. Bare breasts were everywhere: on the models in fashion magazines, on the centerfolds in *Playboy*, on the hippie girls bathing in the ponds at

Woodstock, on the actresses in the musicals *Hair* and *Oh,
Calcutta,* not to mention the breasts of movie actresses projected directly onto the American psyche at so many times their
natural size. About the only place you never saw breasts was on
real women in your everyday life—particularly women who
were using them for exactly what God had presumably put them
there for in the first place.

Betsy and a growing number of other women of her generation were quietly changing that. It wouldn't be considered "radical," despite the fact that as late as 1966 only 18 percent of
infants were being started on breast-feeding in the hospital, but a
small network of mostly white, middle-class women were beginning to thumb their noses at their mothers and doctors and, often, friends, to nurse their babies and live out a vision of
motherhood that seemed to follow from that. Your job, as a
mother, was not to impose control on the baby, but to interpret
and address the baby's needs as the baby expressed them. That
was still a job, though, after all—and you needed to think of
what you were doing with the baby as a job, because otherwise
you were just slogging through isolated days and sleepless
nights haphazardly, which might compel someone more like
Donna to shut down emotionally, or someone more like Tammy
to lean a little too heavily on alcohol or pot. Betsy approached it
quite professionally, as sort of a Plan-Within-the-Plan. She joined
the La Leche League, a national association of women who met
locally in small groups to exchange information about breast-
feeding techniques, and to support each other in a world of relatives and professionals who disapproved of what they were
doing. The La Leche philosophy reinforced her instincts toward
Togetherness, too. She was encouraged to keep the baby with
her at all times, even sleeping in the bed with her and Billy at
night; to let him ride around on her body in a front pack or a
backpack or on a hip during the day. If you nursed, the La Leche

women told her, your body would space your pregnancies out naturally, preventing another conception until the baby was almost ready to wean. And indeed, her second baby appeared almost exactly two years after the first; and her third (well, just *one* more, because she had discovered she really *loved* having babies) exactly two years after the second; and her fourth (this is the *last* one, I promise, but how could you stand not having a baby in the house?) two years after that.

So Betsy was very, very busy all through the seventies, bearing those babies, taking an active role in the leadership of the La Leche League, making sure the children didn't ever sit glassy-eyed in front of a TV but were educationally stimulated by library story times and baking oatmeal cookies from scratch. She was so busy that she didn't have time to think much about the fact that Billy was less and less willing to come with her to the social events organized by the La Leche women, and, later, by the children's schools. She didn't seem to take too much note of the way Billy had begun to refer to them frequently as "your" children. Nor did she dwell on the significance of the construction-worker habit Billy seemed to have picked up of buying a six-pack for lunch and stopping with the guys at a bar for a drink or two on the way home.

Maude wept as Brad's ship chugged off for the Mediterranean. But she was going to see him at Christmastime, only a few months off. The navy was flying a group of wives over to meet the crew in Athens for a two-week holiday. *Europe again!* Maude had always known she'd get back there somehow, and now it was going to happen, with the man she loved. God was smiling on Maude.

It was almost too good to be true. Not only had Brad found his way to God, he'd also found his way to Literature. All those dull months at sea, and he'd taken to passing them in the company of

Tolstoy, Dostoyevsky—men who understood the drama and passion of the human soul. As soon as he got out of the navy, he was going to join Maude in college. They would read together, write together, pray together, and have huge amounts of totally mind-blowing sex.

Turn into her mother? No chance, man. It was as if the whole concept of marriage had been reinvented in the generation between them. There was that saying you saw now, in script lettering, on plaques and coffee mugs against backgrounds of orangy sunsets:

> *I do my thing, and you do your thing.*
> *I am not in this world to live up to your expectations*
> *and you are not in this world to live up to mine.*
> *You are you, and I am I,*
> *And if by chance we find each other, it's beautiful.*
> *If not, it can't be helped.*

That was the essence of what was between them. Neither would dominate, neither would control. They would, in loving one another, also create space for one another so they could each continue to grow personally throughout their lives.

So Brad's next few months at sea would be hard, as a separation, but they would also be Maude's opportunity to confront the future on her own two feet. God had given her everything she'd ever wanted so far, and someday soon, she trusted, He was going to give her Brad's baby. But not yet. Right now, she needed to get back to college. Right now, she needed to crash for a few months at her parents' house while she enrolled as a transfer student at the university in the heart of the City, where she had always expected she would be when all her dreams came true.

Professor Raymond Swagget was scholarship personified. A portly, balding man in his early sixties who spoke precisely and with just the slightest touch of an English accent, he was a world-renowned Shakespeare scholar. His campus office was lined with rare and ancient leather-bound books about the Bard and his contemporaries. Once a semester, he invited students to his home where he showed slides from his travels and uncurled priceless yellowed documents while his white-haired wife served cheap white table wine and cheese. He edited a quarterly newsletter—sort of a Shakespeare fan magazine, really—to which all the other eminent Shakespeare scholars in the English-speaking world contributed tidbits. When radio stations and newspapers needed a quote or a nifty factoid on Shakespeare's birthday, it was Professor Swagget they phoned. And Maude was lucky enough to be among the fifteen students who made it into his fall tragedies seminar.

Maude had a little logistical problem that semester, though. If she was going to be among the navy wives on that plane headed for Athens at Christmas, she was going to have to complete ten weeks' worth of course material in just eight weeks, and her professors were going to have to allow her to take exams early, postpone them till January, or substitute term papers. Her theater prof had balked, which threatened to leave her one class short of a full course load. But since Professor Swagget had been perfectly amenable, Maude had worked up the courage to propose a plan: Could she, in view of her special circumstances, do an independent study with him, in addition to the seminar? Then she could just hand in an early paper rather than having to worry about taking a scheduled exam.

Professor Swagget, who had seemed so unapproachable in his eminence, gave her a knowing wink and said, "Ah, yes. I haven't forgotten what it was like to be a newlywed."

And so, there was another of those unforeseen gifts of her magically abundant life—that she got to spend half her academic hours in the company of a man who knew Hamlet and Lear and

Iago more intimately than anyone then living. With utmost reverence, as though gaining admittance to the Pope's study, she would bring her sandwich in to eat with him at lunchtime, as he sat at his desk and told stories about his research trips to England. Then they might talk about the project she was doing on Ben Jonson, and he might remember the very book she must look at—a hundred-year-old volume he would pull down from a high shelf and bestow upon her, like a blessing, to take home. Sometimes he would ask about Brad, and it was a sign of what lofty place his mind lived in that he might, on hearing her say some inarticulate thing about her love, pluck from the air a wisp of antique poetry, which he would recite in his baritone British cadences, without so much as blushing:

> Drink to me only with thine eyes,
> And I will pledge with mine;
> Or leave a kiss but in the cup
> And I'll not look for wine.
> The thirst that from the soul doth rise
> Doth ask a drink divine;
> But might I of Jove's nectar sup,
> I would not change for thine.

I am his protégeé, she would tell herself happily, lugging her knapsack of books to the bus stop for the long ride back to the suburbs. He had obviously seen something in her mind that commanded his respect, perhaps understanding that she was a person for whom life and literature were not so separate; her mind spun visions of how the two might sprawl out, intertwined, over the coming years, how she would continue to study under Professor Swagget through graduate school, and when Brad returned home they would have long wine-filled evenings with Swagget and his wife in their book-filled study, feasting on gourmet delicacies and bon mots.

But at the beginning of the semester's seventh week, something happened. Professor Swagget's questions about Brad, and their married life, became suddenly more intimate and then uncomfortable. One afternoon he wondered aloud about the Sexual Revolution, all the couples who no longer felt they needed the blessing of marriage to start having sex, but then, Maude wouldn't need to worry about that because she was a *newlywed*. Then abruptly he asked, "Do you like sex, Maude?"

She had no idea what to say. If he'd been a fellow student, or one of the waiters she worked with on the weekends, she'd have had no trouble coming up with something flippant, to defuse it with wit or, if it really offended her, slam it back acidly in his face. But this was Professor Swagget.

"Excuse me?" she said in her most-polite-good-student voice, gathering up her things as quickly as she could, to make a quick escape. But not quite quick enough, because on the way out she heard him muttering something about how *hard* it made him just to think about it.

Well, what you try to do is pretend it didn't happen, and hope it goes away. Because you feel humiliated, and exposed, and trapped. Humiliated, because you have in good faith sought the intellectual respect of a man who has in *his* mind probably got you dancing topless in his private peep show. Exposed because no matter how hard you try to politely pretend it didn't happen, he simply trots along behind you like some kind of horny dog, finding ways to rub against you, touch your breast, pin you to the bookshelf as you're trying to return one of those formerly sacred books. Trapped because, what can you do? Amazingly enough, the onset of this behavior coincides exactly with the passing of the deadline for dropping courses. You cannot drop. You cannot scream at him, "You're a disgusting, pathetic, dirty old man," because he holds two of your four semester credits in his hands. You cannot complain to the college administration because he's an eminent, tenured, married faculty member and you're just a girl, so who's going to believe you? And remember, this is only 1972, there doesn't yet exist a term like "sexual harassment" to frame the episodes as inherently unacceptable and reassuringly impersonal. You think you're the first woman this has ever happened to, and maybe—because you've been trying your whole life to look sexy and attractive, have been told by a thousand magazines that this is your very life's mission—maybe you even brought this on yourself. So you dodge his advances as best you can, reminding yourself that there are only two weeks to get through. But now along with the load of books you haul back and forth to the bus stop, you also lug the disturbing knowledge that a man upon whom academia has bestowed the custodianship of history's greatest poet has a soul more rotten than Denmark, and treats you as though your soul is of small value compared to your tits and ass.

Athens might have been disappointing had she set her heart on finding a city there that shimmered like Paris. Athens sprawled out across the bottom of a broad bowl of blue scrubby mountains, spilling its clutter of unremarkable concrete-block buildings gracelessly into the distant haze. Here and there among abandoned city lots you stumbled across half-excavated, half-overgrown remnants of decomposed glory—the stone floors of the ancient agora, the pipes that had once fed water to a Roman bath. High above Pláka, the Parthenon still sat majestically upon the massive stone shoulders of the Acropolis and its fortifications. But in the cafes and tavernas below, the men just sat and drank and argued while the women scurried from shop to shop filling netted bags with produce. No one ever seemed to glance upward to marvel at the massive crumbling evidence of a long-past Golden Age of Man.

Maude and Brad—newlyweds reunited—were far too drunk on one another to do much looking up either. The other navy couples piled into tour buses marked "Delphi" and "Olympia," or caught boats out to picturesque, whitewashed islands. Maude and Brad held hands and laughed about how they couldn't bear to stray more than a few blocks from the hotel room. They made love late at night and slept through breakfast. They made love in the afternoons and took naps and went out for long, late dinners, walking back to the hotel with their arms around each other's waists while in the sky above them the Parthenon, floodlit by night, downgraded itself to the role of romantic stage prop.

Late the next summer, in 1972, Brad came home from the navy for good, and he and Maude moved into his parents' ugly suburban bungalow and assumed their dirt-cheap mortgage, while his parents retired to their vacation place out at the lake.

Maude had strenuously objected. She wanted to live in the City with the new friends she'd made at school. She'd already put in more than a year of trekking all the way back out to the suburbs every night to sleep in her childhood bedroom.

But Brad was adamant. The American economy was a mess. President Nixon had, not long before, unilaterally imposed a system of wage-and-price controls which, coming from someone else, might not have seemed so alarming. Coming from the man who was known everywhere for his ardent advocacy of the free-market system, they seemed to sound a siren warning for some imminent economic breakdown. It wasn't as though either Brad or Maude had any savings, after all, and they were both going to attend classes full-time, so it really didn't seem like a smart moment to take any risks they didn't have to take.

It wasn't that Brad's reasoning didn't make sense, Maude thought; it was just that hers made just as much sense. After all, they *could* just decide to have less space, for the same money; they didn't *need* a spare bedroom and a basement and a garage, just for the two of them. And half the income was going to come from her waitressing; didn't that entitle her to half the decision-making power? So then, if you didn't have one of those old-fashioned, man-as-head-of-the-family kind of marriages, how were you supposed to resolve these disagreements?

In the end, what decided it was that Brad screamed. He swore at her and yelled at her, and for a moment she thought he might hit her, but he didn't. Instead, he stomped out, slamming the door behind him. Maude was stunned: *her Brad*, who'd loved her enough to wait for her all those years, to find his way to God for her, to major in literature. It was scary to think that maybe now she knew exactly how much he loved her, and where it stopped: *I'll give you this and this and this, but not* that. Or maybe the love itself was stopping, wearing off, wearing out, so that he no longer wanted to give her things at all.

Those thoughts frightened her—those, and the thought that he might get that angry again, and this time really hit her.

So she moved with him into his parents' house and stopped talking about living in the City.

She got Brad a job at the restaurant where she worked. The staff there referred to him as The Flamer. He wasn't a regular waiter, he was the guy in the fancy suit who came to your table with a cart full of flourishes, to toss your Caesar salad or ignite your cherries jubilee. Sometimes she just stood still at her waitress station and watched him, tossing and flaming and flirting, practically levitating the women diners right under the noses of their dates or husbands, and she still couldn't believe her good fortune, that he loved *her*, that he was hers.

In the early summer of 1973, someone at a party mentioned that Betsy, whom Maude hadn't seen in ages, was pregnant. Maude called her up.

"It's so exciting. When are you due?"

"October," said Betsy. "You know, it's funny. I'm five months' pregnant—I mean, I can feel it moving and everything—and I still can't quite believe it's for real!"

"I know," said Maude, "because—" and here she paused for a moment, dramatically, "—I AM, TOO!"

Then they were on the phone a long time, comparing symptoms and planning how they would get together in the fall so Maude could hold Betsy's baby to see what it felt like before her own baby came in December.

Then Betsy's tone suddenly changed completely and she said, "Have you heard about Carole?"

"Her, too?" said Maude.

"No, she's not pregnant. She's divorced."

"What? From *Josh*?" They had all liked Josh. Of course, you always, with Carole, worried about her heart breaking, the way you might worry about someone with a literal medical heart condition dropping dead. Only there were certain men, like Dave, and then Josh, you didn't worry about her with because they just seemed so completely *nice*.

"All of a sudden, he started talking about wanting an Open Marriage. He told her he needed to feel free to see other women and she had no right to be possessive of him."

"So what did she say?"

"She actually tried to go along with it, at first. She said lots of people are doing it these days, so if it bothered her she must be especially uptight and she ought to get over her own hang-ups. And then, she said, one night he was on his way out and he refused to tell her where he was going or when he was coming back, and she said, 'Then you know what? Don't bother coming back, because I can't handle this.' "

"Oh," said Maude. "So is she—okay?"

"Well, she really won't talk about it. But she dropped out of school before she finished the last semester, and now she's living in an apartment with a girl who was a couple of years ahead of us in high school, and they're both waitressing. You should call her."

"I will," said Maude, taking down the number.

*   *   *

But it was a couple of days before Maude could compose herself enough to call Carole. She was surprised at how upset she felt. Was it just her own disappointment? She'd certainly had her doubts, privately, about some of the other Girls' marriages, but Carole was the one—other than herself—of whom she didn't once think: Did she cop out? Carole had held out for True Love, and everyone who saw her and Josh together had been sure she'd found it.

Of course, this kind of thing was hardly unusual, these days. Nobody seemed to be sure what marriage *was* anymore. It was unusual to find someone like Brad, with whom you were so sure you could do all the personal growth you were going to need to do without bumping your head on the ceiling. Either way, you could lose. You could try not to grow, repressing all your real needs and feelings and desires till you ended up like the Louds, robotically acting out empty, meaningless roles, and then one morning you woke up—if you ever did wake up at all—and realized you'd blown your whole life away. Or you could try to give each other perfect freedom, like so many couples who were currently going the Bob-and-Carol-and-Ted-and-Alice route, who joined swingers' clubs and held orgies and talked openly about their affairs. All those couples—usually the men, though—would insist that the sex was Meaningless. Well, if it was meaningless, why were they having it? And if it wasn't, it was very, very dangerous. Everybody knew the story that had been all over the news that spring of the two New York Yankees pitchers, Mike Kekich and Fritz Peterson, who'd switched wives in mid-season. It had started out as a "joke," the couples said, something all four of them giggled about over drinks. But then after a party one night, the wives had actually gone home with each other's husbands. The double affair had gone on all season, and then when they all tried to go back to their original mates, no one wanted to. So now they were all getting divorced, and Fritz

Peterson and Susanne Kekich were going to get married to each other and live with the Kekich children. Only, Mike Kekich and Marilyn Peterson hadn't been able to work things out because, Mike said, " 'Marilyn and I are both under the same sign of the Zodiac—Aries. We butted heads. It fell apart.' "

You felt sorry for the Peterson children. And Marilyn and Mike. And Carole, of course. But the fact was, if the feeling had died, it didn't do anyone any favors to stay around pretending it hadn't. Ultimately, Maude decided, Carole would surely grow as a person because of all this. Maude felt ready to call her now. She sighed as she picked up the phone, and thanked God that He had forced her to wait for Brad until Brad had finished sowing his wild oats, and until she was sure he was the one.

"It's the Libbers," said Maude's mother. Maude had just been fitted for a bridesmaid's gown for her cousin's upcoming wedding, and they were driving home together. "They've got no respect for the institution of marriage."

"Ma," said Maude, "how could it be the fault of a bunch of feminist activists that Carole's husband wanted to sleep with other women?"

"Yeah—what made him think he had the right to ask for that? What made him think any woman was gonna want to sleep with a married man, anyway? She wouldn't, unless she thought she was going to get him to divorce his wife and marry her."

"But, Ma, if she thought that, she probably wouldn't be a Libber. Libbers aren't obsessed with getting married."

"Ha!" said her mother triumphantly. "Libbers are even worse! Libbers act like it's okay for a man to think he doesn't owe a woman anything just because he sleeps with her. Of course they're going to just walk away afterward, if they think they can. That was the whole point of getting married first, in my day. It was for the woman's protection."

Maude was so confused by her mother's logic she wasn't sure where to start. "That's patronizing," she said. "Women don't need to be protected. They're strong enough to take care of themselves."

"They're strong enough to take care of themselves and the whole rest of the world, too," said her mother. "And that's what they've always done. You think Carole wasn't waiting on that Josh hand and foot, cooking his dinners, typing his term papers, washing his socks?"

Maude, who personally would have drawn the line at typing term papers, said, "Yeah, so?"

"So, what does she get in return? Does he take care of her? No, he goes out looking for a new woman. In my generation at least you didn't have to worry about that till you got fat or lost your looks."

"Ma, you're missing the point. Marriage can become a trap for a woman, too. You must understand that. Isn't that what happened to you, in your first marriage?"

"That wasn't frivolous," her mother said firmly. "That wasn't so we could go out and fool around with other people. He was mean to me. He *hit* me."

"So then why did you want to get married again? What made you think it was going to work out the second time if it hadn't worked out the first time?"

Her mom thought for a while. "Your father was very different," she said finally. "He was a Good Man." The way she said it, you could hear the capital letters, as though men came with labels like that affixed to the backs of their necks, where you could check if you weren't sure what they were made of.

"Besides," she added with a small smile, "you were on the way."

"MA!" said Maude, astonished. "You never told me that."

"Well, it's time you knew. Actually, we might not have gotten married if it hadn't been for that."

Maude wondered whether that meant that her father wouldn't have asked if he hadn't had to, or that her mother wouldn't have said yes if she hadn't felt cornered. She was about to ask, when her mother abruptly terminated the intimacy, and said, in an entirely different tone of voice, "The dress was nice, but it's too bad she had to pick something so fitted at the waist."

"Let's hope," she added, taking her eyes off the road for just a moment to glance at Maude's belly, "let's hope you still fit into it in August."

She did still fit into it in August—perfectly. The other bridesmaids exclaimed enviously over how slim and energetic she was, how she didn't seem to be showing at all.

But her mother frowned, and asked when her next doctor's visit was.

The visit was scheduled for the Friday after the Thursday when her very last paper for her very last semester of college was due. She was exhausted from staying up most of the night to finish it, but as she deposited it in her professor's box she felt a great rush of exhilaration: She was done now, she had earned the right to quit waitressing, and just sew and cook and read and wait quietly for her baby to be born.

But on Friday the doctor said, "Your uterus is not the size we would expect it to be at five months." He took blood to send to the lab for another pregnancy test. But, because it was already Friday and the lab would be closed all weekend, they would not have the results till Monday.

Maude went home and cried and prayed, alternately. Brad said there was nothing they could do: Either the baby was okay or it wasn't. Maude thought that he didn't really understand. *My baby is on death row*, she thought, *but maybe I can still save it.* And so she prayed and prayed to God, and waited for him to return a last-minute stay of execution.

On Monday the doctor called and said the pregnancy test had been negative. Her body had stopped supporting the pregnancy hormonally. They would wait another day or two to see whether she would miscarry spontaneously. If not, she would have to have a D & C. "An abortion?" she asked anxiously, as though the doctor were proposing ending something that was not already over.

She went on praying for the whole two days. The test might turn out to be mistaken, after all. She kept praying right up until the awful afternoon that became a jumble of nightmare images in her mind: the woman shaving her pubic hair—why had she done that? it was so humiliating—and had she introduced herself as *Sister*, was she a nun? And then the doctor, only moments afterward she thought, telling her the "tissue" they had removed from her had been severely malformed—just *tissue*, not a baby. Nature had misfired, and let her fall in love with a baby who would never even come to be.

After that, Maude just cried and cried, and entirely stopped praying. No God that she could love, she told Brad emphatically, could do something like this to her. Brad lost patience pretty quickly, saying, "Hey, it was my baby, too. How come everybody acts like this terrible thing just happened to you, and it's okay if you just sit there and go all to pieces but I'm supposed to just keep going about my business?"

She didn't know what to tell him. She knew her own grief *was* deeper than his, because it was within *her*, literally, that this terrible thing had happened; she was the scene of the accident. He might be hurting, but she was too decimated to hold out any comfort to him.

Brad being Brad, it didn't take him long to find a woman who could. He began getting phone calls from Liza, a waitress they had both worked with.

"She's just a friend," Brad insisted. Then he added, reproachfully, "She *listens* to me. And she's fun to be with."

This is the wake-up call, thought Maude. *If I don't get up and pull myself together . . .*

So she went back to waitressing, and to smoking, which she had quit for the sake of the baby, and she found an attractive waiter to flirt with at all the parties they went to, just to show Brad that his blatant flirtation with Liza didn't really threaten her. If he wanted space, he was welcome to it.

In November, she went to visit Betsy, and held her small, warm, pink baby boy and exclaimed over how cute he was and didn't even cry till she was safely outside again in her car.

On the last day of 1973, she and Brad gave a New Year's party for the crowd of students, bartenders, waiters, and waitresses they hung out with. After a while, she noticed that Brad had disappeared. Liza was gone, too. She started asking people: "Have you seen Brad?" Finally someone said, "Check the spare bedroom."

The spare bedroom was locked. Maude rattled the knob and yelled, "Brad, are you in there? Would you let me in, please?"

No answer.

"Brad, are you in there? Is Liza in there with you?"

A circle of people was gathering nervously around her. The attractive waiter, with whom she was no longer interested in flirting, said, "Maude?"

"WHAT?" she snapped, spinning around. "What do YOU want? Did you know they were in there? Did everyone know they were in there? Why the HELL didn't anyone tell ME?"

She turned back and began pounding on the door. "Open up the door, you son of a bitch. Open up the fucking DOOR!" She gave it a hard kick and then burst into tears. Finally, someone took her by the arm and led her, sobbing, gently down the stairs.

After a week of virtual silence between them, Brad announced that it was really his house and he wanted her to move out.

"Brad," she said patiently. "We are married. We took vows. We promised to stick with each other, to try to work things out."

"I can't," said Brad. "Not unless you leave. I can't think with you here."

"Leaving would be wrong. If I leave, *she'll* want to come here and be with you."

"You don't understand," said Brad. "I want her to be here with me. I want to see her every day. I don't want to have to sneak around. I don't want to have to be—*dishonest.*"

Oddly, Maude didn't get angry with him. She got angry at Liza—she *hated* Liza, she fantasized about *murdering* Liza—but she couldn't think that it was Brad's fault. She still loved him, and she thought the thing would run its course. *Think carefully,* she wanted to tell him, *before you kill this; you don't even appreciate what it is you're killing.* It was what she had tried to tell God about the baby, but God hadn't listened either, because the baby was already dead by then and God had already moved on to something else, and her words had dissolved in the pool of her own tears.

Carole took her in. "Next victim," she said cheerfully when Maude's car pulled up, because she'd just seen the roommate Maude was replacing through an unwed pregnancy. She hugged Maude and helped her carry in her suitcases and a few wilted plants, and then she made her a gin and tonic and offered her a Marlboro.

"I didn't know you smoked," said Maude.

"I didn't," said Carole. "I took it up when I was getting over Josh."

"Oh?" said Maude. "What else did you take up?"

"Well, I took up yoga. I took up macrobiotic cooking. I took up astrology."

"Is that all?"

"Welllll—" Carole took a long drag, and giggled. "For a while I took up this real cool guy named Mark."

Maude regarded her gloomily. She had expected to find Carole more forlorn and plainly damaged. But Carole had more than a year between her and the loss of Josh. In another year, Maude thought, maybe I'll have a sense of humor, too.

But then, because banter was usually the dialect that sprang to the Girls' tongues when they were together, she heard herself say, "Yeah? So of all that, which would you most heartily prescribe for a fellow traveler with a totally shattered heart?"

"That's easy," said Carole. "Smoking, for sure. But don't worry, hon. We'll do some serious drinking, too."

For a while after the loss of Josh, Carole had simply been stunned. She just went on, though, like those cartoon characters who run off cliffs yet remain suspended in midair, their legs cycling frantically, because they haven't discovered there's no longer anything beneath them. She did all the things women do to transcend humiliation in love. She drank too much, smoked too much, ate alternately too much and too little. She fell in love again too impossibly fast with Mark, who'd been a friend of Josh's. He was into a guru called Baba, whose teachings admonished him to be vegetarian, and celibate. When he got involved with Carole, she became a vegetarian, and he faltered in his celibacy.

Carole, too, tried to follow Baba. He had "dropped the body," as his disciples phrased it, in 1967, so of course she never got to actually meet him. But the disciples ran a retreat in South Carolina, and Mark took Carole there for a while, and they ate brown rice and vegetables and got up at dawn to do yoga under the orange sunrise. But Carole really wasn't a morning person.

Carole's family never said anything remotely resembling I told you so about Josh, but they eyed Mark warily. When her uncle, visiting her apartment, saw her shrine to Baba, with its picture of him in his gauzy white garments, he said, "Hey, Carole, who's that fat guy in the underwear?" Her mother, with the air of making sure a potential lifeguard knew CPR, cornered Mark right off the bat and said, "I know how my daughter feels about you, now why don't you tell me how you feel about my daughter?"

He had to think about it for a moment. Too long a moment, really, before he said that he *really cared.*

A short time later, he reminded Carole that Baba said those who love carnally cannot experience the more perfect spiritual love of Baba.

She went on struggling through her senior year at college. When her mom called, she could just chatter away as though everything were fine, but then her dad would get on the phone and say, "How's it going, hon?" and somehow she would deflate just a little.

"Oh, Dad, it's *so hard,*" was all she could say.

Her dad would say, teasingly, "Well, you know you can always just quit," and that would comfort her and reinflate her, because it would remind her that he was always a safe haven, but at the same time, that she was not a quitter.

But frankly, she didn't see what the point of this education was. At the beginning she had decided to major in psychology, with the vague intention of ending up in one of the Helping Professions. But whatever it was that made her want to help in the first place—her desire to connect emotionally with others, to sense their needs and feel their pain and make of herself, through the simple presence of her own openness, a sort of pillow for their weary heads—was not at all addressed in the courses she took. You didn't get academic credit for being a pillow for weary heads, not unless you could accept and memorize certain authorized truths about Freud and conditioned response and a host of pretty upsetting pathologies. It seemed as if you couldn't even get personal credit. What Carole was really suited for—what she would most have liked doing—was getting married and taking care of her husband and a house and kids. But you couldn't say that anymore, not in college; Carole was even afraid to think it to herself. Everyone would have looked at you like you were some kind of freak. Hadn't you ever heard of Women's Lib? Didn't you understand that without a career, you would never have any kind of *identity*?

So Carole drifted into sociology, thinking maybe she'd be a social worker. But halfway through that year, the drinking and the vegetarianism and Mark suddenly wore off, and the next time her father told her jokingly, "You know, you can always quit," she burst into tears and sobbed into the phone, "That's good, because I just did."

In the safety of her childhood bedroom, Carole decided that she needed a year to back off from the pressure of college work, to get her head together. She didn't know exactly what was going to cause that to happen, probably not a crummy job waitressing at the nearby hotel that was capped with a round restaurant that actually revolved.

But on the first day of waitress training, she made friends with a girl named Cindy, who said she liked to party. She looked mousy, with light brown hair that was pulled back and big glasses that hid her eyes, and she seemed timid. But the first night she showed up at Carole's door to go out drinking, her hair was down and she had some nice makeup on and she was a total knock out. When you got to know her, her pixie face lit up easily with laughter, and it turned out she'd been a couple of years ahead of the Girls at St. Mary Magdalen High School, so there were people they knew in common. She and Carole quickly developed a routine. They signed up for the same shifts, then clocked out together and headed for the hotel down the street where they drank at the bar, often till one or the other couldn't stand up. They had been doing this for less than two weeks when Cindy excused herself to make a phone call and then returned to her bar stool visibly pale and shaken.

"So," she said, lifting her vodka and tonic in a mock toast, "Here's to me. I'm pregnant."

Familiar story: used to live with him, he couldn't make a commitment, he wanted to see other women, she still loved him. He told Cindy that of course he would help pay for an abortion, but if she chose to have the baby, he wanted nothing more to do with her.

Her mother told her essentially the same thing.

"And what do *you* want to do?" Carole asked her.

"I'm adopted," said Cindy. "Someone didn't abort me."

"Then you'll have it," Carole said, as though that solved everything.

"I can't keep it," Cindy whispered, choking on the words. "I'm not—a responsible person."

That's what her mother told her: She was impulsive, selfish, self-destructive, noncommittal. She couldn't stay in school, couldn't hold a job; she drank too much and she was slutty and the only men she fell in love with were the ones who didn't fall in love with her. Hardly motherhood material. And her mom didn't want a baby dumped on *her* to raise, at her age, whenever Cindy got to feeling that she was sick of playing house.

For the first time since the disintegration of her marriage, Carole was filled with a sense of mission, of vocation. She went out and rented an apartment, and both of them left the bedrooms of their daughterhood and set up housekeeping together. Carole got Cindy the phone number for Catholic Charities, and instantly there was a couple out there who would be thrilled to adopt this baby. So it *was* settled.

The months went by. Cindy, growing larger and grouchier and more depressed, sleeping on their days off sometimes until one or two in the afternoon, would get up to find Carole in the kitchen, humming a show tune and making Cindy a bowl of pastina, because that's what her gramma had always made for her when she was a little girl, and it would definitely be good for the baby, and you bet it would cheer Cindy up, too. They continued to work the same shifts and to go out afterward. The handsome hotel chef, out on the loading dock smoking cigarettes with the manager, would watch them as they left the back way, great-bellied Cindy waddling awkwardly beside pert, petite Carole, and would call sardonically after them, "Remember, girls, try to stay out of trouble."

Six weeks before her due date, Cindy quit work and moved back home with her mom, who grudgingly agreed that she could return as long as she was positive she was definitely giving up the baby. Meanwhile, her mom was planning on taking a two-week vacation that would be timed so all the unpleasantness would be over before she got back. So it was Carole who picked Cindy up from the hospital, tucked her into bed at home, and went poking around in the kitchen for some Italian caloric agent powerful enough to neutralize the tragedy of an empty-armed mother. Cindy lay in bed and cried while her breasts swelled with the milk of futility, until finally it dried up and went away. Good for nothing.

Cindy just kept crying. Carole stayed with her a week, ten days. Finally, as her mother's return approached, Cindy took Carole's hand and whispered, "She's going to kill me."

"Why is she going to kill you?"

"Because I'm going to get that baby back."

"Hon," said Carole, "if you want that baby back, we'll get you that baby back. And we'll make sure your mom doesn't kill you."

The Catholic Charities caseworker said the family was *expecting* the baby, they already knew she was born. But yes, if she insisted, if she was sure she was doing the right thing, she could still have the baby back. But one thing she'd better know, the caseworker warned—*the witch's curse at the cradle of the first-born daughter:* "We sometimes find with women who keep their babies in circumstances such as yours that the children pay hell for the mother's resentment at having been left by the father."

Cindy vowed that this would never happen. Then she went to see the parish priest, telling him her only hope for raising the baby was to have her mom behind her, and her only hope for getting her mom behind her was if the Church was behind her.

So the priest went to see her mother, who agreed to let Cindy stay. Provided that Cindy did all the shopping, all the cleaning, and all the cooking, and that she went on welfare and Aid to Dependent Children.

And she reminded Cindy, whenever the baby cried, not to pick her up, because everybody knows babies who get picked up when they cry grow up spoiled.

Cindy secretly disagreed with her about that, but she followed the advice anyway, because she wanted to keep her mother's goodwill, such as it was, and because, despite what she had sworn to the caseworker, and even though she had just turned her entire life irrevocably upside down to keep the baby, the infant's cries never provoked anything from her other than an unwelcome glimpse of an unsuspected coldness and emptiness within.

By the time, in the winter of 1973–74, when Cindy went home to her mother and Maude showed up, newly shipwrecked, on her doorstep, Carole was herself again. She didn't know why, because as far as she could tell, the things she really *had* to do, the important things—the things she had had to duck for lack of strength—were still before her: the college degree to be completed, some career to be chosen, an actual job found. She thought of the time she had just spent as aimless drifting, because there was no dean or adviser there to sanction the period as a junior year abroad in the American suburbs, where someone still might become fluent in the idiom of friendship, and earn high honors in the independent project of being the pillow for someone else's weary head.

IV

The Woman in the Closet

1974–1977

Fractured Fairy Tales

In early February 1974, a nineteen-year-old Berkeley student stood in the tiny kitchen of the apartment she shared with her twenty-six-year-old fiancé. She was fixing them a dinner of canned chicken soup and tuna sandwiches. She always did the cooking. She did all the cleaning up, too. He decided what time meals should be served.

In high school, when she was just seventeen, he had been one of the teachers. He was very, very smart. He had graduated from Princeton, and now he was getting his Ph.D. in philosophy. And he wanted her to be his wife.

Wasn't it cool? Except now, to be honest, she was having doubts. Funny—when they were just living together, it had seemed so important to extract a commitment from him. But now that she had one, what with all the recent talk about Women's Lib, she was starting to question what marriage would mean to her own identity. Would she become, simply, Mrs. Faculty Wife, a woman whose best years might be consumed by deference to the whims of the wives of deans and tenured faculty members? She'd gone straight from her parents' house to his, without ever stopping to discover who *she* was. How would she ever find herself?

It seemed very important to her to figure all this out, and pretty soon, because she expected that the decision she made about it would determine how happily the rest of her life turned out.

But as a matter of fact, she was wrong about that, because at around nine P.M., the doorbell rang, and when her fiancé went to answer it, into the apartment burst two men and a woman. They beat him senseless, tied her up, and carried her, screaming, out into the street, where, under cover of gunfire, they threw her into the trunk of a Chevrolet convertible and roared off into the night.

For the first two months, the kidnappers kept her tied up and blindfolded on the floor of a tiny dark closet lined with carpeting that stank of sweat and mold. Right outside the closet door, they performed noisy gun drills, loading and unloading their weapons and warning her that they would shoot her instantly if the cops came to rescue her or if she tried to escape. One morning she awoke to find that the bonds had slipped off her wrists in the night; terrified that they would kill her when they found out, she sobbed uncontrollably until one of the nicer—female—kidnappers appeared, and then she apologized profusely and asked to please be tied up again.

They brought a tape recorder into the closet and made her record messages to her parents and to the media, explaining that she was a "prisoner of war." For a large part of every day, the kidnappers lectured her: Her father, a rich and famous "corporate enemy of the people," didn't care about her enough to meet their ransom demands; she had been arrested as part of the revolution on behalf of oppressed people of all races, in retaliation for all the "beautiful people, oppressed poor people forced into a life of crime by the capitalist system and then thrown into prison, where they were beaten and tortured and kept in solitary confinement in order to prevent them from starting a revolution." She was not allowed to urinate or defecate in private. After a while, she became so weak she could barely stand up unsupported. After a while, two of the male kidnappers occasionally came into the closet and raped her. She was told that this was because they had all begun to feel much more "comradely" toward her, and comrades in their revolutionary cell must take care of all of each others' needs, including sexual ones. Also, she was told that these acts of intercourse promoted her liberation as a woman and the liberation of all women, because she was helping to smash the idea of monogamy. "Monogamy only serves to reinforce male supremacy and the oppression of women," the kidnappers told her. "Monogamy means that 'men wear the pants.' "

No one came to rescue her. Not her parents. Not the police. Not her fiancé. So day after day, night after night—barely knowing which was which, and it didn't much matter anyway—she lay on the closet floor, wondering if and how she was going to die.

Then one day, one of the male kidnappers came to the edge of the closet and told her, "The War Council has decided that you can join us, if you want to, or you can be released, and go home again."

This is a trick, she thought. How could they possibly return her now, with all she knew about them? If she said she wanted to go home, it would prove that she had rejected their education. It would prove she didn't honestly care about the plight of the oppressed people, and that would prove that she really was, as they had often called her, a bourgeois bitch, and then they would certainly not hesitate to execute her. The real choice, she thought, was: Join, or die.

She joined. Then, to prove her loyalty, they made her participate in a bank robbery. They gave her a weapon. While they waved their guns around—at the tellers, at the customers, and, she just assumed, at her—she stood in the middle of the bank waving her gun and trying to remember the political speech they had made her memorize for the occasion. "This is Tania . . ." she said finally, using the nom de guerre with which they had christened her, ". . . Patricia Hearst." Then she stopped. That was all she could remember.

Patty Hearst's participation in the robbery of the Hibernia Bank in April of 1974 converted what had been an outpouring of public concern for the kidnapped heiress into a gathering wave of outrage. No one knew for sure whether her tape-recorded messages of solidarity with her captors were genuine or coerced, or whether she had been the victim of some insidious sort of "brainwashing." Nevertheless, in the two years that she was—depending on how you felt about her—"at large," or "still missing"—she came to magnetize all the public anger at the American kids of her generation: ungrateful kids who rewarded their parents' sacrifices and loving care by dropping out, doing drugs, joining religious cults, rejecting patriotism, espousing radical political notions that mocked everything their parents had ever struggled to achieve.

In the cruelest of ironies, she came to symbolize something else as well. The image of "Tania" robbing the bank—grim-faced, holding a carbine in combat-ready posture, often superimposed on a silhouette of the six-headed cobra everyone recognized as the symbol of the violent Symbionese Liberation Army she appeared to have joined—embodied exactly what had been suggested by the militaristic-sounding phrase which in those years was used interchangeably with terms like "feminist" and "women's libbers": *the forces of women's liberation.*" When people looked at that photo of Patty and her machine gun, they saw an incarnation of the Aggressive Woman, a human I-told-you-so, the vindication of everyone who'd insisted that if women ever stopped being traditional and docile and submissive, all hell was gonna break loose. When, around the time the FBI finally tracked Hearst down and arrested her in the fall of 1975, two mentally unstable women were arrested in quick succession for attempting to assassinate President Gerald Ford, *Newsweek* lumped the three women together and concluded that they constituted "a connection between the recent flowering of the feminist movement and the dramatic upsurge in violent crimes attributed to women since the 1960s." And, in case that wasn't sufficiently explicit: "And now, with the liberation of women, female Americans seem to have finally reached equality with men in acting out . . . rage—not just against themselves, but against society at large."

No one knew that it was docility that had saved Patty Hearst in the closet, that an assertive sense of self probably would have gotten her killed right off the bat. No one knew she had been raped into adopting a concept of "feminist" sexuality, and converted at gunpoint into the army of the "people's liberation." No one looked at the photo of lank-haired, undernourished Tania and the machine gun and exclaimed, "My God, she's had a makeover!" It's not a makeover if you don't come out prettier; it's not a makeover if no one falls in love with you afterward.

Patty Hearst's 1976 trial for waving the gun around in the Hibernia Bank robbery was one of those trial-of-the-century media circuses in which F. Lee Bailey was, inevitably, the high-profile attorney. Patty was led back and forth from the jail in chains, her eyes sunk deep in the black sockets of her pale, emaciated face, her fleshless frame drowning in the pastel suits designed to remind the jury of her good-girl upbringing. Bailey argued that she had been "brainwashed" into joining the SLA. Was there such a thing as brainwashing? wondered the media. Experts were interviewed and quoted, psychiatrists who trained soldiers not to crack under the tortures that Chinese and Viet Cong captors were said to practice on American prisoners of war. But then the judge instructed the jury: The fact of Patty's kidnapping in no way mitigated her participation in the robbery; she was to be judged on the facts of the robbery itself. So the most notorious unwitting women's liberationist of the decade was convicted and sentenced to seven years in prison. By then she was in love with one of the bodyguards her parents had hired to protect her.

After President Jimmy Carter commuted her sentence in 1979, she married the bodyguard and retired behind the walls of a Connecticut home with a crackerjack security system to have children and live in peace. The book she published about her odyssey in 1982 is curiously dry and unemotional, and doesn't tell us whether she still does all the cooking and the cleaning up, or whether she thinks she would ultimately have been able to confront her first fiancé, Steven Weed, about doing his share of the dishes.

Real Life

On Valentine's Day, a week after the kidnapping of Patty Hearst, Maude and Carole decided to take each other out to lunch. They made an appointment at a City salon, where Carole had her waist-length hair cut to her shoulders, and then they went into a department store and bought Maude a sexy, low-cut black leotard, and then they went into a fancy restaurant and ordered shrimp salad and big goblets of cold white wine. It was too bad, they agreed, slathering big crusty rolls with creamy butter, that some women got all tangled up in love very young and then wasted the best years of their lives immersed in domestic

trivialities. Oh, boy, you should hear Tammy and Betsy, although
you literally couldn't, because whenever you called them there
was a baby screaming in the background, and both of them said
that with babies in the house you practically didn't even have
enough time to yourself to get into the shower. But luckily, that
hadn't happened to either of them, and if they were smart,
they'd take advantage of it.

"Like, for instance," said Maude, "this would be an excellent
time to go back to Europe."

"Can't afford it," said Carole. "Are you going to have dessert?"

"There's a three-layer thing that looked good, and a four-layer
thing," said Maude. "And we could afford it if we took double
shifts between now and July and flew one of those airlines that
goes through Iceland. The four-layer thing was chocolate."

Carole looked thoughtful. "Remember Donna? We could pick
up the mayor's key from her and take it back to that awful little
town we stayed in."

"What?"

"Didn't you know about that? During the mayor's reception,
when Sister Mary William got mad at us because they had put out
champagne and we were all drinking it and she couldn't stop us?
Donna got tipsy, and she saw a bunch of keys hanging from one
of the doors and she just kind of sidled up when no one was looking and took one. She used to brag about it. She said it was one of
her earliest mortal sins. I wonder what ever happened to her."

"Tammy and Betsy see her sometimes. When Tammy had her
first baby and she was feeling really isolated out there in the suburbs, she tracked Donna down. And apparently Donna was having babies and feeling isolated, too. So she told me now the three
of them get together for lunch once a month or so, and I guess
they bring all the screaming kids with them."

Maude cast a glance around the restaurant, at the waiters in
starched white shirts delivering elegant arrangements of grilled

fish and baby vegetables on fine china. "As I said, it kind of makes you grateful to be single."

"You know," she added after a moment, "my favorite picture from that trip is this one where I'm sitting in the lap of that statue of Zeus at Versailles, without a phone book. Remember, the nuns used to tell us that it was a mortal sin to sit on a boy's lap, that if you ever *had* to sit on a boy's lap, which I can't imagine why they thought we might *have* to, you should always be sure to put a phone book between your butt and his crotch?"

Carole laughed, and took a sip of wine, and looked a little dreamy. "Remember Dave?" she said.

"Yeah, whatever happened to him, do you think?"

"You know, after all that stuff about how hopeless it would be to have this long-distance relationship, he ended up moving somewhere pretty near here. He called me up one day, totally out of the blue, and said, 'Hey, Carrie, whatcha doin'?' And I just took this huge gulp and said, 'Aaaaaah, writing out wedding invitations, actually.' I couldn't believe his timing."

"So he's still out there," Maude said. "Maybe he's still single. Maybe you could track him down."

"Oh, I dunno, Maude, you really think you can go back like that?"

"Probably not," said Maude. "You'll find somebody better, anyway."

"And you?" Carole said, as nonchalantly as she could. Actually, she was a little worried about Maude, who had taken to going into the City late at night and hanging out in jazz clubs by herself. "Not by myself," Maude would insist. "I make friends." She always took along a fat little baggie full of pot, and in the breaks she'd go up to the musicians and engage them in conversation, and then invite them into the back alley for a joint. She told Carole the music spoke to her, and she said it in the same reverent tone she used to use when she talked about being a Christian, as though it was

going to be her new *thing*. She said it was deeply sexual, the flirta-
tious way the melody began, and you relaxed slowly into it and let
the musicians take it through playful twists and turns, sweeping
you up into the passion of their crescendos and then letting you
slowly, ever so gently down. She said she could feel it sometimes
as a tingling in her groin, and it thrilled her, like her solitary walks
down the dark, shiny, city streets her parents had always warned
her not to travel alone. She said she thought a man who knew how
to make music like that must surely be able to coax unearthly
melodies from women.

Brad had taken Maude to her first jazz club, so Carole
couldn't really tell if this was Maude's way of hanging on to him,
or her strategy for filling the crater he and God had left in her life
by running away.

"You mean," Maude said now, "do I think I'll ever find someone better than Brad? You know, it's not out of the question that
he'll come back. I wouldn't be at all surprised if he just got sick
of this woman, now that he can see her all he wants. I worked
with her, and I have to say, there just wasn't very much *there*."

"Josh tried to come back once," Carole said thoughtfully.
"But it was awful, because I didn't trust him anymore, and he
acted like he didn't understand why."

"Yeah, you know why he probably came back? Because you
got interested in Mark. They can always sense it when you get interested in someone else, and that's when they come sniffing
around again. But I'll tell you, it just doesn't happen if you sit
around and cry over 'em. So I think that's an excellent reason for
us to go to France as soon as possible."

Maude waved at their waitress. "And I also think—it being
Valentine's Day—we really deserve four layers instead of three."

On the way out of the crowded restaurant, they had to squeeze
past several cocktail-happy tables in the bar, and at one of them

a middle-aged woman and a moon-faced businessman flagged them down as though they knew them and yelled at them to sit down and have a drink. Carole smiled her polite smile and said, "No thanks, we've got to get going," but Maude grinned, sensing adventure, and plopped down in a chair and introduced herself.

The moon-faced man introduced himself as Roger and said he was a lawyer. He wanted to know if by chance they played handball. "No, we don't," said Carole. "Sure," said Maude. He bowled, too. He had a truck and a snowmobile and a boat. He traveled a lot. He said he was twenty-nine, which surprised both of them, because with his suit and his short thinning hair and his rather stony-faced reaction to Maude's mocking dramatization of President Nixon saying, "There is a time to fly and there is a time to fight—and I'm going to fight like hell," his mere six additional years of chronological age didn't quite account for why he was in some mysterious way that they knew they weren't, a *grown-up*.

The middle-aged woman was his office manager. The moment he excused himself to go to the men's room, she gushed conspiratorially, "Isn't he adorable? And so eligible. I was telling him, he just doesn't meet the right kind of woman, if you know what I mean. As soon as I saw you girls I said to him, 'They look like *nice* girls, and look, they're all by themselves on Valentine's Day.'"

Outside, the girls dissolved into laughter. " 'So eligible, if you know what I mean,' " mimicked Maude. "Oh my God, Carrie— maybe you shouldn't have cut off so much hair. Do you think we're starting to look like the kind of girls who would date a . . . a . . . *Republican*?"

The next morning at eight, the phone in their apartment rang, and both of them held their breath, hoping that the other one would haul herself out of bed to answer it. Finally, Carole sighed, pulled the covers off, and went to pick it up.

She poked her head into Maude's room. "It's that guy we met

yesterday," she said. "He wants to know if we wanna play hand-ball."

"Oh God," said Maude, "does he know what *time* it is? Tell him to call back some time when normal human beings are awake."

Carole padded back to the phone. "Um, could you call back some other time? Okay? Thanks."

The next morning at eight, the phone rang again.

So they met him for handball, and it didn't seem to discourage him that obviously neither of them had ever played it before, because when they were done he asked if they'd like to go bowling next time.

Maude said, "So what do *you* think accounts for the eighteen-and-a-half-minute gap on the tape?"

But Carole said, "Sure."

A few days later, the phone rang at eight in their apartment, and Maude, waiting for Carole to get up and answer it, realized she wasn't there. When she finally picked up, Carole's voice came spilling over the line. "Maude, I'm over at Roger's, he just left for work, you *gotta* come over here and see this place, you'll just die."

Carole answered the door in her slip, and waved Maude into Roger's apartment.

"It's a condo," she said, almost reverently. "He owns it."

"Oh my God," said Maude. It was white, as white as an arctic landscape, and entirely immaculate. White walls, plush white carpeting, white leather sofas, an all-white kitchen. There was a shiny, black, state-of-the-art stereo system, a fully outfitted bar, and a sprinkling of potted plants that appeared to be meticulously cared for.

"But what you really gotta see," said Carole, "is this."

She took Maude into the all-white bedroom and slid open the closet door, and there before them was the most organized display of menswear either of them had ever seen outside a department store. A row of freshly laundered dress shirts hung above a row of neatly pressed suits; there were stacks of carefully folded sweaters in vertical shelving, special racks for ties and belts, all neatly hung, and along the bottom, two slanted shelves of polished dress and white leisure shoes on shoe trees.

Maude said, "You've found him: the anti-Josh." She looked a little stunned. She reached into her purse and pulled out a baggie full of pot, and the two of them went back into the living room and rolled a joint on the immaculate glass coffee table, taking extra care to sweep up all the crumbs.

They each took a nice long drag. Finally, Carole said, "He sure *lives* like a grown-up."

Maude started to giggle and then stopped, looking at Carole suspiciously, because from the expression on Carole's face Maude got the idea that Carole meant this as a compliment.

Maude made it clear in the face of what turned out to be Roger's very aggressive courtship that it was more important than ever that Carole make this trip to Europe. Roger was appalled that she would even *consider* spending six weeks away from him.

"You know," said Maude, "it wouldn't be so bad if he didn't act like he *owned* you or something."

Roger said, of Maude, "Why does she need to keep dragging you out to jazz clubs? She knows you're not looking to date anybody else. She's just trying to stir up trouble."

Carole felt miserable. She noticed she was spending an awful lot of time trying to explain to Roger how wonderful Maude really was, and explaining to Maude why Roger was not, as Maude more or less immediately decided he was, an asshole. But the fact was, Maude *was* trying to stir up trouble, and Roger *was* embarrassingly possessive. He insisted on knowing her whereabouts at all times. He phoned many times a day, and whenever she was out, with Maude or anyone else, she seemed to be constantly excusing herself to phone Roger and tell him where they were, how long she thought they'd be there, when she could be expected at his place. If she didn't make these phone calls, she was likely to find waiters, bartenders, and maître d's hunting her down like parole officers, saying there was a gentleman who wished to speak with her on the house phone.

It was humiliating, but it was also deeply reassuring. Wasn't it? As long as he was obsessed with knowing where to find her, she could tell for sure that he wasn't thinking how nice it would be if she would just quietly fade into the woodwork so he could concentrate on chasing other women. That's the kind of reasoning past pain induces, when it hasn't quite expired.

"I dunno," Maude said skeptically. "It's perfectly possible for them to be possessive and still cheat. It's not about love, necessarily. It could just be about, you know—marking his territory. The real question you might wanna be asking yourself is, how do *you* feel about him?"

But Carole had no idea. She liked Roger—she had a good time with him, she got along with him easily, she admired his gusto in work and play, and she thought it served as a healthy balance for her introspectiveness and her tendency to mope about. But was she *in love* with him? Not the way she had been with Josh, or with Dave—not with that rush of pure passion that stopped you dead in your tracks and consumed you, that filled you up with longing for the other person and emptied you of your fears and your separateness, that heightened your awareness of everything around you and blurred the outlines of your self.

The more she thought about it, though, the more she became convinced of one thing: If she didn't turn out to be in love with him, she would always regret having sacrificed to him the chance to go on this adventure with Maude in Europe; and if she was in love with him, she didn't want to end up among the things he owned, well tended but nevertheless distinctly possessed, a cashmere sweater stacked with all the other sweaters in the ever-so-neat piles of his tidy closet.

In the south of France, you could buy bottles of rich red wine at the side of the road for a dollar. You could lie on a blanket gazing at the landscape that had seduced brilliant painters and understand, as they had, that the sunlight loved the earth here more than any other place. The bread seemed crustier, the tomatoes more succulent, the cheese more pungent, and time itself more benign.

In a little rented car they drove along winding country roads, avoiding hotels and cathedrals, stopping in campgrounds and keeping their eyes peeled for the local bar, where they would sit for hours with the *vin du campagne* and a deck of cards, playing gin rummy and talking to anyone who condescended to speak English. Maude was looking for action; Carole didn't know what she was looking for, exactly. One rainy night they stayed up very late drinking with an Englishman they met at a campground, where he and his young son were staying in a trailer. Carole gave up early and, yawning, said she was heading back to the tent to sack out. Maude and the Englishman kept drinking till they agreed it would be a delightful night for skinny-dipping in the campground pool, and raced shrieking through the downpour, peeling off their clothes, to see who could dive in first. On the way back to his trailer, peeking in on Carole, Maude found her snoring soundly, curled up in her sleeping bag, soaked to the skin, an island in a great river of water that was flowing through the tent. So they picked her up, took her back to the trailer, dried her off, and tucked her naked into the bunk with the Englishman's seven-year-old to sleep off the storm and the rest of the wine.

"I can't believe this," Carole said when she awoke, which

became something of an anthem of theirs all the way up through the Alps. Maude's souvenir from the Englishman was a urinary tract infection. So up the tiny spiraling roads they drove, looping around the hairpin turns with their frighteningly precipitous drop-offs, just managing to squeeze past a caravan of crawling trucks, before Maude would moan, "Oooooh, Carrie, I gotta go, could you pull over?" And when Carole finally found a slice of shoulder, Maude would go shooting off into the bushes while the caravan of trucks rumbled slowly by, and Carole knew it would take another hour to get around them again.

Well, they were in no hurry, really. They stopped at Evian to visit the chateau where they had stayed on the high school trip. It was empty for the summer and looked strange and unreal, like the Hollywood stage set for a movie about their teenage days. It had only been seven years, actually, which didn't sound like much but felt to Carole like an entire lifetime. College, marriage, all that waitressing and drinking: the difference between the life you had dreamed for yourself and the life you actually encountered. It was so improbably beautiful here, the way the blue lake sparkled and the villages nestled in the crannies of the snow-dipped mountains, like the wrapper of a bar of rich Swiss chocolate, like the setting for a fairy tale. It reminded Carole that once she had thought she couldn't live without Dave, that once she had thought she couldn't live without Josh.

At the end of the six weeks, Carole was tired of campgrounds and strangers and of washing without ever feeling completely clean. She missed her parents. She missed her own bed. She missed Roger. She was ready to go home.

But Maude wasn't done yet. She took Carole to the airport, saying she didn't think she'd be getting on that plane, but she had to make a phone call just to be sure.

She caught Brad at home. "I'm just calling to tell you, I met some real nice guys who say it's not that hard to get a work permit in London, and they can help me get real cheap housing, so I'm thinking of staying on for a while." That sounded pretty light and breezy, didn't it? She didn't want him thinking she was trying to pressure him. She took a deep breath and continued: "But I know we're still married, Brad. So if you want me to come home, if you feel like you're ready to talk things over, then I could still decide to come back."

There was a long transatlantic silence, a crackling of dead air. Finally, Brad said, "Hey, if you're having a good time, I think you should stay."

Okay, thought Maude, it's very important not to cry now.

"Brad, honey, could you do me one favor? Has my tax refund come in? Could you send me the money at the American Express office in London? Because I'm running kind of low on cash."

"Sure," Brad said, adding, before he hung up, "have fun."

Here is how many men it took, in swinging London, to almost fill the crater:

Eddie Baboe from Ghana, six foot two, an ebony Adonis. He could eat fire. Maude watched him put a whole flaming stick into his throat, just to entertain his friends, and that very evening, after everyone else had gone home, they listened to jazz records and he danced Maude slowly, slowly around the room until he danced her right into the bed.

Salim, who claimed to be an Ethiopian prince, one of the many great-grandnephews of the emperor Haile Selassie. He was small and wiry and starting to go bald, but he had a flat in a posh neighborhood, and the flat was usually filled with posh people whose photos you saw in glossy magazines. He actually said things to her like, "Cook my dinner, woman," and offered to make her his official mistress. She thought about it seriously, because getting a work permit had turned out to be virtually impossible, and the money from Brad hadn't come, and it looked as though she was going to have to get through the winter in London with one secondhand wool dress and no coat. But Salim would only take her to bed once a week ("When I fuck you, it lasts a week," he maintained), and she thought, To be someone's mistress I would really *need* to be sexually *enthralled*.

Julian, a jazz pianist she met at a pub, who took her out to the country for a few weeks while he played out a theater gig. Between his pay and what she picked up as a barmaid talking to the local drunks all afternoon, they managed to keep a cute little flat. Five or six of his band mates and the trumpeter's girlfriend would come over to drink and play cards, and the makeup and wardrobe guys, a pair of queers, would fuss around making sandwiches and emptying the ashtrays. Julian made love to her every single night, and twice on Sundays, when he was off.

But after six weeks of that, her visa was expiring, and the money from Brad still hadn't come, and when Julian put her, regretfully, on the plane home, she thought her life was at a dead end. Déjà vu: Here she was again in tears on a plane returning from Europe, possibly the only American aboard not eagerly anticipating the outstretched arms of whoever showed up to meet her at the airport. Carole had given up their apartment; it was a waste of money, she had explained to Maude on crinkly airmail stationery, since she was practically living at Roger's these days. Well, Maude had been tired of the suburbs, anyway. It was only because of Brad that she'd ended up there in a bungalow instead of in some bohemian city flat with sunlight streaming in and big overflowing bookshelves and Keith Jarrett on the stereo and a homemade soup simmering fragrantly on the stove because friends were dropping by for supper—smart, artistic friends, actors and photographers and artists like the people she'd known in London—and when she leaned back in the seat and closed her eyes, she could picture every last detail. The trouble was, she was broke. She could reach into her jeans pocket and pull out her entire net worth: two dollars and thirty-five cents, and a key. It was the key she'd never given back to Brad, the key to his ugly ancestral bungalow. The house where he had had the gall to lock himself in the bedroom with *that woman* in front of all their friends; the house, she suddenly recalled, her waitress wages had paid half of for two years; the waitress wages for which her income tax refund had mysteriously disappeared. Maude eyed the key. There were doors, she decided, that Brad had the power to keep locked, and some he didn't.

When Carole met her at the airport, she asked for a ride to Brad's house, where she didn't bother using the doorbell. He appeared in the hallway, startled, sleep rumpled, and as sexy as ever in his cotton boxers.

"You know, honey," she said, with the sweetest smile she could muster. "That tax refund check never did get to me. So I'm just flat-out broke. But we are still married, you know, so I guess this house is still technically my home, and I guess I'm just gonna have to stay here till you think you can help me out with the security deposit on a place downtown."

"Aw, Christ, Maude," he said.

"Now, now—I'm not planning to cramp your style. You just go ahead and do your own thing, and I'll find myself a new waitress job and a boyfriend and you'll hardly know I'm here."

He held out for almost a month, slamming doors behind him and whispering into the telephone before coming home one day and wordlessly dropping a check for five hundred dollars into her lap. And by then she did have a lucrative new waitress job and a new boyfriend, Harry, the house jazz pianist, who told her he flirted with all the waitresses, but when he looked into her eyes, he could tell there was someone really home. It's such a relief, when a man can recognize that. She and Harry made love almost every day, and when he practiced, she would smoke a joint and just lie on the couch and listen. Sometimes she sang, and although she'd never thought much of her own voice, he looked at her with so much love and appreciation she got the idea that maybe with a few lessons, she'd be good enough to make some music with his band.

Newsbites

Meanwhile, Patty sang. Over and over in the winter of 1975–76, she told lawyers and psychiatrists and jurors what had happened to her in the closet, and afterward, when she had tried to come out. Over and over, reporters and producers and editors relayed her story to the public, duly noting that she appeared "wooden and robotlike" as she talked. Did that mean she was truly brainwashed? Or just that she was lying, to steal our sympathy—to avoid taking the consequences for dressing up, armed and dangerous, and scaring us out of our wits?

But Patty had been misfiled in the wrong social trend. It wasn't with the Armed and Dangerous Women that Patty belonged; it was with the women all over America who had suddenly begun singing, women who were fed up with being pigeonholed or closeted or bullied into being something they weren't; women who were only just beginning to sort out the difference between what they had been told in the closet and what they really believed; women who would never have identified with Tania, that Guerrilla Barbie, because she came with such ugly accessories.

Betty Ford has been named 1975 "Woman of the Year" by *Newsweek* magazine for changing the way "a nation schooled in bland, blameless public behavior from its Presidential consorts" views its First Ladies. Mrs. Ford's unprecedented honesty and outspokenness have earned admiration from many but have also at times provoked public outrage and apparently embarrassed her husband. Her openness in discussing her 1974 radical mastectomy for breast cancer earned praise for inspiring other potential victims to seek early diagnosis. However, her comment to *60 Minutes* earlier this year that she "wouldn't be surprised" if she learned her 18-year-old daughter Susan were having an affair elicited denunciations from sources including the Women's Christian Temperance Union, the Los Angeles police department, the Dallas pastor of the world's largest Baptist congregation (who decried her "gutter type of mentality"), and a Chicago viewer who commented: "If Jerry Ford can't control his own wife, how can he run the country?" Mrs. Ford has also publicly admitted to seeking psychiatric help and using tranquilizers to cope with the pressures of being a Congressional wife and *de facto* single mother of four children; as well as to sleeping with the President "as often as I can."

Recently hospitalized for psychiatric treatment, the wife of Canadian Prime Minister **Pierre Trudeau** blames the pressures of political life. **Margaret Trudeau,** 26, told Canadian TV interviewers in the fall of 1974 that she feels cramped by the "posturing" and "formality" required of a political wife. She claims to dislike the constant presence of servants and bodyguards, and also complained about "those damn, those brown boxes" full of official papers her husband brings home and reads every night, when Margaret would "just really like to go out dancing or go out and have a pizza or just go out and drive around in the rain at 2 in the morning."

The psychological and alcohol-related problems of his wife **Joan Kennedy** are widely believed to have been one of the factors contributing to **Ted Kennedy's** October 1974 announcement that he would not seek the presidential nomination in

1976. Mrs. Kennedy told *Good Housekeeping* in 1972 that she had been seeing a psychiatrist for 16 months, explaining that "It's very easy to feel insecure when you marry into a very famous, intelligent, exciting family." Mrs. Kennedy denied at that time that her difficulties had anything to do with the 1969 incident at Chappaquiddick, in which **Mary Jo Kopechne,** a 23-year-old political volunteer, drowned when the Senator accidentally drove them off a bridge on the way home from a party in the middle of the night and then abandoned the scene.

Six months after the death of second husband **Aristotle Onassis** in May of 1975, former First Lady **Jacqueline Kennedy Onassis,** 46, showed up for her new job as editorial consultant at Viking Press, the New York book publisher. It was her first day of salaried work since her stint as the Inquiring Photographer for *The Washington Times-Herald* in 1954—the job she left to marry then-Senator John F. Kennedy. Jackie, who was rumored to have received $3 million in tax-free bonds from Onassis, in addition to an annual lifetime income of $250,000 (adjustable for inflation) and a 25-percent interest in his yacht and private Greek Island, told friends she was ready to face life as an independent woman. "I have always lived through men," she reportedly said. "Now I realize I can't do that any more."

Ann Landers, the columnist whose advice to readers considering divorce has often been less than sympathetic, was forced to acknowledge that not all marriages can be saved when she confessed to her readers in a July 1975 column that her own 36-year union with Jules Lederer was drawing to a legal close. **Dear Abby's** 56-year-old twin sister had often bragged about the "unselfish, supportive, responsive man [who had] enabled me to live life as few people get the opportunity to live it," and sometimes autographed copies of her own books with the signature,

"Jules' Wife." Ann Landers did not enlighten readers as to the causes of the break-up, commenting only that "the lady with all the answers does not know the answers to this one."

Erica Jong, the 33-year-old author whose *Fear of Flying* has sold 3 million copies in the six months since its November 1974 publication, is filing for divorce. Jong, who like her fictional heroine Isadora Wing is an Upper West Side Jewish writer, denies that the break-up has anything to do with the novel's unflattering portrait of Wing's fictional husband, who—like Jong's real-life husband, is a Chinese-American psychiatrist. The author, who has referred to her image following the book's publication as "the matron saint of adulteresses," is already living in a Malibu, Calif., beach house with **Jonathan Fast,** a writer and the son of novelist **Howard Fast.** Jong is at work on a second novel titled *How to Save Your Own Life*, about how Isadora Wing copes with her sudden fame and the stress it places on her marriage by falling in love with a more sympatico lover, who happens to be the son of a famous novelist. *Newsweek* recently hailed Jong as "the most visible star" in a new galaxy of female literary figures who are "the mapmakers of the new female consciousness, sending back firsthand reports on the real—and hitherto unmentionable—terrain of feminine experience." The magazine equated her impact with that of **Colette** (whose husband published her first books under his name) and **Virginia Woolf,** who "speculated that if women ever stopped politely acting out the roles imposed by men and began telling the truth, civilization would shudder to a halt."

Prominent feminists **Gloria Steinem, Kate Millet,** and **Robin Morgan** were among those on hand at Lincoln Center recently to applaud conductor **Sarah Caldwell** as she led the New York Philharmonic through a landmark concert: an evening of music written entirely by women. Co-sponsored by the Philharmonic and *Ms*. magazine, the November 1975 event raised money for the musicians' pension fund—but was also intended to raise the consciousness of the music world. Feminists argue that this establishment of largely male-run orchestras and recording studios has systematically discriminated against women's works— leaving the impression that there must not have been many talented female composers. But Caldwell, director of the Opera Company of Boston, says there was no dearth of material to choose from. "I must have studied well over 150 scores," she said, before selecting works by **Grazyna Bacewicz, Thea Musgrave, Ruth Crawford Seeger,** and **Lili Boulanger,** among others. What she was searching for, Caldwell said, was "music that had a face of its own."

The popular singer and one-time Miss America runner-up whose commercial jingle cheerily exhorts America to "come to the Florida sunshine tree" for fresh orange juice has recently begun using her voice for another cause: a crusade to stop homosexuality. **Anita Bryant,** 37, said her narrow escape from death in a three-car collision in January 1977 convinced her that God had spared her life so she could lead a fight to repeal the Dade County [Fla.] Commission's ordinance that bans discrimination in housing, jobs, or public accommodations based on sexual preferences. Gay activists maintain that the ordinance—the first of its kind in any major city—is a test of whether America is ready to extend civil-rights legislation to homosexuals. It is because of strenuous objections by activists that The American Psychiatric Association only recently dropped homosexuality from its list of mental disorders. But Bryant sees homosexuality as a moral evil that can be resisted or corrected through therapy or prayer and says she knows that "homosexual[s] can be liberated from these hideous chains." The mother of four, she also says the Dade County ordinance is an attempt to "legitimatize homosexuals and their recruitment of our children."

Real Life, 1977

The housewives got to the restaurant first. Tammy, already on her second vodka and tonic, joked about it: "Well, of course— we're the ones who don't have a life. Maude and Carrie, they probably go out all the time, to those fancy downtown places. They don't have to sneak the money to pay for it out of the god-damn cookie jar either."

It was true, this suburban steak house was as fancy a place as any of them had been inside for years. There were thick white cloth napkins folded inventively on the tables, and spider plants hanging from the ceiling, and shiny brass railings around the bar area. You could die waiting for your husband to suggest coming to a place like this, or kill yourself trying to talk him into it. At a certain point, complaining about it during one of their now frequent afternoon get-togethers with their growing collective brood of preschoolers, they reached the logical conclusion: Forget the husbands—let's just go together.

"Ya know, I gave Forman about a month's fuckin' notice that I was comin' out with you guys tonight," Tammy continued. She had recently begun referring to her husband by his last name only. "And you know what? He comes home from work today, and he gives me this totally blank look, and he says, 'Whaddya mean you're goin' out with the Girls? You mean I gotta baby-sit these kids?' So then I remind him that I've mentioned this, oh, five, six times just to make sure he'll be ready for it, and he stands there lookin' at the boys eatin' the grilled cheese I cooked for them so he wouldn't have to go to the trouble of actually fixing their dinners, and he says, 'Ya hear that, boys? Your mom's leavin' you all alone for the night.' "

Betsy laughed and took a sip of ginger ale. That's how you could tell she was pregnant *again* because normally she'd have white wine. She wasn't showing yet, though. Sometime in her fourth month she'd start to inflate, till by the eighth month she would look like a huge walking beach ball with Betsy's perky, smiley face peeking out over the top, still with the same bangs she'd had in second grade. Then, as soon as she gave birth, the weight dropped off instantly and you couldn't tell she'd ever been pregnant—let alone that she seemed to be making a career of it.

"Billy does that, too, when I go out," Betsy said. "I'll be halfway out the door and he'll still be asking me questions, like, where are their pajamas? Like, your average junior high school baby-sitter can figure out to go into their bedroom and look in the dresser, but their dad can't."

Oh, there they go again, puttin' down the husbands, thought Donna. She just wished Maude and Carole would show up already so they could order some appetizers. She had just seen a platter of stuffed mushrooms go by that looked really good. Or maybe they could get some of those little pastry shells with whatever it was that was inside them. Donna always looked forward to seeing the Girls, but for some reason, once they got together, she always found herself wanting to eat everything in sight. Maybe it was because she was trying so hard not to drink, because she had discovered she was the kind of person who, once she had one drink, tended to drink the whole bottle till she got drunk and got dizzy and got sick and passed out. Another one of her immoderate appetites, it seemed. So she tried very hard just to not start. But it made her even more nervous that Maude was coming tonight. She was in graduate school in the City these days and married to this jazz musician and indoctrinated with Art and Feminism the way she used to be indoctrinated with Jesus in college, and she didn't seem to think she had that much in common with them and their ranch houses with all the goddamn Fisher-Price toys you tripped over on your way in. (Only Donna must remind herself not to say goddamn, because Stan didn't like it when she swore, or when someone used bad language in front of her. Once they had been driving on the highway and someone had cut him off and he'd rolled down his window and given the guy the finger and yelled, "You asshole," and then he'd pulled over onto the shoulder and turned to her, looking stricken, and apologized.) Maude had this way of making you feel stupid. Like you were supposed to have opinions about all this bullshit (excuse me) political stuff that *she* had opinions about. Donna could not for the life of her follow politics enough to have opinions about it. She'd had the TV tuned to the Watergate hearings every day for months on end without ever getting the slightest idea what they were talking about. Finally she'd asked Stan, but he had said it was too complicated to explain and gone back to reading the *TV Guide* with Fonzie on the cover. Donna was getting *really* hungry. She reached over for the pack of cigarettes in front of Tammy and lit one. Oh-oh. A couple of the Girls' cigarettes and she'd be back to smokin' like a chimney in no time.

"I betcha a million dollars I know just what he did as soon as I pulled outta the driveway," said Tammy. "He took the kids over to his mother's house and dumped 'em on Delores and went out to a bar. Oh cool, here comes Carrie. What's she doin'?"

Carole was standing at the hostess station, staring at the wrist of her upraised arm.

Donna said, "Either she's tryin' to figure out how late she is, or she's calculatin' how many minutes of freedom she has left before Roger comes huntin' her down."

Maude arrived three quarters of an hour late, kissing everyone on the cheek and murmuring about the traffic on the freeway. As soon as she'd ordered a drink, Tammy stood up, cleared her throat, and said, "Girls, girls, shut up everyone. I get to be the master of ceremonies tonight because I called it before anybody else. Also because I brought a surprise. Now I know we have many important news events to discuss tonight, including Carole's upcoming wedding"—here, the Girls gave a little *yay*—"and Betsy's upcoming—hmmmn, have I lost count? Um—*third* baby"—"*Yay*," went the Girls—"and of course my upcoming move out of the state." The Girls went, "*Boo!*"

"But before all that, I want to point out that tonight we are all reunited on the anniversary of a very important occasion." Here, Tammy paused, reached down next to her chair, and picked up a small bulging canvas tote bag. "I was out shoppin' with Thelma last week, and I saw somethin' that reminded me that now is exactly the ten-year anniversary of our high school trip to France." She reached into the bag and pulled out a clear plastic bottle with a pink label that said "Evian." "And probably, if we hadn't all made that trip together, we wouldn't all be gathered here today. So I bought five of these so we could drink a toast to still bein' friends. And now that we're grown-ups, I guess we're not allowed to add Kool-Aid."

The Girls clapped, and yelled "YAY," and passed the bottles around the table. Carole, who had tears glistening in her eyes, said, "Aw, Tammy, what are we gonna do without you? Do you *have* to move?"

Tammy shrugged. "Well, Forman's got a job offer, and I don't think we could afford to turn it down. I mean, the guy loses his job about every five minutes. I feel like we spend more money paying the fee to get our phone service reconnected after they've disconnected it than we do on our regular phone bills."

Betsy said, "I know that feeling. You guys, Billy's been talking about quitting the union. He says he's sick of sitting around on the bottom of a waiting list while they give the jobs out to guys who are supposedly ahead of him, when he could be out rustling up jobs himself. But if he goes out on his own, we'll lose all our health coverage. Can you imagine, with three little kids? All those ear infections, and immunizations, and antibiotics, and glasses and braces, and no health insurance? I don't even see how we'll be able to pay for my delivery in December."

Donna was digging with relief into the platter of stuffed mushrooms that had finally arrived. Didn't the Girls have anything else to do besides bitch about their husbands, excuse the language? Donna was the only woman she knew who didn't go around doing that. In fact, her friend Sally from the neighborhood play group had said to her several times, "Donna, you're either the happiest woman I ever met or the dumbest." Because she just didn't complain about Stan. He adored her. He worked his ass off to support her and the kids, insisting on makin' it on his own even though her dad coulda got him a cushier job, and he sent her flowers for no reason, and kept on makin' sure she always had an orgasm. It kind of annoyed him when she tried to change the channel to a PBS show once in a while, but he worked so hard all day she couldn't blame him if he wanted to relax by watching *Gomer Pyle* reruns. Donna lit another of Tammy's cigarettes and wondered whether she should have seconds on the appetizers—the mushrooms were real soft and buttery—or try to wait for the entrée.

Tammy said to Betsy, "Can't you get him to at least hold off quittin' till the baby comes?"

Maude, pulling out a pack of her own cigarettes, said quite offhandedly, "Oh, Betsy, why don't you just try giving that uterus of yours a rest?"

There was a stunned silence. Betsy giggled once, and then, like someone who only feels the impact of a bullet a few moments after the actual hit, stopped short. Everyone at the table understood that Maude had just stepped across a line, but no one was quite sure what that line represented—whether what

Maude had just dragged out into the open against some tacit
agreement they all shared was a judgment she had no right to
make about Betsy's choices; or whether it was simply the truth.

Maude, oblivious to the transgression, took advantage of the
silence to embark on one of her inevitable political lectures
about the population explosion, and how, philosophically, didn't
they all think it was really impossible to justify doing anything
more than at most reproducing yourself and your husband?
Hadn't they all seen the photos from Africa, from the massive
famine there, the little bald children with the big sad eyes and
the bloated bellies? And then the difficult moment passed, because Maude was so outraged that the Pope thought he had any
business opposing birth control, and Tammy said, hey, a good
natural method the Pope never mentioned was feeling so pissed
off at your husband that you weren't interested in having sex
with him, and that must've worked for her and Eddie over the
years because here they were, married almost a decade, and
only two kids.

"Oh, Tammy," Maude chided. "You've just been lucky. But you
really should take a more responsible attitude toward your own
body. Get yourself a copy of *Our Bodies, Ourselves*. It's not one of
those awful books where a male doctor tries to tell you what's normal for a woman. This is women themselves collecting really real-
istic information. It's great, it has information on birth control and
nutrition and breast self-examination and masturbation . . ."

"Hey, Maude," said Tammy, "you need instructions for that?"

"Well," said Carole, "I think the best thing about getting married again is I'm going to get to *stop* being responsible for birth
control. I can't wait to have a baby."

Then she turned to Donna, who was cutting into a large juicy
steak that sat on a platter-size dinner plate in front of her along
with a baked potato steaming in its foil jacket.

"How about you, Donna? You've been quiet. You guys planning on having any more kids?"

"Hope not."

"So, are you doing anything about it?" Carole persisted. "Or just taking your chances?"

Donna slowly put down her knife and fork, looked around the table, cleared her throat, and said finally, "Actually, I got my tubes tied."

Donna thought her own voice sounded really loud, like maybe everyone else in the whole restaurant had stopped talking. Then suddenly Maude stood up. "Yay," she cried, and started clapping, and then, one by one, all the other Girls pushed back their chairs and followed suit. A standing ovation. People all over the restaurant turned to look.

Finally, they sat back down. "Why didn't you ever tell us?" Carole asked.

Donna felt that she might burst into tears any second. She cleared her throat again, shrugged, and said, "I dunno. I guess I thought you guys would judge me. I mean, we're all good Catholic girls, right?"

There was a chorus of demurrals: Donna, *no, how could you think that?* But of course, Donna thought, they *were* judging her. And they were getting it all wrong—at least Maude was. She hadn't gotten her tubes tied as some Big Feminist Statement about controlling your own fertility. She had done it to save her ass. She had almost died twice bearing children. The doctor told her that in any future pregnancy, she was likely to go through something at least as bad. So she had gone to the parish priest and explained the situation, and he had said, "Well, if you think that's what's necessary, go ahead and get it done." Donna was appalled. "But it's against the Church," she insisted. The priest had replied: "This is your life. You have two very small children to care for. If this is what the doctor says is necessary to keep you alive so you can care for them, get it done."

So Donna had gotten it done. Of course, Stan knew about it, but she had never told anyone else, her mother or her sister or any of her friends. She understood that the priest's answer could so easily have been, *Sorry, if I make an exception for you, I'll have to make one for everyone else.* Instead, she'd gotten this under-the-counter, black-market dispensation. And Donna was no stranger to the idea of the black market. As with those vague, shadowy feelings about family business, in which nothing gets in and nothing gets out, Donna understood the price of a good deal to be, *You didn't sing.*

But Donna understood one other thing, too: Lotsa guys got mouths on 'em, but that doesn't mean they got the power. She didn't for a moment think that just because one nice priest had been sympathetic enough to write her an excuse, it meant God wasn't gonna flip His lid when and if He found out. The class, as it were, was required. There were no people on earth who could write you a pass that would prevent you from burning in hell for all eternity if God caught you and decided to enforce His rules.

Dinner broke up well before midnight, at the point where the hostess appeared at the table and said, "I have a gentleman on the phone who's trying to locate a Ms. Carole Bourquin. Would that be one of you ladies?"

So the Girls began kissing one another on cheeks and drifting out into the summer evening, into a parking lot overlooking a highway just like the burger joint parking lots in which they had spent the summer evenings of their youth. It had been so urgent then to talk, to tell each other everything that needed to be hidden at home, when they had all been breaking the same rules, together, in the same way. Confession, with the certainty of absolution. It was just as urgent now, just as tempting to confess—but more dangerous, as well, because the rules had become so much less clear. No mother, no church, no *Seventeen* or Emily Post or infallible husband-god to warn you; only your friends to tell you if by action or inaction you committed your life to damnation (or what damnation was).

Driving home, Tammy got to thinking that it would definitely be a good idea to call the Girls before she moved to the country and get them to start arranging for some kind of class reunion next year that she could come back for. And that kept her from thinking too much about what it was going to be like out there in the country, just Eddie and her and the kids, with no Girls to complain to.

Driving home, Carole got to thinking about how glad she was that Roger had finally agreed to have Maude and Harry at the wedding, even though he had taken an instant dislike to Harry because of something he identified as Harry's "seedy musician lifestyle." And that kept her from thinking about how much of Maude she was really likely to see in the future, now that she was cleaving unto Roger and she was no longer the naive romantic girl who believed marriages worked just because you wanted them to.

Driving home, Betsy got to thinking about how outspoken Maude could be, and how you really couldn't take it personally because their heads were in such totally different places, and how it was actually really amusing, if you thought about it. And that kept Betsy from thinking too much about how she was going to pay for the dinner she'd just charged, or the groceries she'd put on the charge card yesterday, hoping that by the time the bill arrived Billy would've gotten called for a new job.

Driving home, Maude got to thinking about how Harry, despite being an artist, was turning out to be a *man* first, like any other man; how, despite her willingness to help support his musician's lifestyle, he was showing no signs of wanting to help support her while she went for her Ph.D. And this kept her from thinking about what she'd said to Betsy. Or about the second baby she'd lost, about a year ago—the baby whose fleeting presence in her womb had convinced Maude and Harry that marriage was a good idea.

Driving home, Donna got to thinking about those Girls complaining about their men, and how sorry she felt for them, and how tired she got sometimes of hearing it. And that kept her from thinking about the strange fantasy she had sometimes, that Stan would take the kids to the zoo and there would be a car accident and they would all die. Or the recurring nightmare she had, where they would all be in the car, and she would be driving, and she would drive them all off a bridge into the water by accident. And then she, being the only one who could swim, couldn't decide which of them to try to save.

V

Fractured Fairy Tales

He didn't want anyone to discover what he kept in his closet, buried under the suits and the jeans and the tennis whites. In every other way, he was a Golden Boy: graduate of an Ivy League college, an exceptionally promising resident at a prestigious New York hospital. He dated beautiful, smart women and was a player of some renown on the country club tennis tournament circuit. In short, he had everything normal men dream will make them happy, and still he reported every evening at six o'clock to the office of a prominent psychoanalyst who was trying to help cure him of his . . . problem.

But what he thought would *really* make him happy was—a *makeover.* Even though he made an awfully good-looking woman dolled up in his dress and wig—even though he was vain about his clear, porcelain complexion and his fine, delicate features— he still suspected that his face gave him away. No matter how close and carefully he shaved, within hours the shadow of his beard was visible again beneath the heavy pancake makeup. He became convinced that if only he could have his face done over by a real professional, he would finally look in the mirror and see himself transformed and flawless; fully, deeply, convincingly *feminine.*

After careful consideration, he conceived a plan. Dressed in his normal, manly clothes, he went to an expensive Manhattan salon that catered to wealthy women and told the proprietor that he was attending a costume party disguised as a woman and wanted the most authentic makeup job possible. In that one stroke of genius, his hidden perversion became a bit of innocent hilarity in which not only the salon staff but most of the day's patrons were delighted to play along. The rich ladies hung around after their own treatments to watch the salon's top cosmetician anoint him with masques and cleansers and creams and paints. When he was done, everyone marveled, himself most of all. He gazed at the lovely woman in the mirror—upswept hair, delicate cheekbones, smoldering eyes with long, thick lashes—and felt entranced.

But then, oh, what a letdown. There was no real costume party to go to. There was nowhere at all, really, that he could go dressed like this, where the consequences of his beautification could be let to unfold. Like Cinderella with her midnight curfew, he was under a deadline; the beard would begin to assert itself, giving him away; and, as this was sinful Manhattan and not some childish fairyland, any prince he snagged by his appearance was not going to take very long in discovering the off-putting, much-reviled appendage between his legs. And where was the Fairy Godmother who would help him out of this dilemma?

Well, if you think it's hard to find a Fairy Godmother who can just magically transform ugliness into beauty, try finding one who's willing to chop off a man's penis. Even the eminent psychoanalyst was so disturbed by this possibility that, when he realized his client was seriously considering it, the daily sessions began regularly erupting into shouting matches. So the Golden

Boy spent another whole decade trying everything he could think of to find happiness in his masculinity: He joined the armed forces, grew a beard, indulged himself in snazzy European sports cars, even finally—in a last-ditch attempt to live manfully ever after—married a fashion model and fathered a son.

And yet slowly, his closets were filling up with women's clothes. Slowly he was dropping the pretext he used while cruising the tall-women's clothing boutiques: that he was shopping for his girlfriend. The salespeople had started to recognize him by now and he had run out of oh-so-casually proffered explanations for why his girlfriend wasn't ever once available to shop for herself; but this was Manhattan, after all, and the salespeople hardly seemed to care whose body the clothes were ending up on as long as he kept his wallet open.

He undertook a three-year process of electrolysis in which every individual hair of his beard was painfully destroyed at its follicle. He swallowed estrogen tablets that made his hips swell and the hard, sculpted muscles of his athlete's physique soften and subside. Taking a leave from his now thriving medical practice, he went to Europe and lived entirely as a woman for almost a year. Like any other American woman traveling solo, he discovered himself a magnet for irrepressibly amorous European men. Like any other American woman, he may have allowed himself to be lulled into thinking he would remain, even after crossing back over into America, an object of overwhelming seductiveness.

Finally, he made the irrevocable decision: He would have the radical surgery that would permanently transform him into a woman. By now, in 1975, he was able to find a surgeon in America who had already performed the operation successfully 157 times. In only three and a half hours, the surgeon relocated his urethra, discarded his testicles, and used skin from his penis and scrotum to create a vagina and labia. The Golden Boy awoke from anesthetized slumber like Sleeping Beauty or Snow White, into his yearned-for womanhood. After he had recovered sufficiently to begin exploring his new anatomy, he was delighted to discover that his womanly orgasms were less intense, but longer and more gratifyingly diffuse than his old male ones had been. And look! Like the new, truly liberated women of the 1970s, he hadn't even needed a Fairy Godmother to effect his transformation. He had arranged it all himself, against enormous odds. And now, too, he was awakening his female sexuality from slumber the same way liberated women everywhere were being advised to do it: without waiting around for the Prince, without waiting—possibly forever—to fall under the spell of love.

But then, what *about* love? If sex was all you needed, if you didn't crave the embracing, approving, validating benediction of love, then you could remain comfortably in the closet you had built yourself, couldn't you, secure in the knowledge that the life you led now was fine for you? And at first, she tried this. As though thirty-eight years of male existence could be erased as easily as footprints on a Pacific beach, she walked away from her New York practice and arranged for a job in California. Ten years before, a woman with her medical credentials and experience might have aroused more curiosity, but by the mid-seventies she was well camouflaged, ironically enough, by all the other women trying to model their lives on men's. She got a busy, reputable doctor to take her into his practice. She acquired a cute apartment and a handsome, well-muscled young lover. If only she had listened to the advice of the close friend who warned her to stay off the tennis court . . . but something drew her there, to one of the most visible clubs around, where stars and celebrities regularly hung out. Aware of the risk, she still agreed to play in a few local tournaments, and, inevitably, in 1976, someone recognized her and tipped off the local media.

Before she even realized what was happening, there were national news reporters sticking microphones into her face and demanding to know whether she hadn't once been known as Dr. Richard Raskind, and even before the dust had settled, her young, well-muscled lover had packed up his stuff and fled.

A few years later, Renee Richards would admit in her autobiography that no one—herself included—could say for sure whether it was nature or nurture that had fashioned her transsexuality; whether it had been renegade body chemistry or the sometimes bizarre attentions of his mother and sister during early childhood that accounted for the immutable sense he had of being a woman trapped in a man's body. The mother had been, ironically enough, a well-respected Freudian psychiatrist who inexplicably delighted in watching while his tomboy older sister dressed the little Richard in clothes the sister herself rejected as being too frilly and girlish. Sometimes, when they were alone, Richards wrote, the sister would push the little boy's penis up inside his body till it disappeared, telling him, "See, you're not a little boy, you're a little girl." Eventually, Richards began sneaking into his sister's closet and borrowing her dresses when she was out, and for four decades he continued to indulge this compulsive dressing up in secret.

But the world changed in those four decades. Blacks marched on Southern capitals with the support of white civil rights workers. Feminists staged protests at the Miss America pageant and stormed the offices of *Ladies' Home Journal.* Now gays were openly colonizing Miami, organizing Gay Pride marches, and gleefully baiting Anita Bryant. You didn't need to be a heterosexual white man to be okay in America anymore—in fact, here was Renee Richards on TV, announcing that she'd *been* a heterosexual white man and she *hadn't even liked it.*

Like Patty Hearst and Pat Loud before her, Renee Richards in the media spotlight was like a big movie screen on which could be projected any number of serious issues—and not dull, abstract issues either, but the ones most people in the late seventies were struggling with in their own lives: What were "masculinity" and "femininity," and if we couldn't draw the lines between them that we had drawn twenty years before, then where were we going to draw the new ones? Under what circumstances were men and women going to love each other, and under what circumstances were they going to compete? Was it fair, for example, for a 6-foot 1-inch, 147-pound woman who had until recently had the musculature of a 6-foot 1-inch, 180-pound man to face down an average-size genetically female tennis player on a tennis court at Forest Hills? And what did that say about other allowances we should or should not make to promote "fair" competition between men and women in other arenas? And what, by the way, was "normal" sexuality? And if ours wasn't, did that mean there was something wrong with us, or something wrong with "normal"? And if our neighbor's wasn't, was it any of our goddamned business?

In fact, if you stared hard enough at Renee Richards, she took on the quality of one of those optical illusions in which the foreground forms one image and the background a completely different one. Was she the world's biggest sucker to have bought the notion every born-woman her age was at that exact moment gleefully discarding: that eye shadow and push-up bras and a handsome man seducing you over cocktails were the real key to happiness—a goal worth going to any lengths to attain? Or was she a maverick crusader, willing to face down the ridicule of a conformist universe to live the life she truly desired to live? It was a measure of how confusing things had gotten by the mid-seventies that lots of people couldn't figure out whether to scorn Renee Richards for the ultimate extravagance of her makeover, or admire her almost ruthless insistence on her own authenticity once she had set in motion that frightening, irrevocable process of finally coming out.

Real Life

The City University to which Maude returned for graduate work in the late seventies seemed to have changed since her undergraduate days. A rowdy band of mutinous feminist scholars was attempting to hijack the great and stately ship of Literature. Of course, the bearded men in the turtlenecks and tweed jackets were still steering, still lecturing from on high of the greatness of the white male Western way—singing songs of Milton and Spenser, Wordsworth and Whitman, Joyce and Proust. But you didn't have to look too far belowdecks to find the feminist pirates plotting to blow up the Dead Man's Canon and loading their catapults with heretical contemporary works by women who raged and bled and slept with men not their own husbands and also, increasingly, with each other.

Why, they were even going to hang Professor Swagget, once and for all. The old dog was still around, but now he'd tried his trick on one student newlywed too many. This time there was a name for what he'd done—*sexual harassment*—and instead of culminating in the girl's private humiliation, it became the subject of campuswide discussion as well as of a lawsuit brought by the offended student and her irate husband. "You, *too?*" women were asking each other, relieved and outraged equally, as the details came out and past Swagget victims identified one another. They lined up eagerly, Maude among them, to tell the grim-faced lawyers lurid details for the depositions.

It was just what feminist leaders had said could happen if women stuck together in sisterhood and solidarity: What one could not do singly, they would all accomplish together. Justice would be redefined by those who didn't find fanny-pinching cute.

Literature would be redefined by those who lived their lives out among pots and pans and families, rather than in romanticized isolation on some rugged frontier. Maude was stirred as she had once been stirred by the fellowship of Christians (who'd let her down) and then of Artists and Musicians (who, as far as she had been able to determine, seemed to like the idea of a woman being supportive of them more than they liked the idea of a woman being them). It seemed that *feminist*, finally, was the name for what she was, comprising all the most important principles she believed in and could live a life for.

Of course, feminists were not all-powerful. In the long run Raymond Swagget did not hang, wasn't drawn and quartered or even tried and fired. He was quietly asked to retire early, and was given a ceremonial dinner and a write-up in the school paper, and the irate newlyweds were presumably paid a bundle of money big enough to seem worth the lost satisfaction of prosecuting. Most people probably forgot about the whole thing quickly enough, though if you were the poor undergraduate assigned to call Maude in any subsequent alumni phone-a-thon even decades later, she would tell you the tale from start to finish (on the university's phone bill, of course) as part of her indignant refusal to contribute.

And the feminists couldn't fix your life either—couldn't find a way to make your musician husband understand that after several years of waitressing to help support his playing unprofitable gigs in little jazz clubs, it might be time for him to take up part-time bar-tending so you could earn your Ph.D.

The feminists couldn't *fix* your husband, no, but, oh, did they understand how you felt. "You, *too?*" they asked you, relieved and outraged equally, as they made you cups of herbal tea and told you the story of what *their* husband or boyfriend or father had done to *them*. They stayed up late drinking and trading war stories and endlessly discussing the books they were reading, and it seemed inevitable that Maude would decide eventually to devote her life's work to them. Harry wasn't going to help her, though. He went on telling her they couldn't afford for her to spend years pursuing a Ph.D. He'd already compromised himself artistically, once, for a woman. He'd given up music and gone to work in the post office to support his first wife and their child. He had vowed never to be used by a woman in that way again. Thus he spoke, and then one day Maude came home from a late waitress shift and found him in the living room, feet up on the Salvation Army coffee table, drinking a beer and watching a brand-new large-screen TV set that, without consulting her, he had bought that afternoon.

"And he didn't even *get* why I was mad!" she found herself shouting at her classmate Daria. They were perched on a windowsill at someone's crowded Christmas party, squeezing themselves out of the way of a crowd of exuberant dancers. "I mean, it's not like we didn't already have a TV set."

"Passive-aggressive," said Daria. Daria *always* got it. Daria lived with a man named Peter, in what she said was a "long-term relationship leading to marriage," but she said "long-term" in a way that made it sound exhausting, like a prison sentence or some grueling training regimen leading up to a particularly punishing marathon. She had a wry sense of humor, though, and there was a vague mannishness that was more in her manner than her appearance. She was friendly, but a part of her was always withdrawn, some subtle reserve of strength and absolute self-assurance she was choosing not to flaunt. It was a comforting quality. It made you want to tell her everything. It made you want to sit there in the windowsill with your thigh pressed tight against hers, feeling pleasantly tingly, talking and talking while the other partygoers began to get their coats on and kiss the hostess. It made you stay too long, till finally there were just the two of you walking through the frozen night toward one car, settling yourselves in the front seat with a dawning excitement, and without fastening your seat belts.

All love begins in a closet, that dark and private place where we discover one another's most secret smells and tastes and frailties and yearnings, all that must be deodorized and masked to factor ourselves down to the common denomination that is daily life. And of course we don't mind at first. It's so much a part of what love is: the relief of finally having someone else in the closet with us.

It surprised Maude a bit to discover how unsurprised she felt at finding herself in the closet with another woman. Their love-making, when they could briefly steal the privacy of one or the other's apartment, struck her as neither the unnatural thing most straight people might imagine it to be nor as the "homecoming" described in stories she read by lesbians about discovering their "true" sexual orientation. Daria's body seemed only as unaccustomed as a new male lover's might be, strange as you first explored its particular tastes and smells, but soon almost an extension of your own.

It was definitely not less intense than lovemaking with a man; possibly more intense, because of the necessity of hiding everything. They could hold hands only in restaurants where there were tablecloths to hide them, and neck only in deserted offices on Sunday afternoons or on bush-shrouded park benches after dark. Once, a cop came along and shined a flashlight on them entwined in Daria's front seat, just like teenagers. Once, Maude and Harry went with Daria and Peter to the theater, and when the lights went off Maude and Daria, in the two center seats, held hands.

"It's hypocritical," Maude began to insist after a while. Weren't they both immersed in a literature about women trying to lead authentic lives, or suffering because they didn't?

"You're romanticizing," Daria told her coldly. It turned out to be an aspect of Daria's mannishness that she could withdraw emotionally when they argued, employing that old husbandly tactic that because Maude wasn't being wholly logical, she must be wrong. "You're underestimating how hard it would be to live as a lesbian. It's not some big, happy, feminist study group out there on Main Street, you know."

Well, if it wasn't, thought Maude, it should be. There were gay men marching through the streets of Miami with their mothers, demanding society's acceptance. Why didn't Daria, who had always *gotten it* before, understand that by keeping their love hidden and secret they were only condoning the idea that they ought to be ashamed of themselves?

And why was it that this was always what happened: that you fell in love with someone *because* they understood, and then after you fell in love with them they stopped being able to understand? Somewhere in the back of Maude's mind she began to wonder whether this thing, which she had thought was the problem of always falling in love with men, was actually just the problem of falling in love.

"She's starting a bookstore?" said Donna.

"With a bunch of her classmates from grad school," said Carole. "All-woman staff, and only books by women. 'By women, for women, and about women,' she told me, 'of every creed, color, race, and sexual'... um, what's that word? Not *perversion*, I know that's not it, but that's kind of what it makes you think of."

"Persuasion," said Donna.

"That's it," said Carole. "Anyway, it was kind of a speech, you know, like Maude gives when she's under the influence of one of her..."

"Convictions," said Donna. "I think we should check it out."

Donna had sounded very enthusiastic on the phone, as if Maude had suddenly gotten hold of the keys to Fort Knox. But Donna had insisted Carole call Maude to set up the actual get-together because even now that they were approaching thirty, Donna was still intimidated by the fact that Maude had been in the *honors* curriculum in eighth grade.

And Carole had actually been glad to have the excuse, finally, to set something up. She hadn't seen Maude once in the almost three years since Maude and Harry had attended her wedding to Roger, and had barely spoken to her. They hadn't had a fight, exactly, but Carole hadn't wanted to upset Roger more than she had to, and Maude had understood this without being told, and after a while it began to seem as if they weren't quite speaking, though which one of them wasn't speaking wasn't clear.

Now Roger was following her from room to room like a lost puppy while she rooted around in the dryer for Natalie's pajamas, rescued a beat-up Big Bird from underneath a sofa cushion, and began rummaging through her makeup drawer for the stick of Rose Petal that gave such a nice tint to your lips without looking conspicuously like makeup.

"What time will you be back?" Roger asked.

"I don't know," she said to the drawer. Blushing Belle. Sweet Honey Nectar. Passion Flower.

"Why don't you call me when you get there and let me know."

Ruby Glow. Didn't that sound a little seductive for a woman's bookstore? "Because I might just want to stay out for a while. I haven't been out with Maude in years."

"Aw, Carrie," said Roger. "You know I can't fall asleep unless you're home."

She felt a little burst of anger, and found herself swiping her lips with Ruby Glow. She took care of *everything:* his home, his child, his dinner, his laundry, even his office now that Gloria, the office manager who'd identified Maude and her as *nice* girls in the restaurant that first Valentine's Day, had retired.

"It's not my problem if you can't sleep," she snapped, heading for the door. "Take a fucking pill."

*   *   *

The address Maude had given them turned out to be a small, brightly lit storefront in a seedy neighborhood. Of course, coming in from the suburbs, you thought everything in the City looked seedy. But the Girls felt especially uncomfortable when the closest parking spot turned out to be several blocks away. As they made their way past boarded-up brownstones and over broken bottles, they cast nervous glances around them and wished they weren't so conspicuous: Donna so large and slow, and Betsy hugely pregnant, again (her fourth, now), and Carole with that uncharacteristically loud red lipstick. The bars looked sinister, with filthy opaque windows and broken neon beer signs, but between them sprouted freshly painted shops with track lights trained on brightly colored futons or cotton shawls imported from South American nations. "Look out," Donna said sharply, making them all jump. "Oh, for Christ's sake," she said, "it's just a big pile of dog shit you were about to step in."

Welcoming them at the store's doorway, though, Maude explained that this neighborhood was ideal for the store's purposes. "You need to be where the young professionals are just starting to go for bargain housing," she said, gesturing grandly toward the street as though it were some rich ancestral land expected to produce a bounteous harvest.

The store itself was small, cozy, and crammed to the ceiling with books. The shelves had small, hand-lettered purple signs that proclaimed: "Fiction," "Our Bodies," "Cookbooks," "Violence Against Women," "Spirituality," "Pregnancy," "Herstory." In the center of the room, tables stacked with more books had been pushed aside to clear a space around an old faded armchair where an author sat signing books and chatting with a small group of customers. None of the Girls had heard of her or her novel, but Maude said she had an impressive national reputation and the store had been lucky to get her. Rich, mellow music was playing in the background, a tape of a singer Maude said they should all really be listening to whose name was Joan Armatrading.

"Now, there are twelve women altogether in the collective," Maude told them, "and I just wish you could meet them all. But, unfortunately, tonight only two are here." She introduced them to Julie, a small black woman with a shaved head who stood behind the front counter ringing up purchases. Then she took them toward the back of the store, where a heavyset white woman with short dark hair was sitting behind an oriental screen panel punching numbers into an adding machine.

"And this," Maude said, with what sounded somehow like a drumroll, "is my *friend* Ruth."

Ruth jumped up and reached for each of their hands, grinning broadly and saying in a low Texas drawl, "Hey, pleased to meetcha. Maude talks about y'all the time."

"We're going over to the Mexican place on Broadway," Maude told her, in a voice that sounded a little more musical than Maude's regular voice. "I don't think we'll be out that late."

That could *mean*, thought Carole, *"I'll be back to help you close up at nine."*

Maude chattered so much over margaritas that she must have told them everything BUT. She was still waitressing part-time, she said, because all the women in the collective had to do something else part-time to make ends meet, but they thought by the end of next year they'd be able to take some money out of the business, but whether that meant a couple of them would be able to go on full salary even if everyone couldn't was bound to be a huge source of argument, but in the meantime it was possible that Ruth was going to move in with her, which would save them both some serious money. . . .

"Your *friend* Ruth," Carole interrupted.

"Yeah," said Maude. "My *friend.*"

"But," Carole clarified, "we're your friends, too."

"Of course," said Maude. "You're my *best* friends. My girl-friends. But Ruth's my—well, you know, my *other* kind of girl-friend."

There was a long silence during which no one looked at any-one else. You could hear dishes clattering from the busboy's sta-tion, and in the front window multicolored Christmas lights blinked merrily even though it was July and the air conditioner could barely keep the temperature below eighty. In a moment, if no one was quick, a twenty-year history of friendship and con-fession was going to vanish before their eyes like a tennis ball lobbed over a fence and into a dark wood beyond.

"You bitch," said Donna, just in the nick of time. "And to think we all got naked with you in the showers on that trip to France."

Carole awoke the next morning as in the first awakening after a death or an earthquake or a final break with a lover, when the body senses an irrevocable change in emotional terrain even be-fore the mind can call up what the change was. She heard Roger showering in the bathroom, with the radio tuned to the all-news station, and after a moment the thought fell into place: Oh, Maude.

She carried it around with her all day. Even as she sat Natalie on the potty and chirped, "What a big girl you are! Big girls make *their* poop in the potty, don't they?" she was thinking: *Why should this make any difference in how I feel about her?* She took Natalie to the fancy park with the old fire engine in it as a treat, but really the treat was for herself, so that she wouldn't have to chatter with the women she knew at her neighborhood park, and could concen-trate on her own thoughts while she pushed Natalie higher and higher in the safety swing. She knew it didn't mean that Maude had ever thought about her, or any of them, in that way, or that she ever would. During Natalie's nap, when normally Carole would have checked in with *All My Children*, she just took a can of Tab out to the lawn chair in the backyard and sat staring into the little blue wading pool with the merry white whales dancing around the outside edge. She wished she had a cigarette, too. The thing she didn't understand was, *why* would a woman want to sleep with another woman? Of course, complaining about husbands was a mainstay of female suburban conversation, and that was because by the time they were thirty or so there were very few women who hadn't yet discovered that men are impossible to live with. But you lived with them anyway. Sometimes a wife might develop a big crush on a neighbor's husband, under the mistaken impression that underneath everything he might be somehow different from her own, though a mature woman would know better. But you couldn't just decide, could you, that because men were all pretty much alike, it would be a better idea to fall in love with your neighbor's *wife*?

Though if anyone could, Carole supposed, Maude could. Carole carried the empty Tab can back inside and threw it in the kitchen garbage, then rummaged around in the drawer under the telephone just in case there were any abandoned cigarettes still lying around there. Then she picked up the receiver and slowly dialed Maude's number.

When Maude answered, Carole told her what a great time they'd had and how proud they were of her for opening the store.

"But, could I ask you something?" Carole added, hesitantly.

"Sure."

"Maude, are you—happy?"

"Oh, geez, Carole, you got an hour? I mean, who do you know who's happy?"

"No, I mean—"

"You mean, Ruth?"

"Yeah."

There was a pause. Carole could tell that Maude was genuinely taking the time to think this through.

Finally, she said, "Yeah, I'm happy."

"Okay," said Carole.

There was another long pause. Then Carole said, "We didn't see you for such a long time. Remember how in high school we used to always get dressed up and take each other out for our birthdays? We should start doing that again."

"We should," Maude agreed. "You know, I really missed you."

"I missed you, too."

By the time Roger came home at six, tired and complaining about work, Carole felt much better. She didn't say anything to Roger about Maude for a long time, because she knew she'd just get another earful about what a wacko Maude was. Carole herself would never understand it, but Roger would probably never be nice about it. Nevertheless, as Carole browned a pan of ground beef for spaghetti sauce and watched Roger on the floor, with his tie still on, telling Natalie they were going to go outside now and see if the tomato plants needed a little shower, she felt very lucky to have survived her long-haired boyfriends and Baba and all the other craziness of what she now realized she thought of as her youth, and to have landed in the middle of this very *normal* American family.

So Maude was a lesbian. Betsy was surprised, of course, but maybe it explained some things. Like her crack about Betsy's uterus, for example. Betsy had not decided to give her uterus a rest. When she went in for her first doctor's visit on this fourth pregnancy, the obstetrician had attempted to calculate her due date by asking, "Date of last menstrual period?" and Betsy had considered carefully and replied, "Seven years ago, I think."

Betsy wished she had time to give this whole Maude business some more thought, but really, she didn't, because she was much too busy. Billy was still threatening to leave the union, and that, Betsy thought with grim irony, would make them a No-Career Couple. The ironic part was that her original Plan, which had

seemed so unusual in the sixties and which she had abandoned
in order to have kids, was now a huge national trend, even for
women who had kids. The Two-Career Couple had been in style
for a couple of years already. In January of 1978, in a cover story
on "How Men Are Changing," *Newsweek* had reported that because wives were returning to or continuing in careers, men
were "reassessing their priorities, their ideas about success,
their notions of themselves as omnipotent husbands and lovers."
The article had used as an example an ABC news correspondent
named Ted Koppel, who had decided that he would take a leave
from his usual job responsibilities to look after his four children
while his wife, Grace Anne, went back to law school. Of course,
it turned out that during what *Newsweek* referred to as Koppel's
ten-month "stint as a househusband" he was still receiving half
salary from ABC in return for taping a daily radio commentary at
home (if ABC had been in the least interested in Betsy's opinions
about life, she would have been happy to tape a daily commentary for free), which was supplemented by an advance on a novel
he was writing with CBS correspondent Marvin Kalb. Koppel's
actual "househusband" routine was as follows: After seeing his
wife and children off at 8:30 each morning, "[h]ousework kept
him occupied until 9 (a maid did some of the heavy work)." Then
he spent from 9 to 10 writing and recording his radio commentary, and from 10 to 3 working on his novel. Then his kids came
home and he spent an hour with them before preparing dinner.
The article added that he was "furious" when his wife arrived
home later than she said she would and dinner was ruined, even
though "I had done the same thing to her I don't know how many
times before." After ten months of this, Koppel returned to his
regular job at ABC and the couple hired a full-time maid, and
that was probably a smart move since Koppel then became really famous later that year after ABC invented and handed him
the show that evolved into *Nightline*, aired at an hour when

most adults with the primary responsibility for little children aren't free to sneak out of the house.

Of course, Betsy was now dug into a hole way deeper than hiring a maid could haul her out of. To hire a maid, one or both of you would have to be earning more than the maid would want to be paid, and Billy's construction work was so unreliable, and what kind of job was she going to be able to get with a business degree that was a decade out of date and no subsequent job experience? Anyway, who was this "maid" who was necessary to facilitate the careers of these glamorous Two-Career Couples? Why was the magazine interested in the "plight" of a highly paid, highly visible TV personality who could afford to send his wife to law school and pay someone else to wipe his children's noses, and not in the plight of the maid who undoubtedly got a very small salary for wiping his children's noses and might possibly have had to leave her own children with their grandma or in front of a TV set in an empty apartment to do it?

Betsy was still planning to get a good job in business some day, but for now she was only interested in being the person who wiped her own children's noses. She genuinely enjoyed taking them on outings to story time and puppet shows, and making up games for them, and having them running and tumbling around a house that was so noisy and full of life and so unlike the cold, dark, silent house in which she had grown up feeling so alone. If only Billy were grateful to her for cheerfully shouldering a responsibility most women today seemed to be abandoning. But he was sullen and resentful, acting as though the kids were hogging all the oxygen in a very small, nearly airless room. If only she didn't have to worry constantly that he might, with little regard for any of them, at any moment quit the union and lose all their health insurance. His conviction that he was being passed over for jobs his seniority entitled him to seemed a little paranoid to her. If only he wouldn't drink quite so much, and erupt in such awful temper tantrums whenever she tried to talk to him about anything important.

Well, Betsy had always been a coper. If what they needed now was a little extra cash flow, she would find a way to get it that didn't require her to leave the kids; she would become some other woman's "help." She put up fliers in the neighborhood advertising herself as a provider of "home day care." The woman who responded was, ironically enough, a nurse in a hospital pediatric unit—a woman who needed child care so she could go to work caring for other women's children. Betsy cheerfully bundled up this new baby, Patty, along with her own kids, and fed her and took her along to story hour and wiped her nose and thought occasionally about how it was just this long chain of women, helping bring up each other's children, who paid each other and thanked each other while the husbands went about their business hoping not to be bothered.

But maybe that was too mean to Billy. His worst problem, really, was that he had grown up feeling lonely and unloved, just like she had, and somehow insisted on continuing to feel that way, even though it wasn't still true. Betsy knew that all he really wanted was all that she really wanted: the *evidence* of being loved. If she could only make him *feel* that, she thought, he would stop doing all the things he did to run away, and would finally sit down, surrounded by his family, and act like he loved them back.

And Betsy had a Plan for that. In a kitchen cupboard, behind the granola and the whole wheat flour, where Billy would never have thought of looking, she had hidden a coffee can, a cache for odds and ends of money she collected: the deposits on soda cans she returned to the supermarket; the change that sometimes fell out of Billy's pockets when she was doing laundry; tips the pediatric nurse gave her at Christmas and when she had to work on her birthday. He had always wanted to learn to fly an airplane, and she calculated that she could save enough this way to give him flying lessons for his thirty-fifth birthday.

After that, she thought, when the can had been emptied, she would start saving again, this time for herself. This would be the money she would use to pick up her original Plan where she had left off—the money that, once the kids were all safely in school and competent at wiping their own noses, she would use to return to school to update her skills, and go after the job she'd always meant to have some day, in business.

Donna didn't really give that much thought to Maude's revelation either. At least, she didn't think she did. Christ, that Maude was *always* into something kookie. It was actually the bookstore that interested Donna more. She had started reading recently, and the appetite she was developing was, as always, voracious. She had signed up for an evening class in psychology at a community college, and she loved the books, and she was getting an A so far.

"Hey, Ma," she said on the phone, "it turns out I'm not so dumb after all."

"I always said to you, Donna, don't be a nurse when you could be a doctor," said her mother mournfully. "But you wouldn't listen. I told you marriage would be a prison, Donna, but you refused to go to college."

"Ma, what I refused was to be locked up in a women's college for four years," Donna said. "That's the only place you would let me go."

"Aw, Donna," said her father into the extension, "whaddya need this kinda crap for? You're a mother, a mother belongs at home with her kids."

But Stan didn't seem to mind being left at home with the kids. There was a TV show practically every night that he couldn't stand to miss, anyway, and he always said that anything that made his Donna happy made him happy, too.

Of course, if he'd actually been paying attention, he would
have noticed that, most of the time, Donna didn't look all that
happy. What she really resembled was one of those quiescent
volcanoes that have remained dormant for so long that everyone
for miles around has long forgotten it was anything other than an
ordinary mountain. So even though she had begun to smolder, to
rumble and emit occasional puffs of steam, whatever Stan saw
was apparently no more alarming than what the villagers on the
slopes of Mount Vesuvius glimpsed out of the corners of their
eyes in the spring of A.D. 79, and then placidly continued going
about their business.

Tammy certainly wasn't alarmed, at least not early on. Donna
came over to say hi one evening, after Tammy and Eddie had
returned from their stint in the country and were living in a
rented town house nearby. The kids were in bed, and Eddie was
out somewhere ("Getting drunk," Tammy said, with a careless
shrug), and they were just sitting at the kitchen table talking
while Tammy brought out a little plastic bag and some rolling papers and began to roll a joint.

"It was kinda nice out there in the country," Tammy said as
she worked. "Lots of grass, you know? The other kind. Both
kinds, actually. And cows. And no Delores."

Donna watched her for a moment. Her face was still very
pretty, with those incredibly long lashes fringing her sky blue
eyes, and the freckles spilling across her milky white skin still
giving her an air of freshness, even though she had put on weight
with her two pregnancies (not as much as me, though, thought
Donna) and her lovely dark brown hair was already peppered
with gray.

"So how come you guys came back?"

Tammy shrugged. "I dunno. Just didn't work out with Eddie's
business, I guess." Donna got the distinct feeling there must be
more to the story than this, but Tammy wasn't a blabber.

"D'ya hear about Maude?" Donna asked.

"Jesus fuckin' Christ," said Tammy, "sometimes I can't believe that girl. But that reminds me. Did you hear the one about the lesbian who goes to her gynecologist for her annual checkup? And the doctor gives her the whole exam, and she gets her clothes back on and goes and sits down in the doctor's office, and he says, 'Well, everything looks just fine. As a matter of fact, if you don't mind my saying it, I gotta tell you, you got one of the cleanest vaginas I've *ever* seen.' So she says, 'Oh, thanks a lot, Doc. I have a woman who comes in twice a week.' "

Donna laughed. Well, Tammy didn't necessarily want to go that deep with anything either, whereas Donna, especially since taking the psychology course, had started to think it was very important to get to the bottom of everything. For example, Donna thought, what Tammy is doing right here at the table is indulging in a *criminal activity*. Donna was making the distinction, here, between the behaviors Tammy engaged in that Donna merely disapproved of, such as drinking in the middle of the afternoon when you were the sole caretaker of your small children, and those that actually broke the law. But Tammy didn't seem to make those distinctions. Tammy didn't do one damn thing that she *should* have done, from following the law, to going on a diet, to putting that incredible sharp intelligence of hers to some constructive use, to leaving that asshole husband of hers who was always drunk and out of work. And why was that? Why could she get away with not having to follow all the rules of life that everybody else worried all the time about following?

Donna suddenly understood that it was not just literally that she spent most of her life trying to stick to some unpleasant strict diet that required her to live on heads of iceberg lettuce and cups of chicken bouillon while most of the people she knew could help themselves to spaghetti and chocolate chip cheesecake. And it was because, she suspected, they all knew a secret that she herself had never been given the chance to learn: They knew when to STOP. Her mom had always stopped her before she'd even had a chance to start. Her mom, and her dad, and the diet doctor with the amphetamine shots, and then, just to make sure there was always someone there to stop her even after she left home and her parents couldn't stop her anymore, there was Stan, with his arms tight around her—stupid protective Stan squeezing every last drop of imagination and daring out of her and never saying one damn interesting thing.

Tammy was raising the joint to her lips.

"Gimme one of those," Donna said.

"Whaddya, nuts?" said Tammy. "You don't smoke."

"You smoke with Eddie, right? I'm gonna take one home and get Stan to smoke it with me."

Tammy shrugged. "How about you just smoke it here with me?"

So they smoked together, and at first Donna didn't feel anything. "I guess it didn't work," she said, and got up to go. But by the time she was actually on her feet, she felt like it had been a very, very long time since she had started to get out of the chair, and she started to ask Tammy if, in fact, it had been a very long time, only it seemed to take such a long time to ask the question that Donna got very tired and had to sit back down.

"I better call Stan," she said finally. "Listen, honey," she said into the phone, "I was just on my way home. But I can't come home now because I . . ."—she stopped and tried to think of something that might sound like a plausible explanation—"be-cause"—nothing came up but the truth—"I'm stoned and I can't waaaaaaalk!" At this, she dissolved into laughter. And she just sat in the chair, laughing and laughing into the telephone, vaguely hearing Stan's voice yelling at her from a great, great distance till finally she heard him hang up.

After that, it became harder and harder for Donna and all the people around her to keep not noticing the signs of an imminent eruption. She went to the doctor for a facial tic she thought might be related to a viral infection she'd had years before; he politely suggested, with a series of confusing euphemisms about "being exhausted" and "needing a little more attention," that she was having a nervous breakdown. He suggested a little hospital stay, so he could "run some tests," and while they were at it, he added—noting that according to the nurse's records Donna had weighed in at more than 350 pounds—they could staple her stomach.

Donna took him up on the little hospital stay, because deep down inside she sensed there was something not just a little wrong, but horribly, terribly wrong, and wasn't it possible— wouldn't it be an enormous relief?—if it turned out to be just that she was fat? Understand, she wasn't just a little fat— "chunky" or "big boned," as she had been in high school—but really fat, the kind of fat that makes you different from other people, that makes them stare at you and whisper unkind things, and disqualifies you for all life's prizes: admiration, affirmation, love. But what if all you really had to do to win those things was, say, cut yourself in half? Then it was really under your control. Then it had rules you could follow, a little trail of pebbles that would lead you back from the dark forest where you were lost and abandoned to the place where everything was fine.

She decided not to let the doctor staple her stomach, though. That would be cheating, for one thing, and for another, she was tired of having things done to her when maybe the problem was that she needed the experience of doing. She went on a new liquid diet that consisted of one solid meal and two milkshakes a day, for a total of about three hundred calories. A near starvation diet, but she liked it because the rules were simple and you never had to worry about which foods were okay and what was actually a portion and did those few little Tater Tots you ate off

Jack's dinner plate while clearing the table really make any difference.

The pounds began melting away immediately. Suddenly she was under 300 pounds for the first time since getting pregnant with Donny. Then 270, 240, 215, and she was down below 200. Starving wasn't hard this way. She felt euphoric, as though all that disappearing flesh were sucking with it into oblivion every doubt, every pain, every inadequacy that had ever diminished her spirit. At about 180, Stan began to look nervous, and encouraged her to eat "real food." But this babe emerging from fat old Donna was too powerful, didn't want to stop not feeding herself, was being noticed by other men for the first time in her life.

One night, at around 160, she went out bowling with her girlfriend Candace. Candace's husband was out of town, but her brother Ted was visiting for a few days and he agreed to watch her kids for the evening. When Candace and Donna returned from the bowling alley, the three of them sat around the bar in Candace's finished basement and drank whiskey sours and played old Frank Sinatra records. Ted was a big man, dark and overly handsome, like a soap opera star, and married. And he kept asking her to dance.

Donna excused herself and went up to the kitchen to call Stan and tell him she was going to be home a little late.

"No problem," said Stan. "But listen, while you were out, I took the kids to the mall and we went into one of those places that does eye exams, and they tested Donny and said he needed glasses. So I bought him glasses."

Those were his exact words. That wasn't exactly what he meant, of course, as Donna understood. What he said in "Family," the dialect in which people related by love address each other when they mean to communicate something more unpleasant than the actual words for which they wish to be held responsible—and what Donna, performing simultaneous translation in her head, actually heard—was: "Fine. Lose weight. Go to college. Go out and have fun at night—*while I do the things with your children that a Good Mother ought to do.*"

But it might have seemed somewhat irrational, both to Stan, who hadn't heard himself say this, and to Donna, who hadn't heard herself hear it, when she shrieked into the phone, "I AM THEIR FUCKING MOTHER!" and then slammed the receiver down.

Anger erupting. Some old fight she had never quite finished having: *You wanna fight? I'll fight witcha.* Donna knew what Ted wanted, even though until tonight she'd been naive enough to think that only Other People did things like this. She sat at the bar and drank some more whiskey and bided her time till finally Candace got up and, looking uncomfortably from one of them to the other, announced that she was exhausted and was going up to bed.

"We'll just dance one more dance," said Ted. They danced two or three. Then they lay down on the couch, tangled and furtive like kids, and took off only so much of their clothing as was absolutely necessary in order to fuck.

Ted hadn't given Donna his phone number, but she assumed this was because he was going to call her. When a week passed without the call, however, she called information for the phone number of the car dealership where he'd said he worked. She could tell by the way his voice didn't warm up at all when she said who she was that she'd made a mistake.

"Whaddya nuts, Donna?" he yelled into the phone. "You had a fling, that's it. I can't keep seeing you, I'm *married.*"

It took Donna a few more barren fucks with strangers to figure out that there weren't a whole lot of nice guys out there looking for an affair, not even for the short-albeit-doomed relationship that Donna was hoping might be the key to making everything bearable, since, obviously, losing weight had not been it after all. Donna was down to 150 pounds by now, as thin as she'd ever been, and she'd proved to her own satisfaction that it made her more attractive to men, but who would ever have predicted—when generically imagining the Men to whom one would be attractive when one finally looked the way one should—that all the Men would be creeps?

Things were bad enough now that the doctor had thought to supply her with a bottle of Valium before they got any worse, and she had the bottle with her at a New Year's Eve party at Carole's house as 1981 turned into 1982, and no one kissed her at midnight. Stan was home with the kids, and none of the other Girls had come, and Donna suddenly felt she just couldn't face this whole new year, so she went into the bathroom of Carole's master bedroom and swallowed the entire bottle of pills, chasing them down with a glass of champagne. Then she started to feel sick and dizzy, so she lay down on Carole's bed, thinking she'd feel better after a little nap.

Then she realized with a start that she wasn't going to wake up feeling better, she was going to wake up dead.

The ambulance was there within minutes. Donna had already made herself throw up, though, and didn't want to go to the hospital, but on second thought, she sure felt like shit and it was clear that she had pretty much ruined the party. Her last thought as they carried her on the gurney out through the front door was, Roger is gonna be *really* pissed about this.

She woke up New Year's Day in a psych ward. Stan was there with a big bouquet of carnations. She could see that his face was pale with concern as he held the flowers out to her and said, "I want my Donna back," so she wasn't sure why it was at that exact moment that the top of the volcano finally blew off, and she spat in his face and spewed out every vile truck driver obscenity she could think of, till even he, gentle soul, skinny little Stan, backed out the door and fled down the hospital corridor.

"Why'd she pick *our* house?" Roger would demand periodically for a long time after that.

"I don't know," Carole would say. "I guess she felt safe here."

"Safe, like this was a safe place to check out? Or safe, like she thought we would save her from checking out?"

That, Carole didn't know. It did seem that Donna had checked out, though. For a couple of years in the early eighties the Girls barely saw her, barely knew where she was. She was in and out of the hospital. She tried going back to live with Stan and the boys, and when that didn't work, she tried renting a studio apartment nearby. Then one day the phone rang and Donna said she was calling from California.

"What are you doing in California?" Carole asked.

"Well," said Donna, "for one thing, I'm in love."

She said she'd never felt anything like this: They were soul mates, they could finish each other's sentences, he would reach over just at the exact moment when she felt her glasses get ready to slip down the bridge of her nose and push them up again. He was brilliant, passionate, larger than life; a match for her bigness.

Later she called to say he was in jail, some little episode where he'd knocked out a couple of store windows when he was drunk, nothing major, but while she was waiting for him to get out she was having a little fling with this woman she'd gone out on a date with one Saturday night and not come home till Tuesday morning. Her name was Cass and she was very tall, "Five foot fourteen" was how she phrased it. Donna sounded elated. "Make sure you tell Maude!" she yelled into the phone before hanging up.

Then still later, another phone call from California, only this

time Donna was crying and she sounded scared. He'd gotten out
of jail, and the first night out he'd gotten drunk and whacked her
around their hotel room a couple of times, and now she was hiding out at a friend's house, hoping he didn't track her down.

"Call Stan," said Carole. "He'll come get you. He still loves
you, you know."

Then an operator broke in on the call. "Excuse me," she said,
"but I have an emergency phone call from Mr. Kimball for Mrs.
Kimball, is this she?"

"Fuckin' Roger," said Donna. "Carole, don't go, I need to talk
to you."

"I'll call you right back," Carole said. "He's off camping in the
middle of nowhere, it might really be an emergency."

"Don't bother," said Donna, and hung up without leaving her
number.

"Hey," said Roger. "You were on the line a really long time. I
got worried."

Carole sighed, and reassured him. Then she tried to call Stan,
but couldn't get through. Later she discovered he'd gone out to
the Coast to get Donna, who was back in the hospital on antide-
pressants, but it was a long time before Carole heard from
Donna directly again.

In 1982, Billy finally did quit the union, so Betsy's family lost its
medical benefits. Betsy would have liked to stay in home day
care, but four kids develop an awful lot of ear infections, so she
went out and looked till she found a job in a retail clothing store
where they gave her a health plan for only twenty hours of work
a week and let her work all the hours on two evenings and one
weekend afternoon. They paid only minimum wage, and half the
time she was sorting hangers, but it didn't inconvenience Billy or
require that the children ever go unsupervised by at least one
parent.

Billy's thirty-fifth birthday came, but the flying lessons turned out to be more expensive than Betsy had anticipated, so she gave him a nice sweater instead and went on saving in the coffee can for his fortieth birthday, and thought to herself that the Plan could wait for an extra couple of years.

Tammy never wasted much time worrying, period. How much stuff was really worth getting worked up over, if you thought about it? So she had to call Donna a whole bunch of times before she finally had a funny feeling and thought to call Carole and ask her where the hell Donna was.

And, well, frankly, Tammy found the whole story pretty fucking incredible, maybe even more incredible than Maude's, because from Maude you expected something half-assed. But it had seemed like Stan was such a nice guy, and took such good care of Donna, and she had seemed to appreciate it.

But you know, you could never tell about somebody's marriage from the outside. Tammy's mom, Thelma, who often refused to speak to Tammy's dad over some teeny little offense she had, in her own imagination, magnified into an assault, liked to sit at the kitchen table with a cup of coffee and tell you about the neighborhood wives.

"Lois, in the house with the green awning? Fred was always drinking, *always*, and in the summer, when the windows were open, you could hear him yelling at her all the way down the block. And, God bless her, *they* were married forty-five years."

God bless her? It was dawning on Tammy that she'd grown up taking for granted her mother's vision of marriage as a big endurance test where God assigned you the biggest obstacle He could find in the warehouse at that moment, and then you staggered along trying to carry it for as many years as you could. You got instantly disqualified if you staggered too much or dropped dead too early or certainly if you dropped out (which was un-

thinkable), and it was good to gossip with the other wives because that's how you found out if your husband was worse than
theirs, which gave you extra points. And if he was *really* unbearable—a nasty drinker, a wife beater, a flagrant womanizer—and
you bore him anyway, that was the big jackpot, because the
neighbors were sure to know, and they'd tell other neighbors, till
maybe one day you'd become the stuff of legend, and maybe
even the Pope would hear about you and make you into a saint.

Maybe Thelma's real beef with Tammy's dad was that he gave
her so little to complain about. He wouldn't be drawn into the
emotional tempests that were always swirling through a household where three daughters and their mother and *her* mother
perpetually supplied each other with less evidence of mutual
adoration than all the others expected was appropriate. The only
calm spots in Tammy's memories, aside from those Sundays in
the stables she had given up so Eddie wouldn't think she stank,
were the Saturday mornings in the car, when she and her father,
under the pretense of doing errands, escaped feminine turmoil
driving around town in a wordless cloud of his blue cigar smoke.
They didn't need to talk about anything, analyze anything, prove
anything to one another, ever. To this day, he still phoned from
time to time, separate from her mother's calls, and asked simply,
"You okay, Tammy?" And she always said, "Yeah, fine," no matter
how awful things were, because no matter how awful things
were, she always felt better when she heard his voice.

Somehow, she thought, that must have been what she'd had
in mind when she married Eddie: the two of them driving somewhere, it didn't matter where, not necessarily talking, probably
drinking and smoking, just keeping company, like pals. Instead,
she'd gotten the raw material of sainthood: a bully, a baby, a
nasty drunk. His pals were other guys, like his friend Murray.
They had fun. Her role was supposed to be to make their sandwiches, keep an eye on the kids, and keep her mouth shut about

certain aspects of reality that Eddie wished to be protected from.

Like the time he decided he wanted to have a boat.

"Whaddya mean, a boat? Eddie, the goddamn phone is getting shut off three times a year because we can't pay the bill, so how are we gonna afford to pay for a boat?"

"Easy. We charge it. So you pay a little at a time, you know?"

No, she didn't know. All she knew was that if she kept fighting it, he would get mean and nasty, because when he wanted something, he didn't like hearing anything that suggested he wasn't fully entitled to it. It was easier not to make a big deal out of it. Anyway, wasn't it really his job to worry about the money? To her, money was a thing that came to you because you played your part in a family. Her job now was wife and mother, just as it used to be being a daughter, and you didn't think about how money followed from that any more than you ever thought about just getting fed up and quitting.

So all that summer of the boat, they packed up the car with the kids and their clothes and their diapers and strollers and groceries, hitched the boat to the back, and drove up to a cabin on a lake. Murray would drive up to visit, and Tammy would spend the weekend cooking and diapering and sweeping sand out of the cabin and kid-watching, just like at home only here with no TV to distract any of them, while Eddie and Murray went and got sunburned speeding around the lake with a case of beer in a cooler.

Tammy especially missed the Girls that summer. She hadn't made any friends out in the country, hadn't really even tried. Truth be told, she didn't seek out other women generally. Her feeling was, they came fraught with all the kinds of crap she was always trying to get out of dealing with in Thelma and Delores and her sisters: whining, competitiveness, jealousy, emotional demands, doing stuff behind your back designed to punish you or get the best of you. Except the Girls. They had so much history together, you knew you could trust them. They were like the sisters you *should* have had, people who knew you really well, cared about what happened to you, and completely stayed out of your face, because except for the times they chose to get together, the paths of their everyday lives didn't cross that much anymore.

It wasn't as if she would have talked to the Girls about Eddie, though, because that just wasn't her style, to go deep into private things. She would've listened if someone else had talked, though, and if that someone else had described anything like life with Eddie, she knew what she would've advised: *Get out now.* Fine, but where was there to go? Not home to Thelma. Hadn't she married Eddie to get away from Thelma in the first place? Not out on her own, with two little kids and only a high school education and no job skills to speak of. And she certainly wasn't running away like Donna, abandoning the kids to Eddie and Delores.

But the fights kept getting worse. Once, out in the country, Eddie said it was fine with him if she went over to his friend's house and watched a football game with him, and then when she came home he asked, sneering, if she'd had a good time with her *boyfriend.* And then, with Delores, who was visiting, sitting right there on the couch watching, he'd just started yelling and screaming and pushing her out the door and telling her she'd better never come back.

She'd checked into a motel and spent the whole night lying awake, planning how she'd pick the boys up the next day after he dropped them off at school and take them back to Thelma's with her and find some way to support them all. But then, first thing in the morning, the phone was ringing off the hook. Eddie had called every hotel and motel in the area to track her down, and he was falling all over himself to apologize and beg her to come back, and of course she did, because she knew all along that no matter how badly somebody else took care of her, it was better than she could ever take care of herself.

One night, Eddie came home to the little house in the country and snapped, "Pack up. We're leaving." They packed all night and pulled out of the driveway just before dawn, leaving behind their down payment, which was all the money they had ever managed to accumulate. Tammy never learned exactly what had gone wrong with Eddie's business opportunity, but there was something about some loans he'd taken out in her name without consulting her, forging her signature.

Back in the suburbs, he got Delores to buy them all a bungalow with two unfinished rooms in the attic he promised to fix up so they could have some privacy from his mom, and vice versa. But nothing ever got fixed up, not the attic or the drab green paint on the downstairs walls or the leaky shower fixture a previous owner had installed in the bathtub that squatted on four stubby legs in the bathroom. In the summer they bought a secondhand air conditioner for the downstairs but every time they plugged it in all the lights in the house went *pfffffft*. Eventually the attic rooms were claimed by the boys, now eight and four, who were tired of sharing. But the rooms weren't heated, so in the winter, no matter how many old comforters Tammy heaped on them at night, they always woke up in the morning with their teeth chattering.

The grown-ups worked out a livable schedule under which they were rarely home at the same time. Delores had a part-time job during the day, and Eddie did what he referred to as "job hunting," which consisted of going out in the morning with Murray, also currently unemployed, buying the paper and a case of beer, and taking them back to Murray's house, where they read the classifieds and the sports section, occasionally made a few calls, and shared the beer. Tammy got herself a job in the deli department of the local Food King. It paid $3.65 an hour and got

her out of the house three evenings and one weekend day, while
Delores watched the kids.

"Carole, didya ever wonder about their ham salad?" Tammy
said into the telephone.

"I didn't, Tammy, till this minute. Are you gonna tell me something horrible? Does it involve, like—hooves?"

"No. No hooves, no snouts, no lips, and no assholes."

"Body parts, though, right?"

"Okay, I'll give you the recipe: You know, the deli counter has
all these different meats, right? Baloney, ham, spiced ham,
chicken loaf, roast beef, whatever. So when you get to the ends,
and you can't really slice off any more, you throw 'em in these
big plastic buckets. Not the olive loaf, though."

"How come not the olive loaf?"

"Carrie, it would change the flavor."

"Oh. Gotcha."

"So then you take all these buckets, you get a couple during
the week, you know? And you take them all over to the butcher,
and he grinds everything up together for you, and then you clean
out the sink, and you dump the stuff into the sink."

Carole groaned. "You're making this up."

"I am not. Carole, this is my *career*. So now you go out into the
grocery department, and you pick out two really big Miracle
Whip jars, and a big thing of pickle relish, and then you go over to
the juice aisle and get three big cans of Hawaiian Punch. And you
put the mayonnaise and the pickle relish in with the meat, and
mix it all up, and when you can stick your hand in and scoop
some out and drop it on the counter and it goes *fwopppp*, then it's
done. Except, it's still this brownish color, you know, like ground
beef that's been sittin' out too long, so that's why you add the
Hawaiian Punch, just enough to turn it that nice pink ham color."

Carole laughed and laughed. She forgot that she was worried
about Tammy. But it was virtually impossible to worry about

Tammy, because as surely as she could turn baloney and roast beef ends into ham salad, she could take practically any shit life dished out to her and turn it into a joke.

Tammy had another joke, a private one, that she took to practicing on Eddie. Down the block there was a bar called the Yellow Dog, and when Eddie wasn't drinking at Murray's, he was usually drinking there. It was a neighborhood place, not one of those dingy shacks where married guys hide out from their wives, but a lively joint with a couple of TVs, a couple of pinball machines, a Pac-Man, and a jukebox, all of them usually going at the same time, and a cook who made decent pizza. Most Fridays, Eddie hung out there while Tammy cooked dinner for the kids, bathed them, read them bedtime stories, and put them to bed. Around the time they fell asleep, and the dishes were done, and the toys picked up from the living room floor, and Tammy was just about to settle down on the couch with a paperback from the library sale bin, Eddie would come home loaded and say, "Hey, c'mon, Tammy, let's go out."

"Your mom's already sleeping."

"So what, the kids'll wake her up if they need anything."

"I dunno, Eddie, I had a long day today. I'm pretty beat."

"Awright, fine," Eddie would say, sitting down on the sofa with a thud. "Just don't say I never ask you. Just don't say we never do nothin' fun. You know why we never do nothin' fun? Because you're always TOO FUCKING TIRED."

"Okay, Eddie, how about this? You want some pizza? How about I go down to the corner and get us a pizza and bring it back, and we stay up and watch some TV together, okay? Pepperoni, onions, olives—whatever you want."

"Okay," Eddie would say, grudgingly. "Just come *right* back."

"Sure," Tammy would say. Then she would duck into the bathroom, perk up her face with a little powder, a little eyeliner and mascara, and head down to the bar Eddie had just come from, knowing that within ten minutes he would have passed out in front of the TV set in that way where you couldn't rouse him for hours. She'd have a seat at the bar, order the pizza and a drink, and by the time the pizza was ready she'd be involved in a conversation with somebody, and she'd tell the bartender, "Just keep it in the warmer, okay?"

Then, around one or two in the morning, when she was pleasantly blasted and the place was emptying out, she would take the pizza home, put it on the coffee table in front of Eddie, and eat a couple of slices, or maybe just throw a couple out if she wasn't hungry. In the morning, Eddie would invariably stumble into the bedroom snarling, "Hey, why the fuck didn't you wake me up when you got back with the pizza?"

"Oh I did," Tammy would say, not even bothering to open her eyes. "You said you'd be up in a minute, and then you went back to sleep."

Well, maybe it wouldn't sound that funny to everyone— which is why Tammy kept this particular joke private. But really, it was the best you could do with a man who was always either nasty because he was drunk or because he wasn't, when he wasn't likely to change and when he was yours forever.

Then one day, it just stopped being funny. It was Tammy's thirty-third birthday, and they had gotten into the car to go over to the house of Harriet, who worked with her in the deli, who was going to make them dinner, and she said, very quietly and calmly, that she wished that just this once, since it was her birthday and these were new friends, he would please stop himself from drinking so much that he did something embarrassing.

"You stupid bitch," he said, and she thought to herself, *Here he goes, I can't stand this.* She pulled the door handle, just wanting to get out of the car before he really started up, and he grabbed a handful of her hair to stop her, yanking so hard that it came away in his hand in a little clump. Tammy shrieked with pain. She pushed the door open and leaped out of the car, screaming at Eddie to stay the hell away from her. She was screaming other things, too, and she couldn't stop herself. It was like she was split in two, half of her thinking, *You shouldn't be standing out here in broad daylight in the middle of your own neighborhood screaming all these things at your husband with all the neighbors listening,* but the other half of her was such a juggernaut of pain and fury that she couldn't stop. He was screaming at her, too, and as she backed away from the car, the front door of a nearby house opened and out onto the sidewalk came two women she didn't know, looking concerned.

"Can we help you?" they said. "Do you need some help?"

She realized she was standing there, holding the side of her head, and she could feel there was a bald spot that seemed wet, and might be bleeding. How humiliating. *Mind your own fucking business,* she wanted to scream at them, but something in their expressions stopped her, and she said instead, "No, thanks. It's okay. It's just my husband."

But the women didn't turn away, shrugging, as she expected them to: *Oh, boy, will you get lots of points for that guy.* They just continued to stand there, regarding her, and one of them said, "It doesn't make any difference if it's your husband. He shouldn't hurt you."

Oh, thought Tammy. She just stood there, staring stupidly at the two women. Eddie's screaming had stopped, she realized, probably deterred by the audience of these two strangers, who had just said something kinder to her than anything anyone else had ever thought to say.

"Are you sure we can't help?" one of them said again, and Tammy smiled wanly and told them, "You have helped. Really, I think you have."

*   *   *

After that, she stopped thinking about whether she could make it on her own or not. She just decided that she would. There was a guy at the Yellow Dog, Martin, who seemed to have the hots for her, who was actually nice to her, just nice enough to make her think that some other, brighter future might be out there waiting for her, worth the risk. Secretly she packed up boxes, one by one, of the things that were hers—books, her wedding china, clothing—and took them over to Martin's apartment on the sly. Then one night, she kissed the children good-bye, went out to her annual bowling banquet, and never came back.

VI

The Steps They Took

The Eighties
and Beyond

Fractured Fairy Tales

A girl of her era didn't expect to have to come out more than once in a lifetime, especially when she had managed so superbly the first time.

Then, she had been a lovely, honey-blonde, nineteen-year-old college freshman in a white bouffant ball gown and elbow-length white gloves. Though her lineage was not as aristocratic as that of many of the girls with whom she whirled through the 1954 Gotham Ball, and then, several weeks later, the Debutante Cotillion and Christmas Ball, her beauty far outshone theirs. We know this because the next spring the Bermuda Chamber of Commerce selected her from a pool of vacationing college debs to be queen of its annual floral pageant. At her coronation in 1956, she led a procession of forty-five floats through the streets of Bermuda's capital. She rode in a horse-drawn carriage decorated with five thousand lily blooms, wearing a tiara of pink and white carnations.

Back home, awaiting the arrival of the requisite prince, she was committed by her parents to the safekeeping of the nuns at

a Catholic girls' college, Manhattanville College of the Sacred
Heart. (Boys at nearby colleges referred to it snidely as Man-
huntingville.) And, as parents of her generation often encouraged their daughters to develop a skill to Fall Back On, her
ad-executive father fixed her up with a high-profile modeling
agency. For her first job, a one-minute commercial, Maxwell
House paid her $2,500. Coca-Cola and Revlon quickly booked
her, too. It was all very glamorous and flattering, but still not exactly the kind of validation a girl yearned for most profoundly.

One day, the woman who owned the modeling agency came
in to find her lovely model earnestly chatting with a young man.
He didn't *look* like a suitable prince, but something about the intensity of their conversation made the woman suspect her
honey-blonde girl's career was about to draw to a close.

"Who's that fat kid with Joan?" she asked her secretary as
soon as she reached her office.

The secretary told her that the fat kid's name was Ted
Kennedy.

The second time Joan Bennett Kennedy came out was in 1978, at
age forty-three. She was still turning heads, but the gazes now
were often hostile and critical, or full of pity. Among Kennedy
women, she seemed aberrant: not a loud and thick-skinned
cheerleader, like the sisters and Ethel, not mysterious and allur-
ingly aloof, like Jackie. The whispers were that she was not
weathering the family tragedies well, that she had come
slightly—perhaps even completely—unhinged. As far back as
Ted's 1964 Senate campaign, a reporter had noted that "She
doesn't smile as much and she doesn't seem to give a shit anymore. A couple of times I saw her and she looked like she had
crawled through a rathole." In March of 1969 she attracted national front-page coverage by showing up at a sedate six P.M.
White House reception in a glittering sequined mini-dress that

stopped at least six inches above her knees. "Pat Nixon, usually the model of rigid self-control, stared at her exposed thighs," reported a biographer. "The President shook her hand and, with admirable exercise of will power, looked at her face and said a few words of greeting. A marine in full dress uniform, standing behind the President, stood at attention, eyes straight ahead but, momentarily, lowered." A year later, after she showed up at a White House luncheon honoring Imelda (Mrs. Ferdinand) Marcos in shiny knee-high boots, a midi-skirt, and a lacy see-through blouse with a blue bra plainly visible under it, a reporter for the *Boston Globe* wrote that it would help if Joan would equip her closets with locks and give the keys to a designer "who, from now on, will follow her around and daily give her the right clothes to wear." After a third White House event, which Joan attended in gaucho pants, a tight sweater with a bolero jacket of tie-dyed leather, and suede boots, syndicated columnist Harriet Van Horne proclaimed, "With her long blond wig, she looked like a faded film star on her way to a ranch cook-out."

But the real sin, Harriet Van Horne mused, went much deeper than simple bad taste:

> In her mode of dress, a woman is making a public statement. She is proclaiming her respect—or lack of it—for herself, her hosts, her husband and the milieu in which she lives. Naturally, she is also reflecting her time. But more obviously she is projecting her inner conflicts. One wishes, therefore, that pretty Mrs. Kennedy would discard those cheap novelties and hie herself off to the Paris couture—or to a good New York dressmaker. She can, one may assume, afford to dress well. Her mother-in-law, at eighty, looks elegant and womanly.

A lady did not project her inner conflicts. She got a makeover and then everyone, herself included, forgot that they were there.

Even when one's inner conflicts were widely known to include two assassinated brothers-in-law, several miscarriages, a son who had lost a leg to cancer, and a husband with what was euphemistically referred to as a roving "eye" who had driven a young woman off a bridge under mysterious circumstances and then deserted the scene, one was expected to keep proclaiming one's respect for that husband publicly. Whether one's husband returned the favor apparently depended upon what the stakes were. To the general public, whose political support Ted continued to court throughout the seventies, his office declared that the rumor of marital problems was "so ridiculous it doesn't even deserve attention." But a biographer of Ted's much later reported that when a journalist friend visited Ted at the family's Squaw Island summer house in the seventies, on his way out "Kennedy suggested that the friend say hello to Joan, who he said was at the rear of the house. The friend was aghast when he saw her lying in a drunken stupor in the rear of the car. 'I've seen drunks often enough,' the journalist said, 'but what I was looking at there was the result of a two- or three-day bender.' "

By 1978, it appeared that Joan had done the unthinkable: packed up and left her husband and the one child still at home in their Virginia mansion, and moved by herself to an apartment in Boston. Was she so far gone now that she would abandon a teenage son? That she no longer cared if she trashed Ted's political future? And how was it that the magic family that could charm, bully, or buy anything—elections, Pulitzers, *Jackie*— couldn't stop the public self-destruction of this woman JFK had long ago nicknamed "The Dish"?

When reporters inevitably tracked her down in the Beacon Hill apartment, Joan did the best she could to tread the fine line between the reality she was trying to acknowledge about herself and the loyalty she still felt she owed her in-laws. It wasn't Ted she had left, she told a reporter for *McCall's* magazine, but the fishbowl of Washington life. "I needed to find out about myself," she said. "I needed help on my sobriety. I needed to talk to a psychiatrist. I still do." She went on to admit that she had been drinking too much for many years, that she knew she had embarrassed many friends and loved ones, that she was attending Alcoholics Anonymous meetings in Boston, and that she was also attending graduate school to earn certification for teaching music.

For Joan to come out as an alcoholic (not to mention as a psychiatric client and, essentially, a failed political wife) in 1978 was much more revolutionary than it would be today, and you can see in retrospect that both *McCall's* and Joan Kennedy had very mixed feelings about it. Betty Ford had broken this ground only recently, pioneering a new narrative in women's life stories in which it was possible to be both beloved and troubled—as long as one wasn't currently messed up and clueless, as long as one was admitting one's problem and and seeking help, as long as one was (though it was a few more years before the phrase caught on) *in recovery*. For the popular magazines, this opened up a whole new territory of makeovers where before there had been only the wifely plotlessness of living happily ever after, periodically punctuated by going on a diet or adopting a new recipe for meat loaf. Even since the magazines had discovered, courtesy of Pat Loud, that not all wives lived happily ever after, they hadn't been able to conceive of a future plot for a wife or ex-wife with this affliction, except sending her to a spa to spiff her up so she could find a new husband and start the cycle over again.

But now, right beside Happily Ever After, the magazines had begun to conceptualize a place called On Her Own. This was a place where women went for spiritual and psychological makeovers once cosmetic makeovers had failed them. These psychological makeovers always had steps, or stages, just as diets and exercise regimens did, and gurus and best-selling

authors who told you what they were, and the women who underwent them were always shown to be growing stronger and
more independent as surely as made-over women grew more
beautiful. Women who were On Their Own returned to college or
graduate school, attended support groups like AA, claimed that
their work was paramount and that they didn't care (well, right
now, anyway) whether they found Mr. Right or not. Lynn Caine,
author of the best-selling seventies memoir *Widow*, told readers
of *Ladies' Home Journal* in February of 1978 that a woman
should never remarry within a year of being divorced or widowed because she needed at least that amount of time to discover that "life without a husband could be good." In that same
issue, TV's beautiful twenty-nine-year-old "Charlie's Angel" Kate
Jackson, who dated sexy stars like Warren Beatty and Nick
Nolte, assured readers that she had *chosen* to live alone for now.
Right now, coming home to "just a good book" was preferable,
she said, to coming home to a husband. She, like Joan Kennedy,
was confiding her deepest thoughts to a psychiatrist, not because there was anything *wrong* with her, but because "I wanted
to know if there was anything brewing in my subconscious that I
really ought to know about."

The real conflict—the inner conflict that the magazines didn't
seem to understand they were projecting—was that so many
women appeared to be *in recovery* from the very relationships
with men the magazines had instructed them—were still in-
structing them—to make every hair and pore of themselves over
to snag. Was it a good idea for women—other than those stri-
dent, non-leg-shaving feminists—to explore this conflict? Oh,
dear, not if they could get around it. Not if, for example, Joan
Kennedy could just get her own inner conflicts under control,
start dressing tastefully, and go back to Ted. Then we could all
relax and live on in the Fairy Tale, once again, only this time a little more cautiously, allowing for small bumps on the golden

road, because recovery was a sort of filling station or elegant spa hotel on the way to Happily Ever After, and not in itself the destination.

Certainly, the *McCall's* reporter to whom Joan made her 1978 confession couldn't wait to assert this interpretation. After only one paragraph, she interrupted her account of Joan's interview to tell us that, watching Joan, "my mind went back to a childhood phrase: 'Once upon a time' was the way the tales began, and this one began so easily, 'Once upon a time, there was a beautiful girl with long blond hair and wide blue eyes who met a handsome and very rich prince. . . .' "

"Was it possible," she wondered as she watched Joan across the table, "pouring out her story, innocently, almost pleading for understanding, discovering herself as she talked . . . that her story will, someday, end as fairy stories are supposed to end? Will people ever say, 'And they lived happily ever after?' "

Well, Joan tried. When Ted decided to make a run for the Democratic presidential nomination in 1980, Joan gamely headed out to the campaign trail and crisscrossed the country speaking on his behalf. She told everyone who asked that of course she planned on living in the White House with Ted, though *Newsweek* noted of their first joint campaign appearance that "the two acted more like a pair of strangers on a blind date than a husband and wife of twenty years." Though she remained sober and chirpy in public, her campaign secretary, Marcia Chellis, later painted a bleak portrait of Joan's private life as Mrs. Candidate, which included glimpses of Joan bingeing on ice cream and fast food and holing up in her bedroom for days on end. Chellis reported that Ted almost never spoke to Joan privately but had office staffers call her to deliver messages, and that at least once, when Joan was on the road but Ted was staying in her apartment, Chellis went up to deliver some papers and found a strange woman's luggage parked in Joan's bedroom and the woman herself primping in Joan's bathroom to the sound of rock music on the stereo, "instead of Joan's usual classical music."

When Ted's presidential aspirations finally collapsed for good in a bitter power struggle with Jimmy Carter at the 1980 convention, Joan's marital aspirations collapsed for good as well. She informed Ted that she wanted a divorce. Ted's office, apparently hoping to downplay the public announcement, released it into the flood of other news raging around Ronald Reagan's 1981 inauguration, including coverage of the inauguration festivities, speculation about the role Nancy Reagan would play in her husband's administration, and the release of the fifty-nine hostages from the American embassy in Iran. (Back to househusbanding for Ted Koppel? Not on your life.)*

"Joan Kennedy Loses Her Marriage But Gains Control of Her Life," reported *People* magazine, which quoted Nancy Korman, "a Kennedy adviser during the campaign," as asserting, "She is not going into a vacuum called nonmarriage, but into a life which she has created and can be proud of."

It was Joan Kennedy's third coming out, and this time, as the eighties were dawning, it looked as though On Her Own might be a place where one could dwell forever in recovery, after all. Might have to, in fact. In the same year, 1981, Colette Dowling's

---

*Even though it had evolved from "America Held Hostage," ABC's nightly update on the Iranian hostage crisis, *Nightline* had by this time carved out an independent identity covering other kinds of stories, including homosexuality in the military and the dangers of organized children's football. The show therefore survived the end of the hostage crisis, and *Newsweek*, in a February 1981 story attributing its success to the myriad strengths of its host, "The Unflappable Koppel," trotted out his househusband stint once again as evidence of his personal heroism. "In a business where being seen on camera is the name of the game," the magazine commented, "Koppel's disappearing act was a risky move, but it won him a new kind of admiration. 'Ted had enormous self-confidence and, because of that, he's not a neurotic or paranoid,' says ABC colleague Barrie Dunsmore."

huge best-seller *The Cinderella Complex* chronicled what the author characterized as the myriad neuroses and pathetic dependence of women who pined for Prince Charmings. It was the year a self-abusive dieting disease called the binge-purge syndrome, or bulimia (identified by the American Psychiatric Association as a separate disease only the year before), began to receive significant coverage in the press, suggesting that legions of women were now in need of recovery from their own attempted makeovers. It was the year Jeffrey Masson was fired from his post as projects director of the Sigmund Freud Archives for publicly asserting that Freud had recognized the reality of childhood sexual abuse even while disseminating the theory that such assertions originated in the erotic imaginations of the children themselves. In a lengthy November 30, 1981, cover story on Freud and contemporary psychology, *Newsweek* also documented what it called "An Epidemic of Incest," noting that within the past two years therapists and sociologists had come to estimate that "one of every 100 adult women in the United States was sexually molested as a child by her father—an astonishing figure in itself, and one that many experts think is far too low." It was not, in other words, only the love of their boyfriends and husbands from which some women needed to recover, but also the *love* of their fathers.

It seemed that the Fairy Tale must surely die, that anyone with eyes could see that it led women nowhere except to a land where awesome amounts of self-reconstruction would ultimately become necessary. And yet, within less than a month of the announcement of Joan and Ted's divorce, Britain's Buckingham Palace released the news that Prince Charles, 32, had finally found his princess. And that July, 750 million television viewers watched 20-year-old Lady Diana Spencer float down the aisle of St. Paul's Cathedral and into a marriage that the archbishop of Canterbury and most reporters worldwide agreed was "the stuff of which fairy tales were made," looking every hair and pore the made-over Cinderella and feeling (she only very much later confessed), like "the lamb to the slaughter."

Real Life

What they told you on the airplane was: If the oxygen masks dropped down in an emergency, and you were traveling with small children, you were supposed to adjust your own mask first. Now the reason the stewardesses—no, not stewardesses now, but flight attendants, here for your safety and not for your ogling pleasure—anyway, the reason they have to make such a big point about it is that it goes against maternal instinct. Everyone knows: You see to your children's survival first—and only then to your own.

Donna had plenty of time to contemplate this on the flight home from California, which turned out to be so much longer and bumpier than the literal airplane trip. Stan had come out to retrieve her, and sitting next to him on the plane she felt more like a bandit in the sheriff's custody than a wife returning home with her husband. She felt nothing wifely for him anymore, and she knew that everything of value she had managed to steal for herself on the lam was going to have to stay buried for a while, away from the unsympathetic, uncomprehending eyes of the people at home who "loved" her.

"Leavin'?" her dad had sneered months ago, when she had tried to say good-bye. "You're *leavin'*? You can't even cross the street by yourself."

Donna, instantly the toddler with one hand on the space heater, had snarled back, "Oh yeah? Watch me."

"A woman don't leave her kids," he informed her, and then shook his head sadly. "You know, Donna, you're my daughter, so I love ya. But I ain't got any respect for ya."

"Then keep your love, Dad. I got no use for it."

Donna was in a relatively thin period, around 180 pounds, and most of the time in California she was on the streets, so she must have been living off her father's words, which burned inside her like jet fuel even though she thought she was too numb right then for anything to hurt. The very first night, when she still had money for a hotel, she picked up an Italian in the bar and took him upstairs. The second night, she picked up a German. The third night, she had her period, but the guy she met in the bar that evening said if it didn't bother her that he'd just got out of jail, it wouldn't bother him if she had her period. After they fucked, he looked into her eyes and whispered, "I prayed to God before I got outta jail that He would send a woman to me, someone I could really love."

Well, this was pretty much what Donna had been hoping for, too, when busting out of that marital jail to which she had been condemned after rejecting the alternate sentence of four years of Catholic girls' college. This was it, the very heart of where, as a mother, as a daughter, as a Catholic, as a good girl, you were not supposed to go. Kurt was big and strong, as strong as she was. And he was *bad*, with the immense magnetism of that certainty women so rarely have that he was *entitled* to be a law unto himself. He had no qualms about breaking into rooms inside her that she had always supposed were to be kept pristine and dusted, and sitting down with his feet up on the coffee table like he was ready to watch TV. So Donna learned the secret no truly good girl ever learns: the erotic magic of having your fortifications battered down. They stayed in that hotel room for days, and a decade of wifely orgasms faded into vague insignificance.

When he drank, unfortunately, he battered down other things: real doors, shopkeepers' windows, her face. Still, when he got sent back to prison, she was willing to wait for him. If Stan had been the way out of her mother's house, then somehow

it seemed that Kurt would be the way out of the way out. She
didn't see how she could escape without him, without his batter-
ing ram and the ecstasy he created in her body. Imagine facing
life without that: a long dreary succession of empty white days,
and once a week you shopped for groceries.

Waiting, drifting, not even trying to find herself, even though
here she is in California, which is certainly where all the lost
people can be found. One night in a bar, while she is reading a
book—the best way in a bar of attracting anyone capable of talking about anything else besides sports—a dykey-looking woman
comes up to her and starts a conversation. Well, Donna's not put
off by dykes, because besides knowing Maude, lately she's been
crashing at a commune of lesbian feminists who have adopted
her—a runaway suburban housewife—as a worthy rehab project. The woman tells Donna she's a therapist, and Donna, thinking of her unpleasant stay in the psych ward following the
episode at Carole's New Year's party, says, "Oh yeah? I've known
some therapists. Most of 'em were jerks. Oh, excuse me, I
shouldn't be so quick to name-call. Big *Fucking* Jerks."

Donna casts a sidelong glance at the woman, to see how this
is received, but the woman only shrugs. "Every profession has
its jerks," she says. "But psychologists don't all agree with each
other. There are different sects."

"I don't usually discuss sects with people I just met," says
Donna, and when the woman grins, Donna thinks: Okay, I won't
rule her out. So they chat some more, and before she excuses
herself to go, the woman—whose name is Kay—reaches into a
satchel and pulls out a book, which she hands to Donna along
with her business card. "Read it, and if you like it come see me
and I'll lend you more," she says.

The book is called *Social Equality: The Challenge of Today*, by
Rudolf Dreikurs. Donna takes it into bed that night, in the little attic room the lesbians have given her, and stays up all night reading.

The moving force behind all our actions is an inner plan [wrote Dreikurs] according to which we act and which we hardly know. . . . Our self-concepts shape all our interests, strivings, feelings, and movements. If we accept ourselves as we are, we do not waste energy fighting with ourselves. This "saved" energy is then available for coping with the contingencies of life around us. We ourselves are our greatest problem. We must first make peace with ourselves. Then we can turn to the rest of the world with confidence, courage, and often joy.

Donna devours the book. Rudolf Dreikurs is speaking directly to her soul. He recognizes the little, thin, wifely, motherly person she has always tried to be and the earthy, passionate, loud-mouthed, questioning broad she is, and the battles they have waged and the battleground of her body that has perhaps grown huge as a result, and through his words she suddenly sees both these women clearly. She knows Carole once had her Baba, and Maude has been born not just again but many times, and even Betsy has always had her Plan, but this is the first time in all her thirty-three years that the clouds have parted and the light of heaven has shone down upon her and a voice—so quiet there upon the page but it seems to be booming in her ears—proclaims, *Donna, too, has her own plan.* Page after page, she marvels at Dreikurs's wisdom, at all he seems to understand about parents and children, husbands and wives, the individual and society. But then, some time in the wee hours of the morning, she turns the last wise page and finds only a blank one. The book is over, and he hasn't yet told her how to make this wonderful thing happen, this mysterious transformation, in which by changing she will become more fully herself.

She's at Kay's office first thing the next morning. "It takes time," Kay says, "to really get to know yourself. To try to unlearn things you've spent a lifetime learning. Time, and patience, and support. And sometimes it's very painful." She lends Donna a few more books, and agrees to see her for therapy, although Donna can hardly afford to pay anything.

They don't make that much progress, though, before Kurt gets out of jail and beats her up again, and Stan comes to take her home. She tries not to cry as she watches California shrink and then disappear below the plane, because even though he has hurt her badly, she still wants Kurt and the way he filled her up worse than she wants anything else she believes life has to offer. She is taking it entirely on faith that some other thing she found in California, some thing Kay and Dreikurs say lies buried within her, can be unearthed, and will some day make her richer.

Her dad refused to talk to her when she got back. He just looked right through her, like: *Donna, you are dead to me.* But her mom took her to lunch and asked anxiously, "Donna, what will you do now?"

"I don't know, Ma. I'd like to finish my college course work. I'm thinking about getting my degree in psychology."

Donna thought she saw a glint in her mother's eye: *Me, a girl psychologist? Crazy!* But her mother just asked, sounding neutral, what Donna thought a year's tuition would cost these days.

The next day she showed up at the apartment Donna was renting and handed her an envelope in which Donna found four thousand dollars, cash.

For the next year, Donna lived by herself, visiting her kids on weekends, attending classes during the week, seeing the Girls occasionally. She began to think that people who liked living alone must have very romantic relationships with themselves. Personally, she had underestimated the stress of having an intimate relationship with someone as difficult as herself. It was so much easier, in retrospect, to have bounced off other people,

blaming them for disappointments, resenting them for the con-
strictions their demands placed on your freedom.

Now she was free, and her time was shapeless. She woke up
on the days when there were no classes or deadlines thinking,
What do I do now? A malicious little voice deep inside her would
chirp, "Who the fuck cares?" and she would have to answer it
sternly, "*Wrong.* First, go to the bathroom." And she would get
out of bed, haul herself into the bathroom, sit down on the toilet,
and think, *Okay, now what?* What she really wanted, most of the
time, was to sit down in front of a soap opera and eat chocolate
cookies, forgetting about the world out there; but she also understood, with constant self-reminding, that it was the world out
there that was somehow the antidote to her sickness. No matter
how hard the struggle, she had to keep going out there and en-
gaging in it.

One evening, in a spirit of professional curiosity, she let a
friend from school take her along to an Alcoholics Anonymous
meeting. She sat on an uncomfortable metal chair and listened
as the guest speaker, a professorial-looking guy in a tweed jacket
and blue tie, talked about the moment he recognized his power-
lessness over his addiction. "I went out to the garage to sneak a
drink," he told the audience. "But then I dropped the cup, and
the drink spilled all over the garage floor. And I realized this was
the last alcohol I had in the house. So I went into the kitchen and
got a sponge, and then I got down on my hands and knees
and sponged up every last drop I could get off the garage floor
and squeezed it into the cup, so I could still drink it."

Donna was mesmerized. Something in the story resonated—
not the alcohol necessarily, because with Donna it could just as
well have been food, or pot, or cigarettes, or sex. But she recognized the desperation he described, the compulsion to seek comfort from something secret, something that isolated you from
other people and made it harder to reach them, so you needed

ever more comfort, ever more sneaking. A life sentence of needing to steal what others either get for free or don't mind paying
for. She looked around the church basement at the people on the
other metal chairs—housewives, salesmen, the clerk from Wool-
worth's maybe, and somebody's grandma and grandpa, holding
hands—all so normal-looking, with nothing but their presence
here suggesting the shadows of hidden demons. They came to
these meetings daily, some of them, because time—which always looked so benign in other peoples' living rooms—was as
blank and terrifying and reproachful for them in their sobriety as
it was for her.

She bought the Big Book and went home to work the twelve
steps. They were hokey, she thought at first, but they were also a
plan. They would nudge her whole life forward, minute by
minute, One Day at a Time. She especially liked the steps that involved homework, the making of lists, the sharing of lists; she
disliked the ones that involved God. She didn't know that she
wanted God—the Catholic God, the Him of her childhood—involved in her plan because, after all, He'd been in charge the first
time and look how things had turned out. But her friend said
some people chose to think of it as Good Orderly Direction, and
Donna liked that. For the step that involved turning yourself
over to the will of God, she began to visualize waking up in the
morning and seeing a stream that flowed through her door,
which was the stream of life, flowing along pleasantly in this
Good Orderly Direction. And instead of standing there thinking,
*Is it cold? Is it deep? Am I strong enough? Would I rather get
the hell away from here?*, her job was to step into the stream
confidently and then float on the currents. Not surrendering her
power to it, but drawing power from it; as Dreikurs had said, not
exhausting her energy swimming against the flow, but conserv-
ing it for the struggles of going forward.

After the first year, Stan said he needed some freedom, now, and that he would give her a divorce and the house if she would come back and take over the day-to-day care of the boys, now twelve and ten. The boys were pissed as hell at her for leaving, but she thought that if she hadn't left they would eventually have been pissed as hell at her for being an emotional zombie, or for any of the reasons she was pissed as hell at her parents and their imperfect love.

She took them to her parents' house for Christmas dinner, even though it had been more than two years now since her father had last spoken to her. He refused even to acknowledge her when they walked in.

"Listen," she said to his stony face. (He *was* a scary man, her dad.) "It's Christmas, Daddy, and I think we're all gonna have a real nice time now that we're together."

He stared through her, but she thought she saw a muscle relax almost imperceptibly beneath one eye. "Yeah?" he muttered finally.

"Yeah," said Donna.

Later, as she and the boys were getting their coats on to go, he pulled her aside. "I'm thinkin', now you're back in the house, it probably could use a little fixin' up. I'll send a couple of boys around next week to see what they can do, but meantime, here's this."

He slipped a white envelope into her hand, and when she opened it outside in the car she found that it was filled with crisp, green, hundred-dollar bills.

Tammy had never spent a day alone in her life before she walked out on Eddie. So she didn't have any idea how she was going to make this work out okay, except that she had no choice. When she went to full-time in the deli department, the market paid her a salary of $12,700, or roughly a thousand a month, but only about $750 after you took out taxes and deductions. From that she had to pay $495 on the crappy one-bedroom that had been the cheapest safe apartment she could find. So then there was about $250 left for utilities, food, and clothes for two growing boys. The law said Eddie owed her 20 percent of his income as child support, but the minute Eddie turned the boys over to her, he "lost" his job. And even though she'd given up math long before they got to percentages, Tammy didn't need to do much calculating in her head to figure out that 20 percent of nothing is nothing. She signed the kids up for free school lunches and brought home one-pound packages of ham from the deli that she had weighed and marked as half a pound. But no matter how much she stretched and connived, it seemed like all the week's groceries would be gone by Tuesday or Wednesday.

The other problem was, without Eddie's mom, she had no child care. The one day a week she had to be at the deli at seven A.M., the boys, now twelve and eight, would have to get themselves up, feed themselves breakfast, and get themselves to school. Two days, when she worked the late shift, there wasn't anyone there when they got home from school. Eddie took them weekends, which meant he picked them up and deposited them with Delores while he drank, but even he noticed that what was going on over at her place was not ideal. "I think I could do a better job with the kids," he told her one Friday, and she had to admit that, maybe for the moment, he was right.

But she figured this was only temporary. If she worked another year, she might be able to afford a new apartment closer to the house, so the kids could stop by after school on days she wasn't working. And her life wasn't completely desolate and empty because, after all, she was still seeing Martin from the Yellow Dog on weekends.

But one Friday night when she pulled up in front of Martin's building for a date, there were a bunch of cop cars out front. Some woman was yelling and screaming, and then the cops dragged Martin out of the building. When Tammy asked what was going on, he scribbled his mom's phone number on a scrap of paper and said, "Tell her to get some money and come bail me out."

His ex-wife had found out he was seeing someone, and thrown a fit, and somebody hit somebody, and somebody called the cops. Tammy stood there on the corner dressed up nicely for dinner and a show, and thought: Hey, I've been *here* before.

She did make sure to get her wedding china and other personal possessions out of his apartment before politely informing him that they had nothing in common and, by the way, he was the cheapest son of a bitch she'd ever dated.

But then there was another problem, because back in the rattrap apartment where there was no Martin, and no Eddie, and now no boys, and she should therefore have been all alone, she was finally forced to admit something she'd been trying to overlook for a while now, which was that she was not alone. She was with child.

"Tammy, everything okay?" She is so used to this conversation with her dad, the dialogue etched into stone over all these years, that it never even occurs to her to blurt into the phone, *"No, Dad, I'm in big fuckin' trouble."*

"Sure, Dad," she says as always, "everything's fine."

"Okay, hon. Listen, did you ever find the Christmas present we bought for Howie?"

"No, Dad, I'll be dipped in shit, I can't find it anywhere, I swear I put it in the bag we brought home—Dad, are you okay? You sound like you're breathing kind of hard."

"It's nothing, hon. I just went down and got the mail, you know how steep these stairs are."

"Oh, okay. You know, you should start takin' better care of yourself, Dad. Stop smokin' that cigar, maybe take up joggin' or power walkin' or—"

There was a *thud* on the other end of the line, the sound of the receiver hitting the floor. She waited a beat for him to retrieve it.

"Dad? DAD?"

Her parents' apartment was too quiet. She burst in, listened to the silence, and just knew. There was nothing the paramedics could do to jump-start his blue body, though they loaded it into an ambulance and rushed it to the hospital all the same: Tammy's last ride with her dad.

The funeral was like a movie, something where you saw yourself and everyone else acting completely normal, only you weren't actually there. Tammy phoned all the relatives on both sides and arranged a luncheon for after the burial, executing it all with a strength and professionalism she had never been able to summon up on her own behalf. *I guess I'm stronger than I think I am*, she thought from time to time, watching herself not fall apart, except for the moments when she caught herself thinking: *As soon as this is all over I will throw myself under a train.*

"Why didn't you *tell* us?" Donna demanded. Betsy had called all the other Girls and told them to get the hell over to Tammy's as soon as Tammy called her.

"How was I supposed to admit it to you when I couldn't even admit it to myself?" said Tammy. "Besides, I don't remember *you* telling us before you decided to disappear to California."

"Oh, well, geez," said Donna. "Next time I decide to have a nervous breakdown and go fuckin' nuts, I will definitely give you guys advance warning."

"The cake is Sara Lee," said Carole apologetically. "I usually like to make it myself, but this was all we had." She was unloading a shopping bag onto Tammy's kitchen table: vegetables and dip, chips, cheesecake, Tab, Almaden. She had even stopped on the way for cigarettes. "Tammy," she added, hovering, "can I get you a glass of milk?"

"We could have helped," said Betsy.

"Helped how?" said Tammy, reaching for the cigarettes. "Whaddya gonna do, bring up this baby for me?"

"Yes," said Maude.

"We could've helped you think about your options," said Donna. "You still have options, you know."

"What, you mean, like, an abortion? It's too late, I'm six months'. Besides, I'd never do that. It hurts."

"I'm serious," said Maude.

"Oh," said Donna, "like having it isn't gonna hurt."

"Well, of course," said Tammy. "But then it has a point. Anyway, look, I was adopted. It was the whole reason Thelma never had to explain sex to us as kids, 'cause me and my sister didn't come from the stork, we came from Catholic Charities."

"*Please shut up and listen to me,*" said Maude. "I said, I will raise the baby. Ruth and I will raise the baby. We've been talking about it, Tammy. We were talking about it before this came up. It makes perfect sense."

"Nothin' here makes perfect sense," said Tammy. "I haven't been seeing a doctor. I haven't been eating right, I haven't been taking vitamins, I haven't stopped smokin'. For Christ's sake, we don't even know it's gonna have the right number of fingers and toes."

"But, Tammy," said Maude, "what about the timing? Ruth and I had just started talking about this seriously, but we couldn't figure out how we were going to handle it. I mean, where do two dykes get a baby? Catholic Charities isn't going to give *us* one. Am I supposed to ask one of my book reps if he wants to be a sperm donor? But it's, like, I'm asking the universe to give me a baby, and here's one of my oldest and dearest friends who's about to give one up."

"Jesus, Maude," said Tammy, taking another cigarette. "Is this gonna be another one of your—enthusiasms?"

Maude's face reddened. When she spoke again, it was in a low, controlled tone, as though she were trying not to yell, or to cry, or both. "You know, I've sat here all these years listening to you guys complain about your—*fecundity.* How many times you *choose* to get pregnant, what you're gonna do so you *don't* get pregnant, what you can't do because of all the children you have, *more children than you know what to do with.* And you know, my body couldn't hold on to a baby, and if that happened twice in my twenties, it's not likely to get any better now that I'm in my thirties. And now I've finally created the kind of home life and emotional and financial stability that I would need to raise a baby, and *there doesn't seem to be any way for me to get one.*"

There was a long silence. The Girls stared into the food and lit more cigarettes, and Maude blew her nose into a square of paper towel. Then she cleared her throat and added, in almost her normal voice, "Unless you just think it would be too weird. If you think it would be too weird, I wouldn't want to lose our friendship over it."

"I think we would lose our friendship if I did give it to you," Tammy said. "What if I saw you yelling at it? What if I didn't agree with Ruth's ideas about religion? You know, Maude, if I'm not going to raise this kid myself, I want him to have a really, really good life. But I just don't want to have to . . . watch. . . ."

"I understand, Tammy, I really do. Only, maybe you could think about it a little more."

Tammy told the doctor, "If you maybe got a couple in your practice who're looking for a baby, here's one you could drop in their lap, probably pretty soon. I just don't want to know anything about it, okay?" She asked for nothing in return, so she was surprised to discover, when she went to check out of the hospital, that her whole bill had been paid by the adopting couple. If they could afford to do that without being required, she thought, they could probably afford to give her baby a pretty nice life.

Her own kids never found out. She wore big loose outfits up till the seventh month, and then told them she was going to visit her cousin in Hawaii for a couple of weeks' vacation. If Eddie noticed anything during their brief encounters while picking up or dropping off the kids, he must have done his math backward to the date of their divorce decree and figured it was smarter, in the interests of legal paternity, just to keep his mouth shut.

The Girls tried to keep an eye on Tammy. She moved in with Thelma temporarily, which gave both of them a warm body to be around during their respective periods of grief and transition, but you had to figure that a mom was maybe not the best party to perform social rehabilitation on a thirty-three-year-old daughter in Tammy's position. She'd need some additional help to get her back Out There.

But by the time they all showed up to meet her at the designated bar for their first postbaby outing, Tammy was already happily ensconced on a stool, smiling her big shit-eating grin, announcing, "Guess what, Girls? We're drinkin' for free!"

"I got here early," she told them. "So I'm just sittin' here drinkin' my rum and coke, and this guy comes up to me. Nice-looking. Well dressed, camel hair coat, gray hair, I'd guess fifty-five. And he just starts talking. So we're sitting here for a while, yakkin', and then he says he'd like to take me out for dinner."

"Now, now," said Maude. "Girls' rule: Never break a date with your girlfriends for a date with a guy."

"Well, *duh*," said Tammy. "I'm here, ain't I? So I says, 'Geez, I'd love to, but I'm meeting my girlfriends here tonight and I haven't seen 'em in a while, so I really gotta stay. But some other night would be nice.' So he goes, 'Okay, tell you what. I'll call you, and we'll have dinner next week, how about Tuesday?' And I go, 'Hey, that's perfect, 'cause I don't have to work Wednesday.'

"So then, he hands his credit card to the bartender and says, 'This lady here is meeting some friends, so whatever they want is on me, and add a twenty percent tip,' and she runs the card through, and he tells me to just bring him the receipt when we have dinner."

"You slut," said Donna admiringly.

"Thanks," said Tammy. "And I'm thinking: I could get used to this. I could *do* this. I mean, assuming he's not a total asshole. Even if he's only a *partial* asshole, look how many years I put up with Eddie, and he couldn'ta bought a matchbook on time."

"But not if he's a *total* asshole," said Maude. "Tammy, I am mighty happy to hear you have principles you're planning to stick to."

"But seriously, Tammy," said Carole. "You be careful. Even if they seem nice, you can't be sure from just one conversation in a bar."

"That's absolutely true, Carole," said Maude, "because, as I recall, that's exactly how we found you Roger."

"Hey, girls," said the bartender. "Last call, and you're only running around sixty bucks on the tab. Drink up, will ya?"

But the guy never called Tammy to make a date for dinner, and she was really disappointed. Because he'd seemed so nice, she thought as she *fwopppp* dropped a fistful of minced assorted deli meats onto the stainless-steel counter to test for doneness, and for about a week there he'd had her thinking there might be a way out of all this.

A couple of weeks later, her friend Harriet from the deli said she and her husband, Bill, were drinking at the Crow's Nest that night, and did Tammy want to join them? And when Tammy got there, they were chatting with another guy they introduced as Ernest. He was in his mid-forties probably, and there was nothing real remarkable about his appearance or his attitude—no expensive clothes or air of entitlement like that guy who had never bought her dinner—so she was surprised when he mentioned being a pretty high-up executive of a famous fast-food company. The two of them hit it off immediately. He knew how to make good drinking talk, nothing too deep but a fantastic mind for jokes and statistical trivia, and the jukebox was playing oldies, and after a while he asked her to dance. As soon as the music slowed and he pulled her close she could feel his hard-on. "You know," he said into her ear, "there's a motel just down the street, if you'd be interested."

Tammy was not uninterested. But then she thought this would not look good, particularly to her mom, who had just watched her bear and give up that fatherless baby about six weeks ago.

"Geez, I can't really stay out all night tonight," she told him. "But if you just wanted to go out to the parking lot for a bit, I could give you a really nice blow job."

This time, Tammy prepared herself psychologically for the possibility that he might not call her. They can seem really nice and still not call, she reminded herself firmly throughout the week, every time she caught herself thinking: *Call, you motherfucker.* She cut out an article from the Style section of the newspaper that showed you "How to Get the Man You Want in 10 Easy Steps." Blowing him on the first date was not on the list, Tammy noticed. Rule number one was: "Look him straight in the eyes when you talk to him. His mother looked at him that way, and he'll love you for it."

It took him five days. Then, when he showed up at the deli to pick her up for their date, she hardly recognized him. He could've been any of those middle-aged men you see in supermarkets shopping for orange juice and TV dinners on a Tuesday night after work. Had she noticed before that he was completely bald? Maybe she'd been too busy looking him in the . . . well, anyway, this time she was careful to look him straight in the eyes—which she noticed were somehow very kind—as she told him, "The air-conditioning hasn't been working too well all day, and I've been sweating like a pig. Do you think we could stop by my house on the way to dinner, so I could take a quick shower?"

"Better yet," he said, "I'll give you a bath."

Jesus, thought Tammy, remembering Carole's warning, I hope my mom doesn't come home and find the bathtub full of blood. But she let him give her the bath, and then they went and made love on her bed, and by the time her mom got home they were sitting in a nice, air-conditioned restaurant, drinking and eating steaks and trading stories about their marital catastrophes. "I tell you," he repeated several times, "I am not saying the 'M' word to any woman ever again."

By now, Tammy had forgotten about the article, and was just looking him straight in the eyes anyway, and listening.

About two months later, while they were standing in line for a movie on the evening of his birthday, Ernest turned to Tammy and asked her to marry him.

"I thought you weren't gonna say the 'M' word ever again," Tammy said.

"I wasn't," he said. "So don't make me say it twice."

"Okay, I won't," said Tammy. "But look, I got some stuff in this big suitcase that I've been carrying around since I got married the first time, and I want to marry you, but I don't want to carry all this shit around through a whole 'nother marriage."

"Yeah, like what?"

"Okay, like, number one: I do not shave my legs very often. Or my pits either."

"What about in summer, for a bathing suit?"

"Well, yeah, for a bathing suit I would, but I mean just—in private."

"Okay," said Ernest. "What else?"

"Okay, see this? This is MY hair."

"Yeah," said Ernest. "It's very nice."

"And I will do what I want with MY hair."

"Tammy, what the hell are you talking about?"

"Once, I got my hair cut real short just as an experiment, and Eddie hit the roof. *'What da fuck did you do to your hair,'* he yelled, and then he said he wouldn't be taking me outta the house again till it grew out. And we went *nowhere* for three months."

"Tammy," said Ernest very gently, "it's not going to be a problem for us. Because I'm not gonna let you tell me what to do with MY hair either."

Tammy smiled, and kissed the top of his shiny head, and said, "One more thing. I've got these girlfriends, and I've known 'em for practically all my life. We get together every month or six weeks, or more often if there's a crisis, and we go out for drinks, or maybe dinner, and sometimes a guy might ask us to dance, but that's all."

"Yeah?" said Ernest. "I got a group of guys I play cards with. And we go to some guy's house around eight at night, and I might not get home till four in the morning. Just cards, though, and shooting the shit. No women."

"Okay," said Tammy.

"Okay," said Ernest. "And my things leftover from my marriage are: No lying. And no sulking. Something's bothering you, you don't walk around waiting for the other person to read your mind about it. You gotta talk."

"Okay," said Tammy. The theater doors had opened up, and the line was starting to move toward the lobby. "You got yourself a deal."

*   *   *

Ernest thought it was significant that they had met on her dad's birthday. "Tammy," he said, "it's like we were *destined* to be together." But it took Tammy a long time to rid herself of the feeling of waiting for the other shoe to drop. He seemed just too good to be true. Not only were they in bed a huge amount of their time together, but he seemed deeply grateful that she was such a slut at heart, and thought the proper way to show his appreciation was to pop up with a little piece of jewelry she had said she liked, or surprise plane tickets to Las Vegas for a four-day weekend. But had the original answer to your naive teenage question of whether or not there was such a thing as true love been Eddie, you might not have immediately recognized an Ernest when he dropped into your lap, or, in Tammy's case, when you had dropped into his.

A few weeks after their wedding, Tammy came awake suddenly one morning, as though startled by a noise. She squinted at the digital clock, which said only 5:30. Ernest lay snoring beside her, apparently undisturbed.

But she thought she heard someone calling, "Tammy." Her father's voice, the voice of a thousand phone calls.

She sat up carefully in bed and peered past the open bedroom door into the hallway and stairs beyond. She thought she saw him standing there, in the weak bluish light that might have been the pale dawn filtering through the miniblinds, or the wispy trailing smoke of a cigar.

"Tammy," he called again. "Is everything all right?"

"Oh, Daddy," she whispered. "Everything's *great!*"

"Okay," he said.

And when she looked again, whatever it was she had seen in the stairwell was gone.

There was another trend *Newsweek* had noticed in 1981, between the divorce announcement of Joan Kennedy and Diana's

celebrated passage down the aisle. Not all women *were* still sitting around waiting for the Prince:

> They have traveled and worked late and dressed to succeed, and
> now they are seeking "something more." Increasingly, women
> over 30 are becoming mothers for the first time—whether
> they're married or not.
>   . . . "I think it's sort of a contagion that's going on," says New
> York psychologist Iris Fodor. "My patients see their friends hav-
> ing babies and they want their own."
>   In some cases, the need to nurture waxes strong enough to
> inspire deliberate unwed motherhood. Some women stop prac-
> ticing birth control without telling their lovers, others turn to ar-
> tificial insemination. A few even advertise for prospective
> fathers in newspapers. . . .

That more or less explained what Maude was doing one
weekend, holed up with her mom at a lakeside resort halfway
between the City and the countryside to which her parents had
retired. That and a little fragment of wisdom Maude had heard
lesbians at the store repeat to one another with rueful smiles:
You can never come out to them just once. No matter how firmly
you put it to them the first time, your parents went right on hoping that it was just a phase you were going through, that one day
you'd get it out of your system and settle down in a *normal* family, to produce the grandchildren they craved.

Actually, Maude's mom had been pretty cool about what she
learned to refer to as Maude's "lifestyle" from the moment she
had first visited the bookstore back in the late seventies. "Oh,"
she had remarked after her initial browsing, "I see you have
some books by lesbians."

There was a pause, in which Maude had tried to gather her
wits for the most productive response, but her mother had then

added, "Well, that's good, because there's all sorts of women."

Maude just nodded her approval, and then her mother gave a little shudder and concluded, "Whoa, I wouldn't want any woman lovin' *me* up, though. I like men."

Her mom had always been perfectly cordial toward Ruth, too, so Maude could certainly understand why she might find Maude's current circumstances somewhat confusing. Why she might think that Maude's lifestyle could use a little bit of straightening out. Why she might keep inquiring, with some hopefulness, about the father of the baby with whom Maude had suddenly, miraculously, revealed that she was five months' pregnant, "Are you planning to marry him?"

Of course, there were things your mom needed to know about you, and things you might not necessarily go into, so Maude didn't share all the little details about Carlos. For example, the way she had met him right under Ruth's nose, in the neighborhood bar where Ruth had encouraged her to hang out, where Ruth herself began spending way too much time following the collapse of the third or fourth "sure moneymaking" business opportunity she'd looked into after leaving the bookstore co-op. Almost weirdly, Ruth had made a big deal of pointing him out. "Construction guy," she had said, "one of those types who comes in for a beer at lunchtime and never seems to go back to work. Good-lookin', don't you think? Cute butt."

At the time, Maude hadn't actually hatched a plan, at least not consciously. After all, she flirted with everyone in that bar, and it was imperceptible the way the particular flirtation with Carlos escalated, until they were suddenly so close to the line that it took only the smallest featherlike push to knock them both over it.

"You don't ever find yourself with free time in the mornings, do you?" murmured Maude, while across the room Ruth traded football commentary with a couple of middle-aged businessmen who were watching the TV.

Carlos gave her a long, assessing look. He wanted it to be known that he stood on his honor. "I like Ruth," he said. "She's my buddy here."

"Well, I like her, too," said Maude soothingly. "She's such a great person. But she's just not—you know, *doing* it for me."

It took only a few more moments of honor before he scribbled his address down on a napkin, and he didn't seem to think it was odd that Maude asked a lot of questions about his forebears, or that, when he revealed that all his grandparents had lived well into their eighties or nineties, she was so pleased that she almost purred.

By this time the bookstore was providing Maude with a modest but reasonably secure living. It had expanded into the space next door, which enabled the co-op to double the number of titles it carried and set up a small cafe. Now, in any given week, a nationally known novelist on a book tour might read there on a Thursday night, while on Friday a locally respected folk singer promoted her new tape. Maude loved the store, and felt more at home in it than she did at home with Ruth. At home, Ruth was in charge of everything: the money, the social life, the choice of what they would have for dinner. If she wasn't in charge, she didn't feel safe, so Maude, who loved to cook, couldn't even surprise Ruth, who loved to eat, with a special fancy dinner, because then Ruth would throw a fit about not having okayed the grocery bill. And under such conditions, when even your generous impulses mysteriously end up threatening your partner, you either begin to erase yourself or to demarcate selected battlegrounds.

But at the store, Maude flourished. There were other members of the co-op who were better at certain things than she was: budgeting, negotiating with publishers and the landlord, devising long-term marketing strategies. But no one was better with the customers. A customer who dealt with any other staffer walked out with the book she came in looking for, but a customer who dealt with Maude walked out with that *and* a hundred dollars' worth of additional books in a neat little shopping bag. Maude read constantly, and she fell in love with books as passionately as she had once fallen in love with high school boys, or philosophies and religions, because they could change everything in your head around, illuminate the world and make it deeper and richer. And because of the many places she had been herself, she could empathize with practically any customer: the fifty-year-old woman confronting her attraction to other women for the first time; the thirty-five-year-old housewife whose husband was dumping her for his secretary; the newly pregnant natural foods fanatic looking for a holistic pregnancy manual; the medieval history professor who was on a murder mystery kick. At the store Maude's promiscuity—her need to connect with everyone and try everything and give it, if possible, her whole self—not only for the first time in her life made perfect sense, but was clearly her greatest asset.

So really, Maude thought, if it weren't for Ruth's suffocating need to control, if it weren't for the several daily phone calls to the store that Ruth said were just "to check in" but Maude suspected were to check on her whereabouts (the Girls insisted, somewhat gleefully, that she was *worse* than Roger), life would have been pretty close to perfect. Whenever she thought about Carlos, an enormous wave of lust cascaded right down her spine and straight into her belly. It had been years since she had felt the heat of a man's body on hers. Wasn't she probably ovulating now? Ruth had said she wanted a baby, too, and she understood that their options for obtaining one were limited. Ruth might understandably prefer some kind of turkey baster arrangement at the local sperm bank, but once it was accomplished she might well decide to stick around to help raise the child.

Or not.

"I'm taking an early lunch," she told the new assistant, a Ph.D. candidate who wore a diamond stud in her nose. "If Ruth calls, tell her I just stepped out."

"He's verrrry attractive," she told her mom now, as they ate chicken salad sandwiches on a wooden deck overlooking the lake. The Indian summer sun warmed them, and the waitress kept their iced tea glasses refilled, and Maude's mind drifted back to summers long ago when she had gone to another lake with Brad and his family and thought that Brad was some kind of God who would shower her with grace and happiness if she were good and prayed. "But, Mom, at my age, you've learned that some of them just aren't good for marrying."

"You don't need to tell *me* that," her mother said. "I'm lucky I even survived being married to your brother's father. Did I ever tell you, I was his *fifth* wife?"

"No, Ma, I don't think you ever did. What happened to the other four?"

"Well, two of them died, under very mysterious circumstances, and it was always my opinion that he had murdered them."

Maude squinted at her mother's face, wondering whether she was really serious. Her mother put down her sandwich and regarded Maude gravely.

"Maude, sometimes I wonder—" She broke off, searching for words, and Maude waited. "Your dad didn't ever—*do* anything to you, did he?"

"You mean—something that would explain why I . . . ?"

Her mother nodded.

"Oh, no no no, Ma. He never laid a hand on me. He's a good man, Ma. A really gentle, kind man."

Her mother's shoulders seemed to relax a bit, and she picked up her sandwich and continued eating. "Well," she said, "I always thought he was. But if you'd ever told me otherwise, dear, I want you to know that I'd have believed you. And I'd have killed him."

Thirty-five years of marriage, thought Maude. They had fought, but they had stayed together, and cared for one another, and the whole time maybe her mom had been practicing something closer to diplomatic relations than to passion. As Ronald Reagan had said: "Trust, but verify."

"Ma," she said after a while, "Carlos was very gentlemanly about sitting me down when he found out, and telling me that it would be fine if I wanted to give the baby his name."

Maude's mother looked out over the lake. "Well," she answered, "there's nothing wrong with our own name, is there?"

"No," Maude agreed. "That's what I told him."

Ruth was torn between her anger at Maude and her genuine excitement about the baby. She went along to Lamaze and learned the breathing patterns, and was there on the long night in January of 1988 when Maude pushed the infant boy into the waiting hands of the midwife. Ruth got up to change Will's diaper in the middle of those first long nights when he cried so much, and when Carlos appeared to view the fruit of his loins (*No flowers!* thought Maude. *No teddy bear!*), Ruth shut herself up in the back bedroom till he left. But being roommates who fought didn't seem to work nearly as well as being lovers who fought, and about two months after Will's birth, Ruth packed up and moved to her own place a few blocks away.

Carlos made affectionate but irregular visits till Will was almost two, old enough to tug repeatedly at the knees of Maude's slacks and demand, "When Daddy come?" Just old enough, Maude thought, for the occasional nature of the visits to have become poignant to everyone. Then one evening, when Maude had arranged for Carlos to baby-sit so she could supervise a reading at the store, he showed up an hour and a half late, and reeking.

"Don't you *ever* show up drunk to see Will again," Maude told him, turning him away at the downstairs door. And that was the last time they ever saw or heard from him.

That left Maude and Will alone in the little apartment in the City. It was a cozy flat, overflowing with books and galley copies sent by publishers who had come to recognize the store's power to attract the right readers for a mushrooming body of women's literature. Ruth stayed involved with Will, taking him on Sundays and for occasional weekends and overnights. Lovers came, both male and female, and Maude would always cook for them and dance with them and wonder, very briefly, whether they might be the right one, but after a while it would always turn out that they weren't, and she and Will would wind up together again in the little apartment, doing just fine on their own.

Newsbites

People readers got the scoop in June 1992, the week right after the magazine's cover story on "Princess Stephanie: Single, Royal and Pregnant." There had been rumors and mutterings for years already, but now, "Dramatic Excerpts from the Book That Rocked Britain" had outed Diana (or, some believed, allowed her to out herself) authoritatively. Andrew Morton, author of *Diana: Her True Story*, had dramatically confirmed that "For Lady Diana Spencer, life as a wife of Windsor was far from merry after she said, 'Yes, please,' to her Prince Charming," and that it had soured, in fact, into A GRIM FAIRY TALE.

It seemed that there had been another woman all along, and that Diana had known this even if at first she hadn't truly comprehended its significance. During the engagement, she had accidentally opened a package containing a bracelet meant for Camilla, which the Prince had ordered with the initials of their pet nicknames for one another intertwined, and which, over

Diana's strenuous objections, the Prince insisted on presenting to Camilla a few days before the wedding.

So, just like Joan Kennedy, Diana had found herself legally and very publicly bound Ever After to a famous man who didn't love her but needed her to act as though he did. And, unlike Jackie or—some said—her own mother-in-law, Queen Elizabeth—Diana wasn't able or inclined to use her vast wealth and unlimited social connections to divert her attention to other pastimes. Instead, she had stared too long and hard into that deep black pool where no love was, and become paralyzed by the idea that what stared back at her was really her own reflection.

Like Joan Kennedy before her, Diana had taken to her closet, where she seemed to be accumulating, among the thousand-dollar ball gowns, a subset of outfits that proclaimed what Harriet Van Horne had so delicately termed lack of respect for her husband "and the milieu in which she lives." Much more shocking, though, were Diana's retreats to the water closet (sometimes five or six times a day, as Morton revealed), where she was apparently trying to drown her sorrows—instead of drinking them away—by vomiting them up and flushing them down the loo.

Grim indeed, and deeply disturbing, that one of the world's most admired women should turn out to be suffering from this bizarre compulsion. But the magazine assured its readers that Diana was now safely In Recovery:

> Diana consulted therapists and sought medical treatment to help control her bulimia. In yet another major step toward rebuilding her self-esteem, she confronted Camilla Parker Bowles about her continued relationship with the Prince, venting, according to Morton, "seven years of pent-up anger, jealousy and frustration."

And it looked as though *People* and Andrew Morton were sending Diana off to live Happily Ever After in (which was now no longer considered an oxymoron or paradox) On Her Own.

Her achievement has been to find her true self in the face of overwhelming odds. She will continue to tread a different path from her husband, the royal family and their system and yet still conform to their traditions. As she now says, "When I go home and turn my light off at night, I know I did my best."

Then it turned out that Diana's syndrome was nowhere near as bizarre as readers might at first have thought, for only about a month later, *People* followed up the Grim Fairy Tale piece with a feature on how "The Princess' struggle with bulimia brings a puzzling disease out of the shadows." Readers learned that "millions of women the world over" were afflicted by "The weight-control urge that can kill." Twiggy's Curse, it might have been called—the fulfillment of the prophecy so casually proffered even as it had been promoted in *Newsweek*'s first profile of the ninety-one-pound fashion phenomenon twenty-five years before: *"Whether the Twiggy look will now sweep across the U.S., emaciating American teenagers as it goes, remains to be seen."* It had done that and more, according to *People*. Not just Americans, but women the world over; not just teens, but adults; not just wanna-bes yearning for fame and glamour, but women who had them both and were now terrified of losing them. Celebrities identified by the magazine as having suffered from bulimia included Olympic gymnast Cathy Rigby, actresses Ally Sheedy and Lynn Redgrave, comedienne Joan Rivers, singer Judy Collins, and movie star/political activist/entrepreneur/bod-of-the-eighties extraordinaire Jane Fonda.

Fonda, then fifty-four, was described in *People* as having been bulimic from ages twelve to thirty-five. "I would literally empty a refrigerator," the magazine quoted her as saying. "I spent most of every day either thinking about food, shopping for food—or bingeing and purging." A reader who did the math could figure that her tenure as America's fitness guru presumably postdated her recovery, or perhaps *was* her recovery, for she had made millions and millions of dollars throughout the eighties exhorting book and video audiences to "feel the burn" of her aerobic workouts.

It was another five years before Americans discovered that Fonda had required a subsequent recovery-from-her-recovery, that during the period in which she had so authoritatively shown us the magical steps that would lead to a Fonda physique—the steps we had made her rich attempting to emulate—she herself had been "obsessively addicted to exercise." This confession came, among other places, in a 1996 interview with *Good House-keeping* that included "surprising talk about putting her husband first, traditional family life—and shorter workouts." Until she had met Ted Turner, whom she married in 1991, she said she had routinely "worked out two or three hours a day and took four-hour bike rides for a hundred miles."

It made you wonder whether those eighties workout tapes, as fanatical as they had been, had still amounted to sabotaged recipes from which your aunt Sue might have left out the crucial ingredient so you couldn't reproduce her masterpieces. Would following those steps to the letter *really* have rewarded you with Fonda's body, or would you have needed to be doing a little something else—a bit of purging, say, or an extra daily hundred-mile bike ride—to get the full effect? Fonda now claimed that with her current only moderate daily half-hour workout, she had gained neither pounds nor inches, and "Now I wonder: What was I doing before?"

Reflecting on the "destructive" nature of a life spent "scared of flesh," Fonda confessed that while she had been acting she would "wake up every morning worrying about how I look, feeling slightly nauseous for fear that I won't pull it off." As a result of Ted's support, though, she had withdrawn from Hollywood, produced a series of new videos based on her more moderate workouts, and pretty much decided, at fifty-seven, to focus on being a good wife. "I was very successful," she said, "but I failed at two marriages. Before it was too late, I wanted to see if I was capable of having a truly intimate relationship. It takes constant tending."

Kind of like mothers had once done, those horrible, boring, stifled, and stifling creatures whom a generation of daughters had sworn never to grow up to be. The women of protofeminist times, who'd made the mistake of not planning for a life beyond the first moment when they discovered a man could look at them filled with the glow of something he called, for the time being anyway, everlasting love.

The weight just creeps up on you. Two pregnancies; thousands of days of little nibbles while fixing breakfast, lunch, and dinner; your metabolism slowing while gravity pulls your tiring flesh quietly downward. And, meanwhile, on the pubescent body of your daughter, flesh has just begun to sculpt a fresh and merciless comparison.

Carole had never let herself get actually fat, but now just over the hump of forty, she looked at her thirteen-year-old daughter and understood that what had once been given to her as a gift was now going to require serious effort to maintain. And it wasn't as though she weren't willing to do the work. She'd been willing to do other kinds of work, had even toyed for some time with the idea of going to law school, but Roger had not been supportive. She managed his office much better than a hired stranger probably would have, and, he pointed out, just because both the kids were in school didn't mean they didn't need someone to come home to at three o'clock. And it wasn't as though they needed the money. By now, in addition to the comfortable house in the suburbs, there was a white-on-white condo in Florida, with a pool and a boat. So it was likely that Carole getting a job was going to damage rather than enhance everyone's lifestyle, and he thought it would be good if she could solve whatever crisis of identity she might be having within this context, and maybe stop bringing home destructive notions from that lesbian feminist Maude and her other pals at what he sometimes referred to as the monthly "circle jerk."

So when a workout center opened in one of the shopping centers nearby, Carole thought maybe signing up for an aerobics class would be a good idea, and before long she had a set of colorful leotards and could shift from a right-left grapevine to a left-right grapevine without missing a beat of "Gloria." Then she started learning to use the weight machines, and was amazed at the definition her body began to take on—more tone than she had ever had even as a young girl. Overall, the exercise was like some miracle drug, like Valium and speed combined in nontoxic, nonaddictive form, because it absorbed both your anxiety and frustration and all the calories you otherwise had to so carefully calculate and ration. And, well, maybe it actually *was* addictive, but only in a very benign sense, because even if you got a little obsessed by it, wasn't it the healthiest kind of obsession a person could have? It wasn't like drinking and being incapacitated for doing anything else—it made you better and stronger for dealing with everything else.

It was about a year and a half that Carole attended the gym religiously, until the morning when the phone rang and her mother told her that her brother's twenty-year-old daughter, Stacey, had had an accident. Her mom's voice sounded weird, she thought, not hysterical and crying as you might expect, but oddly calm and detached, and what she said was, "Somebody said she broke her neck."

Somebody said? What did that mean, exactly, Carole wondered as she sped to the hospital. Somebody said it but it might not be true? Stacey was in intensive care, after all; there must be a doctor who knew whether she'd broken her neck or not.

It was only much later, in retrospect, that Carole understood that deep grief descends on a person gently, like incoming fog, rather than massively, like a piano falling from a window, even when the cause itself is quick and violent. Yes, Stacey had broken her neck; yes, Carole's mother must have been told that already, but her mother had been trying to hold at bay the intimacy with tragedy that would start to enfold the whole family over the next days.

Stacey lay there like a broken bird, hooked up to the machines that kept her fed and breathing while her body refused to respond to any treatment. The family hovered outside the room: Carole's parents, her brother, Greg, and his ex-wife, Karen, who was clearly drinking the whole time and snapped at everyone's attempts at sympathy; assorted other relatives who came and went. It was so unfair, they told each other over and over, as though a silly prank turned catastrophic were less acceptable than the kind of calamity a parent might have thought to put time into worrying about. At a party, on a night when it was much too cold to swim, Stacey had decided it would be fun to dive into the host's pool with all her clothes on. Her best friend had said, "Cool, I'll go too, just wait till I get back from the bathroom," but by the time she got back Stacey had already done it and somehow hit her head, and the friend did jump in after her, screaming for help, to hold her body afloat until the ambulance arrived. They spent days and days outside Stacey's hospital room grappling with the cruelty of that moment, of a child's spirit extinguished by a flash of harmless mischief, and they all knew she *had* already been extinguished, because in all those days on life support there hadn't been a sign in her blank face of the real

Stacey. So why was it such a huge fresh shock, well after they
had thought God had already made that decision for them, to let
the doctors pull the plugs and then watch Stacey's mom clutch-
ing her hand and screaming, "DON'T GO, DON'T GO!"

Carole went home empty, and for weeks afterward they all
walked around like zombies, only periodically Natalie would
burst into tears and clutch at Carole, saying, "I just wish our lives
would go back to normal again," and Carole would say, wood-
enly, "They won't ever be the same kind of normal again," because they had both been changed forever by understanding that
Carole could not protect Natalie from either death or the knowledge of death. Every once in a while Carole thought it might be a
good idea to go to the gym and get her body moving, but she
couldn't work up the enthusiasm. Anyway, it was a long time before she regained her appetite and started remembering to count
calories again, and by then when she looked at her daughter's
glorious, strong young body she felt no challenge, only the deepest, most profound relief.

Betsy tried running for a while, but it didn't make any sense to
her. Why waste half an hour of consciousness running around in
a circle, ending exactly where you started, having accomplished
nothing but freeing up your mind to dwell on how much time you
were wasting? If this was supposed to reduce stress, how come
Betsy's blood pressure went up just thinking about it? Unless
someone could invent a way to get through a thirty-minute workout in, say, ten minutes, Betsy just didn't have the time.

For his fortieth birthday, Betsy had finally saved enough
money to buy Billy the flying lessons. She had given him the little
gift certificate in a manila envelope at breakfast, and, caught off
guard, he had said, "Hey, thanks," and given her a little peck on
the cheek. But then when she got back from work late that
evening, after he'd clearly had a few beers, he cornered her in

the kitchen and said, "I figured out the real reason you want me to take flying lessons."

"I don't want you to," said Betsy. "You've said for years *you* wanted to."

"Oh, yeah, that's nice, Betsy. I mean, I thought about it all day, 'cause I'm thinking: She doesn't even *like* me, why's she gonna get me a present like this? And then, I got it."

He looked triumphant, leaning against the counter with his arms crossed across his chest, his face frozen momentarily into a sneering smile.

"Got what?" asked Betsy.

"You want the FAA to test me."

"Why would I care if the FAA tests you, Billy?"

"For alcohol," he said. "You think you can prove I'm some kinda alcoholic."

Betsy later repeated this conversation to the Girls, expecting her outrage to be echoed and supported by the group, because surely this was the most obtuse, offensive remark ever reported in the group throughout many years of analyzing their spouses' and lovers' obtuseness.

But the story was greeted with silence.

"Oh, come on, you guys," Betsy said. "I've been saving this money for years. I could've spent it on myself. I could have used it to help pay for an MBA."

"We never said he wasn't an asshole, Betsy," said Donna. "It's just, we all kind of thought you *were* saving it for your MBA."

"Yeah, Betsy," said Maude, "whatever happened to the Plan?"

"I was going to start saving for that after I got him the lessons," said Betsy. "It's just that saving for the lessons took a lot longer than I thought it would."

"Betsy, you can sit around till hell freezes over waiting for that guy to be grateful to you," said Tammy. "It ain't gonna happen. I'm telling you, get out now. If I could pull it off, any-body can."

Yeah, Betsy wanted to say but wouldn't, but you gave up your kids in the bargain, and I'm not willing to do that. Instead she said, "I can't. I can't finish raising four kids, work a full-time job, and go back for my MBA if I'm doing it all alone."

Carole refilled Betsy's glass with wine. It occurred to her that of all of them, so quick to have their futures sewn up by marrying before they were twenty, Betsy was the only one still left in the original marriage. "You're doing it all alone right now," she said gently, "and you have been for a long time."

Billy started taking flying lessons. Betsy went to the bank with her oldest son, who was taking out a loan to start college, and took out her own loan to cover the cost of night courses toward an MBA. She instituted Quiet Time at home, so that between five and seven every evening the TV was off and the phone went unanswered and everyone had to do their homework, including her, in total silence. She worked her job while the kids were in school, and reported for an eight A.M. business class every Satur-day morning so that she could even stay on campus and get a few hours' worth of work done on the computers before heading home at noon, when the kids and Billy were just rolling out of bed. On Sundays she cooked the whole week's worth of dinners and froze them along with huge platters of turkey sandwiches that the kids could grab from the freezer, adding their own let-tuce, tomato, and mayo.

Really, she thought, there were no bad side effects to this hectic schedule except that you didn't want to be the driver in front of her going less than five miles an hour over the speed limit, because you would find a sort of wild-looking housewife in your rearview mirror bearing down on your tail and leaning on the horn if you so much as hesitated at a stop sign. And, as she was hardly lingering to watch the scenery, it took a while for the new shopping center she passed on the way to business school to register on her consciousness. It was just rising out of a cornfield near where Betsy knew there were developers building big new houses with cathedral ceilings and master-bath Jacuzzies and three-car garages to lure growing families out from the City. At first the shopping center just had one of those mega-warehouse discount stores and a twelve-screen movie theater, and Betsy thought a restaurant right on the corner would do well, and within a month a restaurant started to go up. Then Betsy found herself fantasizing about how a dry cleaning business could make a mint here, with no inventory to manage and fairly low overhead, and at least in the beginning the kids could work the front counter to save labor costs, and then *bang*, in goes LooKlean Dry Clean.

Not long after this, Betsy found herself pulling Maude aside in the parking lot of a restaurant where the Girls had just met for dinner. "There's going to be a hair salon next," she said, describing the shopping center, "and it might as well be mine."

"You mean, like the place you and I used to wash heads for tips when we were teenagers?" Maude asked, amused.

"Sort of," Betsy said. "Only not a blue-hair place. My concept is: a family salon. Men's, women's, and kids' haircuts. Billy can build it, I'll run it, and the kids can work there. I even have a name, " she added shyly. "It's going to be called The Wild Hair."

"But Betsy," said Maude, "you don't know how to cut hair."

"That's not the problem," said Betsy. "You can hire stylists. The problem is, even though I'm getting this MBA, I'm not learning anything practical, like, how do you set up an account with MasterCard? How do you figure out which suppliers to use? How do you figure out what the store should look like? It just seems like there are so many steps, I don't know where to get started."

"Oh," said Maude. "Well, first you find a couple of books

about starting a business and read them from cover to cover. Then you make a list of all your questions and who you think might be able to answer them. Then it doesn't matter which step you take first, as long as you've really made up your mind to do it. As long as you make sure that you take steps instead of worrying about taking them, after a while you'll find that you're going forward."

That made sense to Betsy. She got Billy to come do most of the construction for her, but once the salon was up and running, he lost interest and refused to do any maintenance without immense amounts of nagging.

He did get his pilot's license, though, and after that he'd try to insist that they fly places on the weekends, places he'd never had any interest in going before. Most of the time, Betsy told him she couldn't, that weekends were her busiest times at the shop and on top of that there were still all the kids' soccer and hockey matches, and parties and dates to make sure they came home from, and she just didn't have the time. That's what she told him, anyway. She wished him the best up there, she genuinely hoped he was happier up there in the clouds than he had ever been in their home, but after all these years she already knew what it felt like to be trapped alone in a tiny hazardous vehicle with him, with no solid ground under their feet and him at the controls.

Sometime in the early nineties, when the Girls were all in their forties and their talk had begun inclining at least as much toward menopause as toward men, Carole asked if they would mind her bringing her old friend Cindy to one of what had now become their regular monthly get-togethers. For the most part, they didn't entertain visitors, and when they did it was on a mutually understood self-limiting basis; for example, Maude's female lovers were sometimes asked along on excursions to movies or plays, or allowed to hang out for a given evening if the gathering was actually at Maude's; and Ernest, whom they all adored, sometimes prepared for them the delicacies he cooked on weekends to atone for a career spent perpetrating flash-cooked hamburgers on an innocent public, and then they would feast on photogenic homemade pizza topped with tomatoes and basil from Ernest's own garden, perhaps, or his fragrant crusty apple pies. Much of the time they weren't engaged in anything all that private or even, to an outsider, all that interesting. Once Betsy demanded that they all go out to a roller rink for her birthday, and once Tammy dragged them all to a karaoke bar and made them perform; every Christmas they went to the same expensive, fancy Italian restaurant where the waitresses not only knew them but sneaked out into the back alley to get stoned with them in the course of the meal; but a lot of the time they just sat around at someone's house, drinking and smoking the cigarettes which by then none of them smoked anymore in real life, and playing long hysterical games of Trivial Pursuit or Scattergories. Strangers were an encumbrance to all this, not only because a fair amount of highly sensitive information about people's marriages and sex lives and children and jobs tended to get dropped into the pauses between eating and the next round of charades, but because after thirty years their conversations had come to be conducted in a complex dialect of jokes and allusions to anecdotes they'd told each other a thousand times and, by the time they'd had to stop to explain them to someone else, they felt, the point would've been long lost.

Cindy had two advantages, however. She had gone to St. Mary Magdalen High School a few years ahead of them, so she knew a lot of the people they were still gossiping about twenty-five years later (because you couldn't resist it, of course, after you ran into them or their mothers in the hardware store and heard the really great story of their divorce or the five Romanian orphans they'd adopted, or how, despite having been known as the biggest brain of eighth grade, they'd only ended up running a doughnut store franchise after all). But more important, Cindy herself appeared in one of their anecdotes, as an alumna of their early High School of the Broken Hearts. They all knew the story of how Carole had nursed her through her first forlorn and un-wed pregnancy, in the little suburban crash pad where Carole was recovering from her marriage to Josh and where Maude went, after Cindy, to recover from Brad.

No one was sure that the chemistry would work, though, and even less so when Cindy, with her pixie face weathered but still intact after all these years, now set off by a pixie haircut, showed up with the air of a skittish racehorse, and announced, lighting one cigarette after another, that this had all been her therapist's idea. "She says if you find the right group of women, the dynam-ics can be very healing. Everybody throws in their lot together, and celebrates and mourns together, and finds some respite from the world."

"I hope," Donna said, "you're not confusing us with one of those groups of women who worship menstrual blood and go out in the woods to howl at the moon."

"Yeah," said Maude, "because, really, we spend a lot of our time eating and drinking and giving each other birthday pre-sents."

"But cool birthday presents," said Carole. "Maude got a leather miniskirt this year, and I got a gift certificate for a mas-sage."

"But it's gonna cost you," said Donna. "Usually we each chip in twenty-five bucks per birthday, but new members, don't you think they should have to pay double, Girls?"

"Hey, did I show you-all the bracelet Ernest bought me on the last cruise?" Tammy said, extending her arm so they could all see the small circlet of gold with a delicate diamond clasp. "And I can't even *mention* some of the things I did to earn *that* one."

Cindy, who didn't know any of them well enough to be sure whether to interpret their banter as hostile or all in jest, lit yet another cigarette. "I have to confess, you guys, that I feel a little intellectually intimidated by you. I remember you were all in the super-smart class."

"Not me," said Tammy. "I've always been a total dumb-head. And Donna here, she didn't develop a single brain cell till she was well into her mid-thirties—am I right, dear?"

"No shit," said Donna. "Hey, Girls, do you-all remember how my mom used to say: 'If you can be a nurse, you can be a doctor'? Well, it looks like my dissertation's gonna be done in another two months or so, and then I'm gonna officially become *Dr.* DeMarco."

The thought of Donna being a certified, professional psychologist stayed with Cindy as a sort of internal counterpoint to her continuing doubt about whether the Girls' sometimes barbed remarks meant they were accepting her, rejecting her, or simply hazing her. She kept showing up at the monthly meetings, but remained withdrawn when the really personal talk began. And then one evening, when they had all gone out to a movie and were driving back to Carole's house in several cars for drinks and snacks, she found herself the only passenger in Donna's car. It was a rainy spring evening, and the blackness and the beating of the raindrops on the windshield created a sense of safety and refuge within the car, like the dark safe silence of the confessional, and suddenly Cindy, feeling tears start to leak out of the corners of her eyes, asked if it would be okay with Donna if she talked a little about the stress she was under right now. And would Donna please promise not to tell anyone else any of this, because it was stuff she'd tried for twenty years to bury that she'd just begun to realize she couldn't bury any longer, but it still made her feel scared and ashamed and very raw to talk about it.

Donna's face immediately assumed the sort of neutral mask that Cindy's therapist wore at their sessions, and this emboldened Cindy to begin her story, reaching back to the end of that summer she'd spent with Carole twenty years before, just after the baby had been born, and Cindy, deciding to keep her after all, had had the twin curses placed upon her by the social worker from Catholic Charities and by her own mother. *"We sometimes find with women who keep their babies in circumstances such as yours,"* the social worker had said, *"that the children pay hell for the mother's resentment at having been left by the father."* And Cindy's mother, piqued to find a wailing infant in her household when she'd thought she'd already served her sentence of maternal toil, would shriek whenever Cindy went to nurse, *"Let that baby cry. You keep pickin' her up and stickin' that nipple in her mouth every time she hollers and she's gonna grow up spoiled and lazy. Like you."*

And though Cindy had vowed not to let them, both the curses had come true. A few years later she had begun dating a man she'd known vaguely in high school, and found herself pregnant again. Mark said he loved her and wanted to marry her, and even though deep down she felt she was still in love with Melody's father (the man who hadn't wanted her), she told herself she couldn't just go around bearing fatherless babies. It was time she got her shit together and acted like a responsible adult. She married Mark without worrying too much about the essential coldness she felt for him, because it was so similar to the essential coldness she felt toward Melody; it was just the way you felt about everyone, she thought, when you'd gotten old enough to have life kick the shit out of you a few times. But then her second daughter, Lizzie, was born, and Cindy was absolutely shocked by the intensity of the bond that sprang up instantly between them. This time, she abandoned her mother's imperatives. She nursed Lizzie on demand and carried her everywhere in a front pack. As Lizzie grew, Cindy had only to look into her eyes to know what she was feeling, and she felt warm and gratified by knowing she could always meet Lizzie's needs. But this only accentuated the fact that she could never meet Melody's, and both of them knew it, and no matter how hard she tried to be scrupulously fair to the girls, never favoring one over the other, it seemed that she and Melody were always fighting, always accusing, always failing to comfort, with Melody growing wilder and wilder as she hit the teenage years.

When Melody was sixteen, Cindy discovered that she was having sex with her high school boyfriend, and this is what had sent Cindy to a therapist, initially. Because Melody was now, Cindy told the therapist, out of control. TOTALLY OUT OF CONTROL. Within a few weeks of starting the therapy, though, it was Cindy who seemed to be losing control. She felt worse instead of better, as though some spell she had been under for an entire lifetime, which had numbed her without her knowing she was numbed, had begun to wear off, and suddenly she was perceiving everything with her raw nerve endings, and it was all quickly becoming unbearable. One Saturday morning she woke up unable to catch her breath, sure she was having a heart attack, and put in an emergency call to the therapist: "I can't breathe and I can't think and I have to see you because I'm having weird images of my father all over the place."

The images were fragmentary, not entirely forgotten, but emerging in little bits and pieces like shards of some smashed pot that had been dropped because it was too heavy to be carried. Her father French-kissing her when she was sixteen. Drunk, he is always drunk, so it doesn't count. No one notices. Her mom hates him anyway. They divorce. Cindy hates visiting him. She has a screaming fight with him and doesn't go for a few years, till after Melody is born. After Lizzie, her dad and his new wife come to dinner. Her dad shows up drunk. They have brought a present: a sundress with a tube top, and her dad wants her to try it on. Her breasts are huge in it, swollen with the milk for Lizzie, and when she emerges from the bedroom, her father bursts into tears, and touches her bosom with his fingers, sobbing, "Oh, those poor little titties." Mark's jaw drops, and he drags her back into the bedroom. "What the fuck was that about?" he demands, and Cindy just stares at him blankly, and says like a zombie, "Huh?"

There were a few years of therapy. Therapy—it sounds so soothing, doesn't it, like aloe lotion on sunburned skin? But what it felt like much of the time was like being skinned alive. That shell we wear is there for a purpose; it grows around us, like the rings of a tree, in response not only to time but also to the droughts and tempests in the air around us, the richness or poverty of the soil that sustains our roots. It can be stripped, to expose scarred tissue, and the tissue can be healed, but only with the experience of this great pain we have arranged our entire lives to protect ourselves from.

Cindy had just finally begun to emerge from this process, convinced that she was stronger for it, that she knew herself better, accepted herself more fully, and was healed, when Melody, just turning twenty, came to her and announced: "Mom, I want to meet my birth father."

Now, Cindy had always known this moment would come. She had never hidden Melody's history from her; had, on the contrary, insisted on it as evidence of how much Melody was wanted. The story, she had always emphasized, was about love: how much she had truly loved Melody's father; how she, while becoming the victim of that great love, had yet redeemed it by keeping Melody when she might so easily have given her away. Cindy herself had always felt enormous shame—the shame of her time, and her mother's, which was so much greater than it is today—at bearing what was then called an "illegitimate" child;

yet she had always told Melody the truth about it, hoping that her honest acknowledgment of what she had done would prevent the shame from being passed along to a daughter who had done nothing to bring it upon herself.

But now, standing there looking into Melody's eyes, opening her mouth to tell Melody the old story one more time, Cindy found herself nervous, and shaking, and swallowing hard. For some reason, she had never noticed before how hard she had to swallow to tell the story. For some reason, this time it wasn't working; no matter how hard she swallowed, up came a few details of the story that for twenty years had stayed so obediently down.

"I—I'm not completely sure," she whispered. "I'm not completely sure who your father is."

It seems, she confessed, her voice cracking at the growing disbelief and disgust on her daughter's face, that there were two other possibilities. The version Cindy had clung to all these years had always made the most sense. It was the only version you could bring home to a mother too furious to help you out of a predicament in which you felt helpless; because having been a fool for love was pitiful but understandable, whereas having had two drunken one-night stands with guys you picked up in bars within two weeks of being rejected by your True Love (because you desperately needed the reassurance that his unresponsiveness hadn't erased you) was just insurmountably stupid and pathetic. Without love, the whole redeeming fairy tale of her life collapsed, because in the eyes of her mother, of her church, of the society in which she grew up—and now, probably, in the eyes of her own daughter—love was the poetic license that elevated base selfish lust into the noble yearning quest for human good faith that all the rest of us could share.

By this time, the car had long since pulled up in front of Carole's house, and through the rain-streaked windshield they could see the other Girls in the lighted glow of the picture window, gathered around the coffee table with their drinks and food and cigarettes. Donna's expression, through the whole story, had remained blank, and Cindy desperately wished she would say something—something wise and from On High, something therapeutic, and forgiving; anything but the shrieking curse of the witch-mother: *You stupid little tramp, you brought it all on yourself.*

"So you can imagine," she concluded, wiping her nose and eyes quickly with the arm of her sweater, "what life in our house is like right now. Melody is still furious with me, and I'm trying to get up enough courage to track down those other two guys and approach them about DNA testing, and here Mark thinks I've been lying him to all these years, and I feel just horrible because—Donna, how is it that a person can really honestly think she's facing the truth about something when deep inside, all along, she knows she isn't?"

She stopped, and held her breath, waiting for Donna to respond. Next to her, in the bucket seat confessional, Donna seemed to be struggling now, to keep her face so blank, and then slowly she seemed to stop struggling. The mask chipped, and Donna was smiling, and then grinning, and then shaking with laughter. "You'll have to forgive me, Cindy," she said, between whoops. "I don't mean to make light of what you're going through. But here we were all holding back with you because we thought you were such a goddamn Goody Two-shoes, and it turns out—" she paused, wiping tears of laughter from the corners of her eyes, "—it turns out: *You're just a slut like all the rest of us.*"

They sat there in the car for a few moments, with the rain beating down on them, while Cindy stared at Donna, openmouthed. Donna finally pulled herself together, put her hand on Cindy's arm, and said, "C'mon, let's go inside and get somethin' to eat." She sounded much friendlier than she ever had before, so Cindy figured she must have blindly guessed the magic open-sesame words, and what Donna had said had been the benediction, after all. Then suddenly, she felt light with the relief of having finally sung, and she got out of the car and followed Donna up the front walk to Carole's door. And as they stood there in the rain, waiting for one of the Girls to let them in, Cindy put her hand on Donna's arm and said, smiling, "You know, you're probably right, Donna. I guess I just never thought of looking at it from that perspective."

EPILOGUE

Sister Luke, singularized pseudonymously by writer Kathryn Hulme in *The Nun's Story* in 1956, was in the hospital room with Hulme when the author died in Hawaii in August 1981. Hulme's *New York Times* obituary (August 28, 1981) described the ex-nun as "the writer's companion and business partner for many years," and revealed that her real, original name had been Marie Louise Habets.

Lynda Bird Johnson Robb appeared in an October 20, 1997, *People* magazine roundup of high-profile women who stood by their "cheatin' " men. The article cited Senator Charles Robb's 1991 admission that he had received a nude massage from a former Miss Virginia-USA who later posed for *Playboy*, as well as a 1994 *Washington Post* report that former aides said Robb had "had 'sexual relations or oral sex' with at least six women during his marriage to Lynda." Lynda was quoted as declaring, "We will celebrate our 30th wedding anniversary this December and I would marry him again tomorrow."

Patty Hearst Shaw and her ex-bodyguard husband, Bernie Shaw, raised two daughters in the Connecticut suburbs before

Patty returned to the workforce as, in the words of an October 17, 1996, *New York Times* profile, "a celebrity." Apparently rejecting quiet docility as a lifestyle, Hearst had already played two campy cameo roles in John Waters films, including *Serial Mom*, was actively publicizing her mystery novel *Murder at San Simeon*, and had just, with "staggering equanimity," faced down schlock radio host Howard Stern, who had asked her on the air what she had been wearing when she was raped in the closet by members of the Symbionese Liberation Army. Alluding both to the genteel way in which she had been raised and to the aftermath of her "Tania" makeover, Patty informed the *Times* interviewer that "If one of my daughters wanted to come out [as a debutante], I'd have to bring in the deprogrammers for *her*."

Pat Loud remained *on her own*. After seventeen years in New York and London, she returned to California where, according to a March 22, 1993, article in *People*, she was working for a small graphic arts studio and sharing Sunday dinners with three of her adult children. She maintained a "civil" relationship with Bill, who at seventy-two was living in Houston and had divorced his second wife. Bill told *People*, "I've finally figured out I just have an adolescent situation going on here, and there's nothing I can do about it. I have kind of a Jack Kennedy complex, I guess."

Renee Richards remained *on her own*, out of the limelight. As of early 1998, she was still a privately practicing opthalmologist in New York City.

Joan Kennedy remained *on her own*. Though reportedly struggling to stay sober, she was arrested for drunk driving in 1988 and again in 1991. Ted Kennedy's 1992 marriage to Victoria Reggie raised the question of whether he had obtained an annulment of his first marriage, a question neither the church nor Kennedy would officially answer, although Kennedy's press office said the new marriage had been "blessed by the church." An annulment would be the Catholic Church's official declaration that the twenty-two-year marriage to Joan had never existed.

Diana, Princess of Wales, was officially *on her own,* a year after her divorce from Prince Charles, when she died in a car crash in Paris in August 1997. One of her most highly publicized actions in the year after the divorce had been the spectacular cleaning out of her closet, which provided seventy-nine outfits from her royal days for an auction at Christie's that raised millions for charity. Though some observers characterized her budding romance with Dodi Fayed as the beginning of a well-deserved happily-ever-after, there were others who suspected it would have turned out badly. Really, it's anybody's guess.

NOTES

Prologue

11 "the mini-girl": Diana Vreeland, then editor in chief of *Vogue*, quoted in "Twiggy: Click! Click!," *Newsweek*, April 10, 1967, p. 65.

11 Mia Farrow at twenty-two: "Newsmakers," *Newsweek*, April 17, 1967, p. 66.

12 Gloria Steinem on the cover: *Newsweek*, August 16, 1971.

Chapter I: Once Upon a Time . . .

Fractured Fairy Tale

Jane Hatch, biographical item on Kathryn Hulme, *Wilson Library Bulletin*, November 1962, p. 289.

Kathryn Hulme, *The Nun's Story* (Boston: Little Brown, 1956).

David Zeitlin, "Real-life Sister Luke found world full of surprises," *Life*, June 8, 1959, p. 144.

Real Life

40 Janis Ian column: *Seventeen*, January 1967, p. 46.

40 "just another gawky": "The Twig," *Newsweek*, April 3, 1967, p. 62.

40 "meager as a wartime": "Twiggy: Click! Click!," op. cit., p. 62.

41 "just a few calories": "The Twig," op. cit., p. 62.

41 "Back in England": "Twiggy: Click! Click!," op. cit., p. 62.

41 "Have a Beauty Happening": *Seventeen*, January 1967, p. 70.

42 "Is a girl": Ibid., tampon advertisement, p. 126.

42 "Someday when I marry": Ibid., china advertisement, inside front cover.

42 "Me, a girl psychologist?": advertisement, *Seventeen*, March 1967, p. 223.

42 "A candid comparison": *Seventeen*, January 1967, p. 98.

47 "How to choose": "Take a Fashion Lesson," *Seventeen*, May 1967, p. 232.

Chapter II: First Comes Love

Fractured Fairy Tale

"White House: The Man in Her Life," *Newsweek*, September 25, 1967, p. 29.

"White House Wedding," *Newsweek*, December 18, 1967, p. 29.

Real Life

72 "The Nun: A Joyous Revolution": *Newsweek*, December 25, 1967, p. 45.

94 the "Bone Test": "Skin . . . and Bones," *Mademoiselle*, January 1969, p. 110.

95 "Rate Your Weight": *Seventeen*, October 1969, p. 144.

Chapter III: The Wives, the Babes, and the Bathwater

Fractured Fairy Tale

Pat Loud with Nora Johnson, *Pat Loud: A Woman's Story* (New York: Coward, McCann & Geoghegan, 1974).

"An American Family," *Newsweek*, January 15, 1973, p. 68.

"An In-Depth Interview by Dr. Rubin: Pat Loud Talks About Love, Marriage, Divorce—and Herself," *Ladies' Home Journal*, July 1973, p. 44.

"A Beautiful Week for Pat Loud," Ibid., p. 90.

Real Life

114 clitoral v. vaginal orgasms: See, for example, "The Female Orgasm," *Newsweek*, October 2, 1972, p. 74. Or "All About the New Sex Therapy," *Newsweek*, November 27, 1972, p. 65.

124 only 18 percent of infants: "Return to Breast-Feeding?," *Newsweek,* January 12, 1970. See also Princess Grace of Monaco, "Why Mothers Should Breast-Feed Their Babies," *Ladies' Home Journal,* August 1971, p. 56.

126 "I do my thing": Frederick Perls, quoted in Barbara Ehrenreich, *The Hearts of Men: American Dreams and the Flight from Commitment* (New York: Anchor Books, 1983), p. 95.

128 "Drink to me only": Ben Jonson, "To Celia."

134 Kekich and Peterson: "The Yankee Traders," *Newsweek,* March 19, 1973, p. 101. See also "Fritz & Marilyn & Mike & Susan in . . . The Summer of '72," *Ladies' Home Journal,* May 1973, p. 124.

Chapter IV: The Woman in the Closet

Fractured Fairy Tale

Patricia Campbell Hearst with Alvin Moscow, *Every Secret Thing* (New York: Doubleday, 1982).

"Kidnapping: The Hostage Heiress," *Newsweek,* February 18, 1974, p. 33.

"Patty on Trial," *Newsweek,* February 2, 1976, p. 24.

"Was Patty Brainwashed?," *Newsweek,* February 16, 1976, p. 23.

"A Psychiatrist's Notes," Ibid., p. 24.

"Patty's Defense," *Newsweek,* March 1, 1976, p. 20.

"What Is Brainwashing?," Ibid., p. 31.

"Three Faces of Patty," *Newsweek,* March 8, 1976, p. 32.

"Patty: Guilty," *Newsweek,* March 29, 1976, p. 23.

"A Songbird Named Patty," *Newsweek,* April 26, 1976, p. 24.

151 *"forces of women's liberation":* For use of the phrase, see, for example, "Day Care: What's a Mother to Do?" *Newsweek,* July 5, 1971, p. 61, or "Feminist Forum," *Newsweek,* November 8, 1971, p. 104.

152 "connection between the recent": "Now, the Violent Woman," *Newsweek,* October 6, 1975, p. 29.

Newsbites

Note: The Newsbites are not directly quoted from any publication, but were composed by the author based on information from the following sources.

166 Betty Ford: "Woman of the Year: Free Spirit in the White House," *Newsweek,* December 29, 1975, p. 19.

167 Margaret Trudeau: "Newsmakers," *Newsweek*, November 11, 1974, p. 72.

167 Joan Kennedy: "Newsmakers," *Newsweek*, May 29, 1972, p. 58, and "Kennedy Pulls a Sherman," *Newsweek*, October 7, 1974, p. 35.

168 Jacqueline Kennedy Onassis: "Jackie on Her Own," *Newsweek*, September 29, 1975, p. 80.

168 Ann Landers: "Don't Ask Ann," *Newsweek*, July 14, 1975, p. 53.

169 Erica Jong: "Mother Confessor," *Newsweek*, December 16, 1974, p. 65, and "Sex and the Woman Writer," *Newsweek*, May 5, 1975, p. 70.

169 Sarah Caldwell et al.: "The Sound of Women," *Newsweek*, November 24, 1975, p. 83.

170 Anita Bryant: "Homosexuals: Anita Bryant's Crusade," *Newsweek*, April 11, 1977, p. 39, and "Battle Over Gay Rights: Anita Bryant vs. the Homosexuals," *Newsweek*, June 6, 1977, p. 16.

Chapter V: Coming Out

Fractured Fairy Tale

Renee Richards with John Ames, *Second Serve: The Renee Richards Story* (New York: Stein & Day, 1983).

"Doctor's Dilemma," *Newsweek*, August 23, 1976, p. 74.

"The Transsexuals," *Newsweek*, November 22, 1976, p. 104.

Real Life

198 The Two-Career Couple: "Working at Marriage," *Newsweek*, November 24, 1975, p. 74.

198 "How Men Are Changing": *Newsweek*, January 16, 1978, p. 52.

198 "stint as a househusband": Ibid., p. 56.

Chapter VI: The Steps They Took

Fractured Fairy Tale

Marcia Chellis, *Living with the Kennedys: The Joan Kennedy Story* (New York: Simon & Schuster, 1985).

Lester David, *Joan: The Reluctant Kennedy* (New York: Funk & Wagnalls, 1974).

Lester David, *Good Ted, Bad Ted: The Two Faces of Edward M. Kennedy* (New York: Birch Lane Press, 1993).

Andrew Morton, *Diana: Her True Story* (New York: Simon & Schuster, 1992).

225 "I needed to find": Joan Braden, "Joan Kennedy Tells Her Own Story," *McCall's*, August 1978, p. 121.

226 "life without a husband": Lynn Caine, "The Case Against Remarrying Too Soon," *Ladies' Home Journal*, February 1978, p. 151.

226 "just a good book": Stephen Decatur, "Kate Jackson: The Feisty Angel with a Marital Game Plan," Ibid., p. 86.

227 "the two acted more": "A Born-Again Politician," *Newsweek*, April 7, 1980, p. 24.

228 "Joan Kennedy Loses": Gail Jennes, "Joan Kennedy Loses Her Marriage But Gains Control of Her Life," *People*, February 9, 1981, p. 36.

228 Ted Koppel footnote: "The Unflappable Koppel," *Newsweek*, February 16, 1981, p. 75.

229 Cinderella Complex: Collette Dowling, *The Cinderella Complex: Women's Hidden Fear of Independence* (New York: Summit Books, 1981).

229 self-abusive dieting disease: "The Binge-Purge Syndrome," *Newsweek*, November 2, 1981, p. 60.

229 Jeffrey Masson was fired: "Finding the Hidden Freud," *Newsweek*, November 30, 1981, p. 64.

229 "An Epidemic of Incest": Ibid., p. 68.

229 Buckingham Palace released: "Prince Charles Finds His Lady," *Newsweek*, March 9, 1981, p. 40.

229 "the stuff of which": "The Wedding: A Fairy Tale Come True," *Newsweek*, August 10, 1981, p. 40.

230 "the lamb to the slaughter": quoted in Andrew Morton, *Diana: Her True Story*, op. cit., p. 65.

Real Life

233 *Social Equality:* Rudolf Dreikurs, *Social Equality: The Challenge of Today* (Chicago: Adler School of Professional Psychology, 1971), p. 4.

249 "They have traveled and": "At Long Last Motherhood," *Newsweek*, March 16, 1981, p. 86.

Newsbites

255 "Princess Stephanie: Single, Royal and Pregnant": *People* cover story, June 15, 1992.
255 "Dramatic Excerpts": "Diana: Dramatic Excerpts from the Book that Rocked Britain," *People* cover story, June 22, 1992.
256 "Diana consulted therapists": Ibid., p. 102.
257 "Her achievement has been": Ibid., p. 104.
257 "The Princess' struggle": "Di's Private Battle," *People*, August 3, 1992, p. 61.
257 "I would literally empty": Ibid., p. 68.
258 "obsessively addicted to exercise": Joanna Powell, "Jane Fonda: Surprising Talk About Putting Her Husband First, Traditional Family Life—and Shorter Workouts," *Good Housekeeping*, February 1996, p. 24.

ACKNOWLEDGMENTS

Many thanks to the Ragdale Foundation in Lake Forest, Illinois, which provided me with the peace and solitude to get this book off the ground.

Thanks also to *my* Girls: Ellen Barish, Cheryl Devall, Lee Reilly, and Mary Ellen Sullivan; Dee Kreisel and Roshanna Sylvester; Becky Saletan, Denise Roy, and Suzanne Gluck.

And to my Boys: Sam and George Booker.